VANDAL HEAVEN

Reinterpreting Post-Roman North Africa

SIMON ELLIOTT

CASEMATE

Pennsylvania & Yorkshire

Published in the United States of America and Great Britain in 2024 by
CASEMATE PUBLISHERS
1950 Lawrence Road, Havertown, PA 19083, USA
and
47 Church Street, Barnsley, S70 2AS, UK

Hardback Edition: ISBN 978-1-63624-287-3
Digital Edition: ISBN 978-1-63624-288-0

A CIP record for this book is available from the British Library

Printed and bound in the United Kingdom by CPI Group (UK) Ltd, Croydon, CR0 4YY

Typeset in India by Lapiz Digital Services, Chennai.

For a complete list of Casemate titles, please contact:

CASEMATE PUBLISHERS (US)
Telephone (610) 853-9131
Fax (610) 853-9146
Email: casemate@casematepublishers.com
www.casematepublishers.com

CASEMATE PUBLISHERS (UK)
Telephone (0)1226 734350
Email: casemate@casemateuk.com
www.casemateuk.com

In loving memory of my brother, Tim. The Big Man.
Thanks for the great memories, mate.

Contents

Introduction   vii

1   The Romans   1
2   The Barbarians   31
3   Vandal Origins   59
4   Vandal Migration   87
5   Vandal Conquest   121
6   Vandal Apocalypse   155

Conclusion   179
Bibliography   190
Index   197

Introduction

The aim of this book is to rehabilitate the reputation of the Vandals, a Germanic warrior people who conquered fabulously rich Roman North Africa in the 5th century AD. They went on to become one of the Later Roman Empire's most tenacious foes, fighting off imperial attempts at reconquest time and again. In so doing, they reinvented themselves as a major maritime power, infamously sacking Rome itself in AD 455 under their great king, Gaiseric. It was this event above all others that sealed their reputation, with Roman chroniclers ensuring the word Vandal is still synonymous with acts of wanton destruction. Indeed, their name is today a noun, the Cambridge Dictionary defining it as 'a person who intentionally damages property belonging to other people'. The chronology here is truly astonishing, with millions of people using this word every day, yet with few aware they are referencing an event that took place nearly 1,600 years ago.

However, this is far from an accurate image of the Vandals. Once settled in North Africa they flourished through a mutually beneficial integration with the existing Roman and Berber population. Much like the Goths and Franks in Europe, they simply replaced the former Roman elites at the top of society with their own leaders, keeping existing political, economic, and social structures intact. North Africa then prospered for a century before Justinian I's heavy-handed reconquest through his general, Belisarius, in the AD 530s.

Retelling the story of the Vandals in North Africa – a part of the world I have travelled through extensively, personally visiting many of the sites I discuss here – also helps reinterpret the history of the region in late antiquity. North Africa was the richest part of the Roman Empire, and continued to be supremely wealthy after the Vandal conquest. In particular, the region from Tunisia through to Morocco was the agricultural heart of the western Mediterranean, with a hugely fertile 250km strip which, in season, stretched north to south from the coast to the Saharan fringe. Here, along the verdant Mediterranean shoreline, the lush green plateaus of the Atlas Mountains, the seasonally abundant high plains, and the purple-fringed valleys of the Aures mountains, grew much of the agricultural produce that fed the wider empire, even after the region fell to the Vandals. It was also home to some of the emperor's biggest imperial estates, which Vandal nobles took over as going concerns, and fat and prosperous cities of all kinds. Some, like Constantine and Djemila, sat improbably high in the Atlas Mountains, while others, like Timgad and Lambaesis, thrived along the desert's edge, controlling access to the Saharan interior.

A key theme in this book will be the end of Vandal North Africa. Its brief restoration to the Byzantine Empire, as the Roman east was by then known, is still widely regarded as a positive development. I argue here that it wasn't, with the accounts of Procopius of Caesarea and others being excellent examples of a late-antique world public relations exercise. Indeed, my new research across many sites in the region shows how the Byzantines weren't welcomed back by a population by then accustomed to a new and fruitful post-Roman way of life where they had come to an elegant accommodation with their Vandal overlords. Here, I then further build on this argument to show how the later Arab Conquest was so successful in the region because its new Byzantine overlords were so unpopular. This is still very relevant today given the region is part of the Arab world, not the Western world.

Chapter Flow

In Chapter 1 and Chapter 2 I discuss the relationship between the Romans and the people they called barbarians, given this informs all we read in the primary sources about the Vandals. First I examine what it was to be Roman, and then their interactions with *barbaricum*, which shaped their view of the world outside the borders of the empire.

Barbarian is a difficult word to use in our age where, certainly in the West, it is deeply embedded as a 19th and 20th century imperial trope which defined a very clear 'us' and 'them'. That was also certainly, and unambiguously, the case in late antiquity when it was very clear to the Romans who was civilized and who barbarian. The Vandal experience here was actually of the most extreme variety given that, unlike their Germanic contemporaries in Europe (for example the Franks or Saxons), they have no surviving voice, such was the scale of their defeat by Belisarius and the later scouring of regional culture by the Arab Conquest. Therefore, fully understanding how the Romans viewed barbarians (and specifically the Vandals) helps benchmark their reputation today, and then allows us to challenge it.

Four further chapters follow, each chronologically tracking the Vandals from their origins on the European steppe (some argue southern Scandinavia), through their astonishing decades-long southerly migration, to their final and improbable conquest of Rome's economic powerhouse in North Africa.

Their specific story begins in Chapter 3 where I detail the origins of the Germanic peoples of northern and eastern Europe, introducing the reader to the Hasdingi and Silingi branches of the Vandals. Chapter 4 then begins with my narration of the complex story of the barbarian incursions through the Western Roman Empire in the 4th and 5th centuries AD, by which time entire peoples from beyond the Rhine were beginning to settle in Roman territory. Here, we see the Vandals crossing the frozen Rhine on New Year's Eve AD 406 along with their Alan and Suebi allies, this unlikely coalition then aggressively driving through prosperous Gaul before migrating en masse over the Pyrenees into Spain in AD 409. There they settled, until Rome cobbled together an alliance with the Germanic Visigoths. The latter, under their King Wallia, then almost wiped out the Silingi Vandals and the Alans who'd travelled south with them. Their survivors then sought refuge with Gunderic, king of the Hasdingi Vandals, who finally managed to repel their Roman and German assailants in Baetica in southern Spain and establish a new homeland there (Cornell and Matthews, 1982, 173).

However, it is in Chapter 5 that the story of the Vandals becomes truly fantastical, and of a scale equivalent to any Tolkienesque adventure in modern literary culture. Here, I next narrate how Gunderic's brother and successor, Gaiseric, led his people even further south, this time to a different continent: Africa. This was the only region of the empire yet to suffer the predations of Germans, Goths, or Sassanid Persians. Crossing the Strait of Gibraltar to Mauretania Tingitana in AD 429, the initial Vandal expedition may actually have been at the behest of the Romans themselves, with the *comes Africae* of Rome's North African *diocese* Boniface allegedly inviting them to North Africa as *foederate* mercenaries. Whether this was actually the case will be tested in this book. Whatever the truth, it soon became a flood of migrants, with 80,000 Vandals and Alans quickly arriving. When the Romans tried to resist this human tide, the Vandals fought back and overwhelmed them, forcing a treaty on Rome in AD 435. This ceded the provinces of Mauretania Tingitana, Mauretania Caesariensis, Mauretania Tabia, Numidia Cirtensis, and Numidia Militiana to Gaiseric. The Romans did retain a rump African territory in the old Carthaginian heartlands around the Gulf of Tunis and in Tripolitania, and though Heather calls the land given to the Germans a Vandal reservation (2005, 288), I argue here this was far from the truth. In fact, the agency in the Roman-Vandal relationship was actually the other way around, as was soon proved when friction between the two erupted again four years later. The treaty quickly collapsed, with Gaiseric leading his mounted warriors on a thunderous advance along the coastal plain to Carthage, *diocene* capital of the whole of Roman Africa. This soon fell to the Vandals, ending the official

Roman presence in the region. The African Vandal kingdom was promptly declared, with Gaiseric its head. Here, the Vandal king's achievement cannot be overstated; he now found himself the ruler of a vast and super-rich territory on which much of the Roman Mediterranean still depended for agricultural produce and commerce more broadly.

In Chapter 6 I then show how the Vandals quickly got to work assimilating local Roman political, economic, and social structures with their own, though here the empire was clearly in denial about their loss of North Africa, with Gaiseric's kingdom not recognized in the west until AD 442 and the east until AD 472 (Hornblower and Spawforth, 1996, 1581). It truly was a Vandal heaven, with the Germanic elite sitting atop a highly organized Roman administration with centuries of experience extracting wealth from hundreds of kilometres of rolling green hills and plains, at least in season, between the coast and the Sahara. Over time a solution was even reached over the most contentious issue that divided the post-Roman natives in North Africa from their new Vandal overlords, namely their respective interpretations of Christianity. Here the former were staunchly Catholic, while the Vandals were Arian zealots.

Sadly for the Vandals, this era of North African prosperity and harmony was not to last. The Byzantine Empire refused to give up its dream of reconquering what contemporary writers still called a verdant paradise. By the early AD 530s the recovery of North Africa had long been a fixation with the emperors in Constantinople. Eventually one emerged who not only had the ambition to succeed where others had failed, but also the means to achieve victory. This was the supremely ambitious Justinian I, a ruler obsessed with legacy, and his general, Belisarius, the leading field commander of the age. After an audacious landing 16km from Carthage in AD 533, a lightning Byzantine campaign secured victory, with the last Vandal king, Gelimer, surrendering in AD 534.

What followed was a brief century-long interlude in which the Byzantine Empire tried to re-assert its rule over territory it now called the Exarchate of Africa. Here my own experience travelling through the region has proved instructive, given the Byzantine phase in most towns and cities includes one common feature. This is a rapidly built fort, some of them huge but many tiny, recycling local building materials. By way of example, that in the former Roman *colonia* of Madauros in the foothills of the Atlas Mountains in southern Algeria was constructed so quickly atop of the city's old *forum* that its north wall is actually the old public theatre, built in the early 3rd century AD by Septimius Severus. Further, all of the many Byzantine forts I have examined in North Africa feature row after row of stone-built internal water troughs, and have surrounding watchtowers, again all built from recycled stone. This has helped shape my view that the Byzantines weren't welcomed back, and spent much of their short re-occupation of the region in a defensive posture behind the walls of their fortifications, with flying cavalry columns darting here and there to pacify the local Berber population.

Finally, in my conclusion I consider the legacy of Vandal North Africa. In particular, I detail how the Byzantine reconquest set in place the conditions which enabled an Arab Conquest of North Africa so complete that the entire region is still part of the Islamic world today.

Geography and Climate

In terms of political geography, the area covered in this book today comprises, west to east, Morocco, Algeria, Tunisia, and Libya (broadly known today as the Maghreb). However, the origins and modern borders of these countries date to recent periods of Ottoman and European colonial rule. As such, they bear no resemblance at all to the administrative structure of the region in the late Roman period, which was retained by the Vandals as a going concern, only changing to the Exarchate of Africa after the Byzantine reconquest.

Following the reforms of Diocletian, North Africa comprised three *diocese* (large units of regional control), each made up of smaller provinces (small units of regional control). The below table details the *diocese* and, within them, the relevant provinces (Cornell and Mathews, 1982, 172):

Diocese	Province
Hispaniae	Mauretania Tingitana (note this key province, on the southern side of the Strait of Gibraltar, was controlled from Spain)
Africa	Mauretania Caesariensis Mauretania Tabia Numidia Cirtensis Numidia Militiana Africa Proconsularis Byzacena Tripolitania
Oriens (modern Libya, Egypt, and Syria). Note here I have only included its western most province.	Libya Superior

Regarding physical geography in North Africa, the area covered here comprises two distinct regions. Today these are Morocco, Algeria, and Tunisia in the west, and Libya in the east. The former region features a layer cake of different geological zones that, broadly north to south, feature a coastal zone, the Tell Atlas mountain range, the high plains (*haute plaines* under French colonial rule), the Atlas Présaharien mountain range in the west and Aures mountain range in the east, and the Sahara Desert. To avoid geographic confusion, I refer to these zones in this book as the coastal zone, Atlas range, high plains, Aures range, and Sahara. Meanwhile, in the east Libya features a fertile coastal zone that quickly transitions to the Sahara, with nothing between.

In terms of regional climate, I well remember the first time I visited North Africa. Landing at Algiers airport in the spring, my travel bag packed with short-sleeved shirts, I was most surprised to find it snowing. Then, as I travelled through the region over the next two weeks, visiting spectacular Roman sites time and again, the word green kept repeating in the back of my mind. There was green everywhere, even in the high plains and through the gorges and gullies of the Aures range as we threaded our way through to the Sahara. Fruit and arable produce grew along every road, with vast fields of crops stretching to the horizon, seemingly unbounded and limitless. The whole experience was eye opening. For me, no longer was North Africa arid. It was beautiful, green, and fertile, exactly as experienced by the Vandals when they first arrived.

The weather systems in North Africa that create these conditions are predominantly easterlies and north easterlies. These pick up moisture as they pass over the eastern Mediterranean. Rain and snow then fall as the systems hit the southern Mediterranean coast. Further south, in the summer months the easterlies and north easterlies meet south westerlies along the Intertropical Convergence Zone over Central Africa, causing the West African Monsoon season.

Broadly, the easterly and north-easterly systems cause mild and wet winters in North Africa, with precipitation continuing into the spring, then picking up again in the autumn, with the summers warm and dry. This summer climate gets dryer as one heads further inland, especially approaching the Sahara. Overall, these weather patterns produce plentiful rainfall, with an ample 400 to 600mm falling annually along the coast.

North Africa's weather systems ensure the coastal zone and Atlas range (which features huge, open plateaus) are fertile all year round, with the high plains and the gorges and gullies of the Aures range fertile seasonally (all year round if irrigated, as in late antiquity in both the Roman and Vandal phases of occupation). Then as now, the Saharan fringe was suitable for only the hardiest crops, mainly dates, which today play a very important role in the regional economy.

In late antiquity the climate in North Africa was much as it is today, if perhaps slightly wetter. In the mid-20th century Rhoads Murphey of the University of Ohio published a highly influential essay in the *Annals of the Association of American Geographers* in which he considered whether climate change had played any role in land-use change in North Africa since Roman times, his analysis based on precipitation and land-use data accessible at the time. He concluded things have changed little, saying (1951, 122):

> …the rivers of Algeria and Morocco still carry, in general, about the same volume of water as they did in Roman times, as evidenced by the fact that Roman bridges and fords are still adequate, and that the rivers are as navigable now as they were then.

Nothing has been published since which seriously challenges this view, even using the most up-to-date data. Thus neglect is largely behind any agricultural land that has fallen out of use since Roman times, though note this is likely to change moving forward due to climate change in our modern era.

Time Periods

North Africa, particularly the western region, featured another layer cake in the classical and late-antique world. This was chronological, covering the dominant cultures there at a given time. The native population in the Roman period comprised various Berber tribes, with Bedouin later settling in the interior following the Arab Conquest. The first historic cultures to dominate the region were the Garamantes, Numidians, and Mauri, indigenous Berber peoples famed across the classical world for their fine horsemanship. All were displaced by the Carthaginians, Canaanitic Phoenician settlers who arrived from the 6th century BC. Their Punic Empire across the western Mediterranean was then destroyed in turn by the Romans through three Punic Wars, which resulted in the final destruction of Carthage itself in 146 BC. Rome then dominated the region until the arrival of the Vandals in the 5th century AD, the latter falling to the Byzantine reconquest in the 6th century AD, and finally the whole of North Africa falling to the Arab Conquest in the 7th century AD. The focus of this book is on the Roman and post-Roman periods, and here I reference four main periods of Roman history. First, the Roman Republic, lasting from the overthrow of Rome's last king, Tarquin the Proud, in 509 BC through to the Senate's acknowledgment of Augustus as the first emperor in 27 BC. Next, the Principate phase of the Roman Empire which lasted from Augustus' accession to that of Diocletian in AD 284. The name Principate is derived from the term *princeps* (chief or master), referencing the emperor as the leading citizen of the empire. While *princeps* was not an official title, emperors often assumed it on their accession, it clearly being a conceit allowing the empire to be explained away as a simple continuance of the preceding Republic.

The final phase of the Roman Principate is today called the 'Crisis of the 3rd Century', when the empire was faced with multiple external and internal threats, including the devastating Plague of Cyprian. The crisis lasted from Alexander Severus' assassination in AD 235 through to Diocletian's accession. The new emperor was then faced with a series of immediate challenges, which he tackled with a fundamental reform of the empire. This featured a new, far more overtly imperial system of administration, which today we call the Dominate. This new title was based on the word *dominus*, or lord, with the emperor now the equivalent of an eastern potentate. The Dominate lasted through to the end of the empire in the west in AD 476, when the last Western emperor, Romulus Augustulus, abdicated.

However, the empire in the east continued to thrive and from that point on is often called the Byzantine Empire (some argue the name should be used earlier, some later, but I find AD 476 an elegant date to make the switch). It should be noted this is not a name the eastern Romans themselves would have recognized. As far as they were concerned, they were still Roman, even if Greek speaking (Haldon, 1999, 1). In fact, the term Byzantine is comparatively modern, first used in 1557 by the German historian Hieronymous Wolf in his *Corpus Historiæ Byzantinæ*, a collection of historical sources covering the later eastern empire. Notably, this was only 104 years after the Byzantine Empire's final collapse after the Ottoman Sultan Mehmed II conquered Constantinople in AD 1453. The name derives from the classical city Byzantium where Constantine I located his new eastern capital, which he rebuilt under the new name Constantinople.

A final chronological phrase I also use in this work, which some readers may be unfamiliar with, is late antiquity. This was popularized by the historian Peter Brown in the early 1970s, and has since become a standard way of describing the transition between the later classical and early medieval worlds. I find it very useful here, where I interpret it as covering the period from the 4th to 8th centuries AD.

Sources

We are fortunate to have a plethora of primary sources that narrate the story of the Vandals, in both Europe and North Africa. However, as already noted, none feature the voice of the Vandals themselves. All are told from a pro-Roman and pro-Byzantine perspective, a factor I take into account when using them.

The Vandals are first mentioned as the Vandali by Pliny the Elder in his *Natural History* (4.28), alongside a number of other Germanic ethnonyms including the Goths, Rugians, and Burgundians. This was published in the AD 70s, shortly before his death in the Plinian eruption of Vesuvius in AD 79. They are then referenced by most subsequent Roman authors writing in the Principate, including Tacitus, Cassius Dio, Herodian, and the anonymous *Historia Augusta*. Into the Dominate, Ammianus Marcellinus then covers their encounters with the later Roman army, though the Vandals only achieve their full notoriety when referenced by the four key Latin chroniclers of the 4th and early 5th centuries AD, Flavius Eutropius, Aurelius Victor, Saint Jerome, and Paulus Orosius. The first three of these (and given their use as sources by the fourth, that too by default) seem to have used as a key resource the so-called 'Kaisergeschichte' hypothetical set of short histories, now lost, which Burgess (1993, 491) argues was probably written between 337 AD and 340 AD. Their common wording and phrasing and facts and errors imply this, including mentions of the Vandals. Note that Jerome and Orosius both wrote their narratives from a purely Christian perspective (for example the latter's best-known work is called *Seven Books of History Against the Pagans*). From this point onwards that becomes a factor in most subsequent primary source references to the Vandals, especially given their adherence to Arian Christianity in a region already well known for heretical conflict within the church, for example with the Donatist schism (see Chapter 1).

Next, St Augustine of Hippo provides unique first-hand insight given he died in Hippo Regius in North Africa while this key city was under siege by the Vandals in AD 430, with his *Letters* being particularly illuminating. Other important contemporary or near-contemporary commentators include his friend Possidius of Calama, Olympiodorus of Thebes, St Prosper of Aquitaine, Salvian of Marseille (who may have visited Carthage just before its fall to the Vandals), Hydatius, Zacharias of Mytilene, and Victor of Vita. The latter wrote one of the most damning accounts of Vandal North Africa. A bishop in the province of Byzacena, Victor of Vita is a principal source for the persecution of the Orthodox Nicene Christians in post-Roman North Africa by the Arian Vandals, though others have since challenged his negative commentary. This is a theme that will be examined in detail in this book.

Moving on, our single most important source covering the fall of Vandal North Africa is Procopius, who devotes two full books of his most important work, *The History of the Wars*, to Belisarius' reconquest there. Usually called *The Vandalic Wars*, the account forms books 3 and 4 in the wider work and is bookended by his accounts of Belisarius' earlier campaigns in Persia (books 1 and 2, usually called *The Persian Wars*), and the later Byzantine reconquest of

Ostrogothic Italy (books 5 to 8, usually called *The Gothic War*). When using these references I will specifically indicate which book is being used given their importance.

Procopius was a prominent scholar from Caesarea Maritima in the Levant. He accompanied Belisarius on many of his campaigns, including that in North Africa where he actually participated in the capture of Carthage. Procopius is often seen as the main propagandist for Justinian I's reconquest of North Africa, Italy, and southern Spain, though this hagiography of the emperor was later somewhat undermined by his *Anecdota*, known today as the *Secret History*, where he heavily criticised the imperial family.

Other key Byzantine sources include the Berber-Roman epic poet Flavius Cresconius Corippus who wrote in the mid-6th century AD when he reflected on the transition from Vandal to Byzantine North Africa (negatively, given he lost his property in the Vandalic War), Jordanes with his *Getica* history of the Goths, and Maurice with his *Strategikon*, a 6th century AD Byzantine war manual. A final important primary source is Isidore of Seville's *Historia Gothorum, Vandalorum et Suevorum* (*History of the Goths, Vandals and Suevi*), written in the AD 620s.

We are equally fortunate to have many high quality later sources narrating the story of the Vandals. However, only in recent years have some sources been more favourable, with scholars even talking of a Vandal renaissance, particularly of their literary tradition in the region. Here I list the key titles used chronologically by date of publication for ease of access by the reader, with the earliest detailed where an author has more than one title included.

In the antiquarian record, one work above all others has shaped our negative view of the Vandals, this being Edward Gibbon's seminal *The History of the Decline and Fall of the Roman Empire*. Volume II, the most relevant here, was first published in 1781. His central argument was that after the death of Theodosius I in AD 395 the empire in both west and east existed '...in a state of premature and perpetual decay...' (2010, 304), succinctly illustrating his overriding viewpoint.

Into the 20th century, Susan Raven's 1969 *Rome in Africa* remains one of the best works covering the entirety of Rome's engagement in the region through to the Arab Conquest, and includes an excellent analysis of Vandal North Africa. Meanwhile, Reginald Pringle's University of Oxford 1979 PhD dissertation *Sixth-Century Fortifications in Byzantine Africa* is still one of the best analyses available of the Vandal-Byzantine military transition in the region, in particular for the insight it sheds on the friction between the Byzantine incomers and the local Berber population.

Archaeology also plays a key role in the story of the Vandals in Africa, though many of the 19th and 20th century archaeological excavations there focused only on the Roman period, destroying later Vandal, Byzantine, and Arab archaeological sequences. However, this was remedied in part by the excavations of the *forum* at Cherchell in Algeria between 1977 to 1981. This was the key city of Caesarea, capital of the Numidian King Juba II in the early Principate and later capital of the late Roman province of Mauretania Caesariensis. These excavations were excellently recorded by Nacéra Benseddik and Tim Potter in their 1993 *Fouilles du Forum de Cherchell*, which shows the city remained a vibrant place of trade and commerce in the Vandal period.

Meanwhile, David J. Mattingly has written prolifically on Roman and post-Roman North Africa, particularly with regard to Tripolitania in modern Libya. Key titles include his 1995 *Tripolitania*, his 2006 co-edited *The Libyan Desert: Natural Resources and Cultural Heritage*, and his best-selling 2011 *Imperialism, Power and Identity*.

Next, John Haldon's 1999 *Warfare, State and Society in the Byzantine World 565 to 1204* is very useful when considering the armies of the early Byzantine Empire. Meanwhile, Andrew Wilson's 2002 *Urban Production in the Roman World: The View from North Africa*, published by the British School at Rome, is helpful when considering the changes, or lack of, that took place in industrial production during the transition from late Roman to Vandal North Africa.

Moving on, an important collection of essays called *Vandals, Romans and Berbers* was published in 2004 that began the process of rehabilitating Vandal North Africa. Edited by Andy Merrills, a number of the papers are heavily referenced in this book. Then in 2005 Peter Heather published his highly acclaimed *The Fall of the Roman Empire*, a true tour de force covering every aspect of the collapse of the Roman Empire in the west, including the Vandal conquest of North Africa. Most recently, in 2018 Heather turned his attention to the eastern Empire with his *Rome Resurgent: War and Empire in the Age of Justinian* covering Justinian I's Byzantine wars of reconquest.

Earlier, in 2009 James J. O'Donnell had tackled the toxic legacy of Justinian I in his *The Ruin of the Roman Empire*, a particularly negative appreciation of the emperor's reign. Moving on, Rome's wider relationship with its Germanic and Gothic assailants was then examined in Michael Kulikowski's 2014 *Rome's Gothic Wars*. This provides excellent insight into the later empire's relationships with its so-called barbarian neighbours.

Meanwhile, Adrian Goldsworthy's many works on Roman political and military history have provided great insight into my research on the later Roman Empire and the Vandal role in its decline, particularly his 2009

The Fall of the West. Next, Belisarius is clearly a key figure in this book given his role as Vandal North Africa's Byzantine nemesis. Here, Ian Hughes' 2014 *Belisarius: The Last Roman General* has proved most valuable.

Few popular historical works deal specifically with the Vandals themselves. However, Simon MacDowall's 2016 *The Vandals* achieves this excellently. Also in 2016, another important work was published entitled *North Africa Under Byzantium and Early Islam*. Edited by Susan Stevens and Jonathan Conant, this features a number of key essays that shed new light on the Vandal-Byzantine transition.

Then in 2018 another important collection of essays was published called *Procopius of Caesarea: Literary and Historical Interpretations*, under the editorship of Christopher Lillington-Martin and Elodie Turquois. This has provided new insight into Procopius' motivations when writing his account of Belisarius' reconquest of North Africa. The onset of the Arab Conquest in the region, and its astonishing success, is then detailed in James Howard-Johnston's recent 2021 *The Last Great War of Antiquity*.

A final mention in terms of modern sources should be made of the current *Vandal Renaissance: Latin Literature in Post-Roman Africa* project, based at the University of Sydney. This aims to highlight the vibrant literary culture in Vandal North Africa which embraced both Classical tradition and Christian theology, helping create a distinct Vandal identity there.

Housekeeping

Firstly, Roman and particularly Byzantine fortifications play a key role in this book. In that regard I have used the size-based hierarchy currently utilized by those studying their respective military establishments as a means of describing fortification size. Specifically, the categories are:

- Fortress, a permanent base for one or more legions, some twenty ha or more in size. In North Africa, Lambaesis is a prime Roman example, with that at Setif an excellent Byzantine example, both in modern Algeria.
- Vexillation fortress, a large fort between eight and twelve ha in size holding a mixed force of infantry and cavalry.
- Fort, a garrison outpost, in North Africa usually occupied by cavalry.
- Fortlet, a small garrison outpost large enough to hold only part of a cavalry or infantry unit.

Additionally, marching camps are also important when detailing the Roman and Byzantine military. These were temporary fortifications built at the end of every day's march in enemy territory. They effectively replicated the permanent fortifications detailed above in their size and layout, but were temporary. Key features included surrounding ditches, and an internal bank with a palisade.

More broadly, regarding the use of classical and modern names, I have attempted to ensure the research here is as accessible as possible to the reader. For example, I have used the modern name where a place is mentioned, referencing its Roman name at that first point of use (unless it is better known by its Roman name, or has no modern equivalent). Meanwhile, where a classical name for a position or role is well understood, I use that, for example *legate* (a Roman general) or *strategos* (a Byzantine general).

Staying with nomenclature, given this work's focus on the Vandals the words German and Goth are frequently used. Both are problematic in that they infer a tribal identity that in reality did not exist. While each grouping may have often shared the same blood and cultural practices, various confederations like the Vandals, Ostrogoths, and Visigoths more often fought among themselves than against the Romans, and indeed later in the empire provided many of the troops and military leaders in the Dominate Roman army. Even the term tribe is itself problematic, given its connotations in the modern world where its use can sometimes be seen as insensitive or demeaning. While acknowledging these issues, I retain the use of the words here for ease of reference.

Acknowledgments

Lastly, I would like to thank those who have helped make this book on Vandal North Africa possible. First, and as always, Professor Andrew Lambert of the War Studies Department at King's College London, Dr Andrew Gardner at the University College London's Institute of Archaeology, and Dr Steve Willis at the University of Kent (where I am an Honorary Research Fellow). All continue to encourage my research on the Roman military. Also Professor Sir Barry Cunliffe of the School of Archaeology at Oxford University, and Professor Martin Millett at the Faculty of Classics, Cambridge University. Next, Dr Sam Moorhead, National Finds Adviser for Iron Age and Roman coins at The British Museum, for his guidance on key sources for late antique North Africa. Finally, my patient proofreader and amazing wife Sara. As with all my literary work, all have contributed greatly and freely, enabling me to complete this work on Vandal North Africa.

Thank you all.

Dr Simon Elliott
April 2023

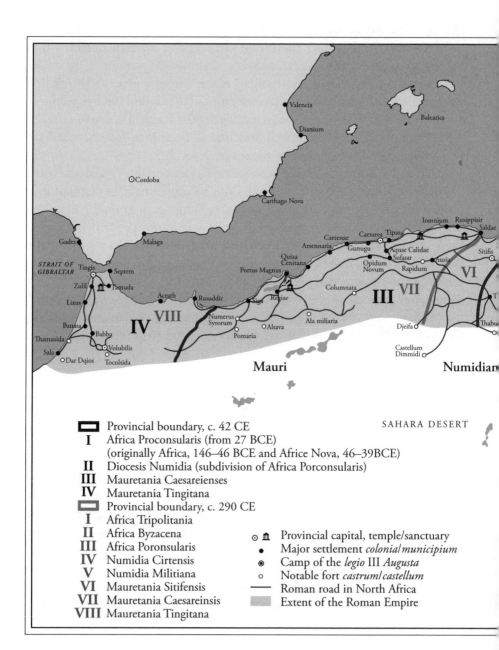

Provincial boundary, c. 42 CE
I Africa Proconsularis (from 27 BCE)
(originally Africa, 146–46 BCE and Africe Nova, 46–39BCE)
II Diocesis Numidia (subdivision of Africa Porconsularis)
III Mauretania Caesareienses
IV Mauretania Tingitana

Provincial boundary, c. 290 CE
I Africa Tripolitania
II Africa Byzacena
III Africa Poronsularis
IV Numidia Cirtensis
V Numidia Militiana
VI Mauretania Sitifensis
VII Mauretania Caesareinsis
VIII Mauretania Tingitana

⊙ 🏛 Provincial capital, temple/sanctuary
• Major settlement *colonia/municipium*
◉ Camp of the *legio* III *Augusta*
○ Notable fort *castrum/castellum*
— Roman road in North Africa
Extent of the Roman Empire

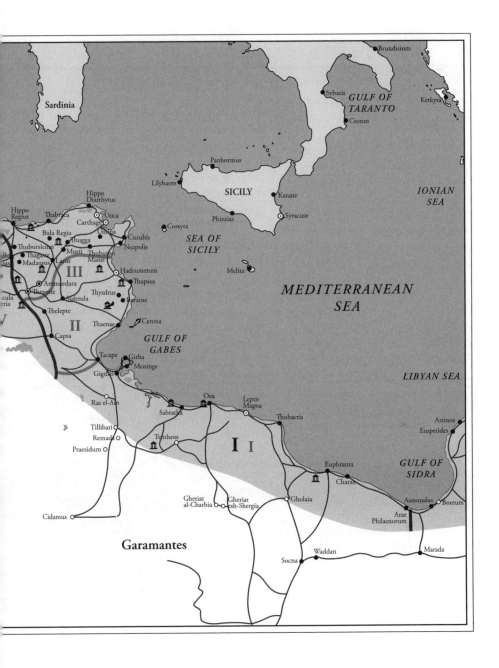

BRITANNIA

Londinium

Rhine River

ATLANTIC
OCEAN

Huns checked by
Gallo-Roman
forces in 451

Huns

Augusta
Treverorum

406 Vandals,
Alans, and
Suebi enter Gaul

402 Western capital
moves to Ravenna

Berdigali

Vandals and Suebi

GALLIA

Mediolanum

Vandals and Alans

Ravenna

Split

Narbo

Toletom

Tarraco

Rome

Corduba

SARDINIA

Taranto

Gades

429 Vandals
cross from
Spain to Africa

410 Alaric
invades Italy
a second time
and sacks Rome

Carthage

SICILY

Vandals

410 Alaric
contemplates
invasion of Sicily
and Africa but
dies of illness

429–39 Vandals conquer
North Africa provinces

439 Carthage
falls to Vandals

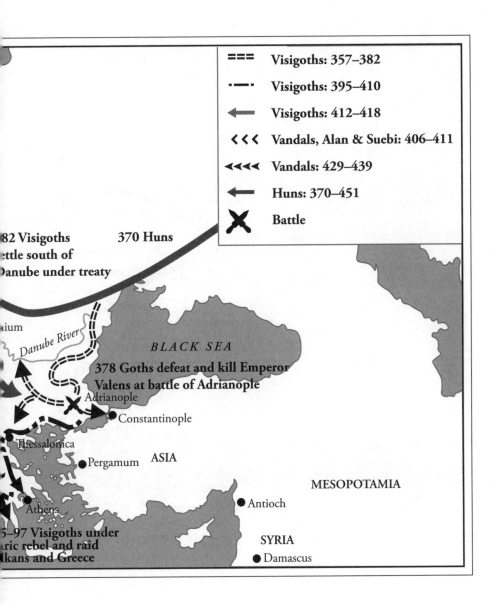

Visigoths: 357–382

Visigoths: 395–410

Visigoths: 412–418

Vandals, Alan & Suebi: 406–411

Vandals: 429–439

Huns: 370–451

Battle

82 Visigoths
ettle south of
Danube under treaty

370 Huns

Danube River

BLACK SEA

378 Goths defeat and kill Emperor
Valens at battle of Adrianople

Adrianople

Constantinople

Thessalonica

Pergamum   ASIA

MESOPOTAMIA

Antioch

Athens

5–97 Visigoths under
ric rebel and raid
kans and Greece

SYRIA

Damascus

CHAPTER I

The Romans

What's in a name? In the classical and late antique worlds, it turns out quite a lot. For the Romans, to be 'Roman' was to be something very specific, and it meant you were 'in'. The alternative was to be a 'barbarian', which meant you were something completely alien, and in every sense of the word 'out'. Even in the late antique world, with its blurring of identities as those from without strove harder and harder to become Roman, and with 'barbarians' rising to the very top of Roman society, the distinction remained stark. This is particularly relevant here given all our primary sources are Roman, or pro-Roman, with the Vandals having no voice at all.

Much later, this even impacted archaeological activity in North Africa where, until recently, attention focused largely on the Roman slice of the chronological layer cake. This proved particularly detrimental for the later Vandal, Byzantine, and Arab phases of occupation, where archaeological data for these layers was often destroyed in the eagerness of archaeologists to access the Roman strata.

Therefore, before tackling the story of the Vandals and their North African kingdom directly, we need to establish how the Romans specifically viewed themselves, and more importantly how they viewed 'barbarians', to benchmark how we access the data in all that follows. This is more difficult than it sounds given many view all Romans as the same, especially in the context of decades-old theories of Romanisation which argued that, once within the Republic or empire, a whole new set of cultural traits was adopted by individuals new to the Roman way of life.

More recently this view has been challenged, showing it was not the case at all. While the Roman system of administration was certainly better than much that preceded (or indeed proceeded) it, control over such a vast geography covering three continents, and with a population of 60 million, was way beyond the means of a pre-modern government. Therefore, by the time of the late Republic, governors were being appointed by the Senate to enact Roman law and control the military in newly conquered provincial territory. With the onset of the Principate, they were joined by procurators, their job to ensure the wealth created in a province quickly found its way into the emperor's *fiscus* (treasury). After all, the expensive process of imperial expansion had to be seen to be *pretium victoria* (worth the conquest). Mattingly (2006, 491), in his stark assessment of the British experience under Roman occupation, is very clear about the economic drivers here, saying:

> ...the desire of the Roman State to extract resources from a province was a constant of Roman imperialism.

However, the staff supporting governors and procurators to carry out their tasks was tiny, usually 80 personnel or less in a given territory. To give context, in Roman Britain this amounted to only 0.0017% of the estimated population of 3.5 million, compared to the 25% in public employ today. Clearly this was an insufficient number of officials to run the province. Therefore, both teams were bolstered by military personnel seconded from the ranks to assist with official duties. Those appointed to the governor's *officium consularis* command team were known as *beneficiarii consularis*, while those on the procurator's staff were called *beneficiarii procuratoris*. A good example of an actual individual fulfilling one of these roles can found in the Museum of London, where the funerary monument of centurion Vivius Marcianus from *legio* II *Augusta* is displayed. Assigned to the governor's staff from his legionary fortress at Caerleon in south-eastern Wales, this man served as a *beneficiarius* based at the Cripplegate vexillation fort in London in the early 3rd century AD.

However, even with their staff strengthened in this way, a Roman province still lacked the political, economic, and social means of control we take for granted in civil society today. Therefore, I believe Rome ruled with a light touch. Effectively, this meant that if you paid your taxes on time and, from the onset of the Principate, acknowledged the emperor as a deity, you could more of less live your life as you wished, especially if you had the money to do so. In that context, on arrival in a new territory, Roman citizens were free to self-express as they wished, providing they acknowledged they were part of the Roman project. This meant the world of Rome was truly multicultural. A fine example is presented by the last ever mention of the British regional fleet, the *Classis Britannica*. This is the tombstone of Saturninus, a *trierarchus* (captain) who was born in Leptis Magna in North Africa, served with the fleet in Britain for 25 years, and then retired to the south of France where he was buried in Arles (Elliott, 2016, 25).

Nevertheless, even with this level of societal diversity and opportunity, it is still important to determine what it was to be a Roman, and so allow us to understand their view of barbarians, and by extension the Vandals. To do that we need to identify specific aspects of the *Romanitas* that were experienced by all within the empire's borders. Here, I choose four. These are Roman societal structure (which set the template for the everyday life of all Romans), the Latin language, Roman law, and religion. With regard to the latter, my focus is particularly on Christianity given the book's emphasis on the later Roman Empire and post-Roman West, with additional detail on Donatism given it played such an important part in the story of North African Christianity, and on the Arian beliefs of the Vandals.

Roman Society

In both Republic and empire, Roman society was highly structured, with movement between its various levels possible, though not common. However, given all levels (excepting slaves at the very bottom) could choose to identify as active participants in Rome's expansionist project, each shared a common view of those from outside Roman-controlled territory; they were barbarians. Therefore, understanding the nature of Roman society helps us view these outsiders (including the Vandals) through the eyes of the Romans. We can then mitigate this very one-sided viewpoint, and begin to understand these various non-Roman peoples far more objectively.

At the top of Roman society were three classes of aristocracy, with the Senatorial class at the apex. These were endowed with enormous wealth (the minimum financial requirement to be a Senator was property valued at 1 million *sesterces*), high birth, and 'moral excellence'. There were around 600 Senators in the mid-2nd century AD. Those of this class were patricians, a social as well as political rank, with all those below (including other aristocrats) plebeians. Note, however, that by the time of the Dominate empire, as the Vandals began their encroachment through imperial territory, the old established Senatorial families of the Republic were long extinct due to the frequency of civil wars in the later Republic and the often-violent transitions between imperial dynasties once the empire came into being. By this time Senators were often appointed by the emperor directly (many still of high birth) through a process called adlection, or were their descendants, though for the latter accession to this highest level of Roman society came with no guarantee of longevity. As Goldsworthy says (2009, 38):

> The ancient prestige of the Senate remained, but very few of its members could boast more than a few generations of Senators amongst their ancestors.

Backing the wrong horse during a usurpation meant only one thing for these *nouveau riche* patricians. A swift death at the hands of an imperial assassin, or the arena.

Next down was the equestrian class, having slightly less wealth but usually with a reputable lineage. They numbered around 30,000 across the empire in the mid-2nd century AD. Finally, within the aristocracy was the *curial* class, with the bar set slightly lower again. These were usually merchants and mid-level landowners, making up a large percentage of the town councillors in the Principate phase of empire. Below the aristocratic classes were freemen who were free in the sense that they had never been slaves. Freemen included the majority of smaller-scale merchants, artisans, and professionals in Roman society.

All of the above classes were also full *cives Romani*, citizens of the Roman Empire, provided they came from Italy. They enjoyed the widest range of protections and privileges as defined by the Roman state, and could travel the breadth of the empire pursuing their professional ambitions. Roman women had a limited type of citizenship and were not allowed to vote or stand for public or civil office. Meanwhile, freemen born outside of Italy in the imperial provinces were called *peregrini* (one from abroad) until Caracalla's AD 212 *Constitutio Antoniniana*, an edict that made all freemen of the empire into citizens. In the first and second centuries AD *peregrini* made up the vast majority of the empire's inhabitants.

Further down the social ladder were freedmen, former slaves who'd been manumitted by their masters. Once free these former slaves often remained with the wider family of their *pater familias* (head of family, former owner), frequently taking that person's name in some way. Providing the correct process of manumission was followed, freedmen could become citizens/*peregrini*, though with fewer civic rights than a freeman including not being able to stand for the vast number of public offices. Their children were freemen. Many freedmen became highly successful, for example Helvius Successus, father of the emperor Publius Helvius Pertinax, who once free made his fortune running a logging business in the Po Valley (Elliott, 2021c, 27). Since freedmen were not allowed to stand for public office, many found other ways to celebrate their lives. A common choice was the creation of monumentalised funerary memorials, a well-known example being that of the baker Marcus Vergilius Eurysaces in Rome.

Meanwhile, at the bottom of society were slaves. Slavery was an everyday fact of life in the Roman Republic and empire. It is first referenced in a Roman context in the Twelve Tables legal codes detailed later in this chapter, which date to around 450 BC, and later in a Romano-Carthaginian treaty of 348 BC which mentions Roman involvement in the Punic slave trade (Hermann-Otto, 2013, 60). As Potter explains, the experience of being a slave in this period could vary enormously depending on personal circumstances (2009, 97):

> The lot of the Roman slave might be quite comfortable, leading to freedom and a decent income. It could also be absolutely appalling.

Roman slavery only began to decline as an institution in the later Dominate period when in some areas wage labourers and land-bound peasant serfs began to replace the slaves, though as detailed in later chapters the institution continued to exist well after the end of the empire in the west, including in Vandal North Africa.

Latin Language

Latin is an Indo-European language, and part of the Italic sub-group that also includes Faliscan (spoken in antiquity by the Falerii from southern Etruria) and Oscan, the latter the language of Republican Rome's Samnite opponents. Latin was originally spoken in the Latium region around the River Tiber in western-central Italy from 800 BC, then becoming the common language first of Italy, next much of the Mediterranean, and finally north-western Europe as Roman power expanded there from the 1st century BC (Spawforth and Hornblower, 1996, 817).

The oldest known example of Latin dates to the early 7th century BC and consists of a single four-word inscription using Greek characters found on a *fibula* cloak pin. This has proved a particularly important archaeological find given it shows early Latin featured a stressed accent on the first syllable of each word, in direct contrast to the Latin written in the later Roman Republic where the accent fell on either the next or the second-to-last syllable of a word. From that point the language is well attested in Italian texts and inscriptions, with three alphabets initially being used. These were Greek as above, Etruscan, and the form that later came to dominate both, the original form from Latium. Once the latter had replaced the former two, there was initially limited dialectal variation, suggesting it was spoken and written in a standardized form throughout the period when Rome conquered Etruria to its north and later Magna Graecia to its south.

However, as the classical period progressed, at least three types of Latin came into use, all based on the now dominant original Latium-based variant. These were classical written Latin, classical oratorical Latin, and ordinary colloquial Latin, this the version used by the average speaker. Colloquial Latin then became the lingua franca of the Roman world as the Republic and later the empire expanded Roman-controlled territory, with the use of Latin a key part of the experience of *Romanitas* in the provinces (Mattingly, 2006a, 66). Given its widespread use across this huge geography (especially in the west, with Greek still the dominant written and spoken language of the Eastern Empire), colloquial Latin continued to evolve, diverging more and more from the classical written and classical oratorical forms in terms of grammar, vocabulary, and pronunciation. This saw the rise of Vulgar Latin, a catch-all term used to describe the various dialects of the language later spoken across the Roman world which coexisted alongside the formal Latin still used by the state, religion, and in literature.

It is from Vulgar Latin that the Romance languages spoken today in many former Roman territories emerged, these the modern forms of the original Latin that are still spoken in the former imperial heartlands, and around the world following subsequent colonial expansion (including North Africa in a French context after a centuries-long interlude following the Arab Conquest).

The success of this language group is shown by the vast number of people making daily use of Romance languages today. This includes 480 million Spanish speakers, 270 million Portuguese speakers, 77 million French speakers, 65 million Italian speakers, and 24 million Romanian speakers. Of these, modern Italian is the nearest in form to the original Latin, then (in order) Spanish, Romanian, Portuguese, and finally French (the most divergent). There are eight surviving Romance language groups still in existence, these being:

- Ibero-Romance, including Spanish, Portuguese, Galician, Mirandese, Leonese, Asturian, Aragonese, and Judaeo-Spanish.
- Occitano-Romance, including Catalan/Valencian, Gascon, and Occitan.
- Gallo-Romance, including French and Franco-Provençal.
- Rhaeto-Romance, including Romansh, Ladin, and Friulian.
- Gallo-Italic, including Piedmontese, Ligurian, Lombard, and Emilian-Romagnol.

- Italo-Dalmatian, including Italian, Romanesco, Corsican, Sassarese, Sicilian, Neapolitan, Venetian, and Istriot. Within this sub-group, Dalmatian itself became extinct in 1898.
- Sardinian.
- Eastern Romance, including Romanian (also known as Daco-Romanian, this considered in detail in Chapter 3), Istro-Romanian, Aromanian, and Megleno-Romanian.

Here we can see the world of Rome reaching out to us directly from the dim and distant past, with the peoples of the old imperial heartlands speaking Romance languages using words that would have been familiar to a Roman citizen (at least in some form) 2,000 years ago.

Roman Law

The Roman Republic and empire featured a highly developed legal system which evolved over a 1,000-year period from the Twelve Tables law code of the early 5th century BC through to the 6th century AD *Codex Justinianus* law code of Justinian I. With its system of elected magistrates and citizen jurists, this legal system seems familiar to us today, and so it should. This is because the influence of Roman law on modern legal systems has been immense, with several of the modern world's major legal systems shaped directly or indirectly by key concepts of Roman law. This is particularly the case with the civil law systems of modern Europe which are largely shaped by 'revived' Roman law (as opposed to their great rival, English Common Law), this trend particularly visible in the former imperial heartlands now comprising modern France, Spain, and Italy. Without the Arab Conquest of North Africa, that would most likely have been the case throughout the region there too.

As stated above, Roman law was founded on the concept of the Twelve Tables, this a legal doctrine physically inscribed on 12 bronze tablets. The laws were created by a board of 10 officials elected to create the new law code who took office in 451 BC, not long after the creation of the Republic with the overthrow of Tarquin the Proud in 509 BC (Potter, 2009, 50). They delivered their findings a year later in 450 BC, with the institution of their new system marking a brand new approach to legal matters in Rome whereby legislation passed by the Senate was then formally written down, allowing all citizens (at least in theory) to be treated equally in legal matters. Though not fully codified, the Twelve Tables were a major step forward allowing Roman citizens the right of legal protection, this for the first time permitting wrongs to be redressed through the use of precisely-worded laws known to all. This innovative approach, which focused mainly on private law and relations between citizens, was then widely copied across the classical world as the power of Rome spread first through the western and then eastern Mediterranean. Sadly, the original bronze tablets were destroyed when the Senones Gauls sacked Rome in 390 BC after the battle of Allia.

Roman law based on the Twelve Tables continued to evolve, for example with the Licinian-Sextian laws passed in 367 BC which addressed the economic plight of the non-Senatorial classes in society, and were specifically designed to prevent patricians dominating the election of magistrates. Significant development continued from that time, particularly in the first 250 years of the Christian era, a time known as the classical period of Roman law. Here, leading jurists made substantial contributions to the body of legal doctrine, particularly Salvius Julianus who around AD 130 drafted a standard form of magistrate's edict which was used from that time to determine if a legal action was allowable, and was then due a defence in court. Later, around AD 160 the jurist Gaius codified all materials detailed in Roman legal cases into three categories, namely *personae* (individuals), *res* (things) and *actiones* (the legal actions themselves), a move which went on to underpin all future developments in Roman law.

This, and the other mentioned examples, are just a few of the many refinements of the Roman legal system that took place over a 1,000-year period of jurisprudence, this the theoretical study of law. North Africa in particular was a renowned centre for the evolution of Roman law, with famous law schools at Carthage, Madauros (Roman Colonia Flavia Augusta Veteranorum Madauerensium), and Timgad (Roman Marciana Traiana Thamugadi). At the latter, the structure of the library associated with the school still exists, and was recently visited by the author.

The wider development of Roman law finally culminated with the *Codex Justinianus*. Formally known as the *Corpus Juris Civilis* (Body of Civil Law), this was the definitive collection of Roman laws and legal interpretations from the earliest days, codified under the sponsorship of Justinian I from AD 529 through to AD 564. Though not a new legal code, and using as their starting point the Theodosian Law Code of AD 438 (compiled under Theodosius II and Valentinian III), his committee of jurists collated in two reference works every past law and opinion in Roman legal history, including all of the ordinances of every Roman emperor, at the same time weeding out anything obsolescent or contradictory. To this they added a basic outline of the law as it stood at the time, this including a collection of Justinian I's own laws.

The two volumes of Justinian I's law code, comprising four specific books called the *Codex Constitutionum, Digesta* (or *Pandectae*), *Institutiones*, and *Novellae Constitutiones Post Codicem*, proved to be Justinian I's greatest legacy, far outliving his reconquest campaigns in North Africa, Italy, and Spain. Indeed, as Heather details, it proved a brilliant choice for a flagship home affairs programme (2018, 99):

> Justinian I's regime...had successfully fulfilled part of the remit of a fully legitimate, divinely appointed Roman ruler by bringing rationale order to part of the written law which, at least according to its own self-understandings, distinguished this unique, divinely supported imperial world from every other society of earth.

As such, in a changing world after the collapse of the Roman west (even taking into account the societal continuity in the imperial heartlands detailed above), Justinian I's *Codex Justinianus* stood out as a beacon of civilized stability. Soon the legal pronouncements of the Germanic and Gothic kings in their new territories in the west (where Roman law as applied to the majority of society continued to exist alongside the Germanic laws of the new elites) were being based on the legal rulings of Justinian. Roman law then continued to evolve in the west over time as regimes came and went, eventually helping merge the pre-existing Roman and new Germanic laws practiced there, with the former largely subsuming the latter given the widespread reach of the *Codex Justinianus*.

Justinian I's law codes then received a significant and unexpected boost around AD 1070 with the rediscovery in a manuscript of lost parts of the code's *Digesta*. From that time onwards legal scholars in the west began to revisit other Roman legal texts, leading to a renaissance in interest at locations such as the law school at Bologna which evolved into Europe's first university. Here students soon realized that many codices in Roman law were better suited to regulate the complex economic transactions now extant as the medieval world continued its development. This led to rulers across the continent employing university-trained jurists who, with their expertise in Roman law, became leading court officials. It was these scholars who resurrected the Roman legal rulings that became very popular with monarchs wishing to justify their sometimes unpopular decisions, for example the concept of *Princeps legibus solutus est*, meaning the sovereign was not bound by law. To give some idea of the longevity of these concepts, this specific example dated back to the Tyre-born Roman jurist Ulpian, murdered by the Praetorian Guard in AD 328 when trying to limit the power of the mad emperor Elagabalus.

Roman-based law proved very popular in Europe because of the structured framework it provided for the legal protection of property, and later the equality which it afforded most individuals in the transaction of their wills. Such was its success that by the 16th century AD, rediscovered Roman law dominated every aspect of the legal procedures in many continental European countries. In fact, only in England and Scandinavia did Roman-based law fail to make a dramatic impact in this period, largely in the former's case because of its very differential experience of the end of Roman rule in the west. In that regard, Germanic-based law was much further advanced as Roman law re-emerged elsewhere in the west, negating the need for the practical advantages of the Roman legal approach. Therefore, instead of Roman-based civil law, the English system of Common Law evolved.

From this point of divergence Roman-based law in the old imperial heartlands and English-based law went their separate ways, and while Roman law is no longer applied in real terms on the continent, its impact is still greatly felt. For example, Roman law is still a mandatory subject for many law students in most continental European civil law jurisdictions. Indeed, reaching out to us today through the codifications of Justinian I, Gaius' 2nd century AD legal categories of *personae*, *res*, and *actiones* can still be recognised in the French *Code Civil*, Germany's BGB civil law code, and the Civil Code of Spain.

Roman Religion

Religion played a central role in Roman and post-Roman society, with dynamic change taking place in belief systems as the Dominate phase of empire progressed. This was largely due to the rise in popularity of Christianity which, through a series of schisms, then created societal friction requiring frequent imperial intervention. Here, to provide context I first detail traditional Roman religion, and then narrate the surge in popularity of Christianity from the time of Constantine I. This is particularly visible in North Africa where, from that time, Christianization on an industrial scale is evident. I then close the section by detailing the two key schisms that particularly impacted this region, Donatism and Arianism.

Traditional Roman Religion

Spirituality in the Roman world originally revolved around the classical pantheon, with worship largely transactional and temple altars located outside the place of worship, rather than within. In the Republic, citizens were encouraged to honour the gods of the Roman pantheon, in particular the Capitoline Triad of Jupiter, Juno, and Minerva. Later, with the onset of the Principate empire, worship of the imperial cult was added. Other popular gods included Mars,

Venus, Vesta, and Mercury. Additionally, worship of other gods associated with a given location within the Roman world was also encouraged, these often local deities appropriated in some way into the Roman pantheon. This was a process called *interpretatio romana* by contemporary writers, with the phrase first used by Tacitus in *The Germania* (43.1). Good examples can be found in Britain, for example at York (Roman Eboracum) where a carving of the god Sol (the personification of the Sun in the Roman pantheon) has been found rendered in the fashion of the local Brythonic sun god (Elliott, 2021, 7). Meanwhile, at the religious small town of Bath (Roman Aqua Sulis) we have another iconic example of such religious cultural transfer. Here, the arriving Romans built a temple complex atop the natural hot spring that already featured a Brythonic shrine to the local goddess Sulis (hence their name for their new settlement), the Romans associating her with Minerva (Mattingly, 2006, 62).

Meanwhile, as Rome expanded its territorial control eastwards, new eastern deities soon joined the gods of the classical pantheon to become popular cults. These were more congregational in nature than the old transactional style of worship associated with the classical pantheon, the worshipper often playing a much greater role in the religious ceremony. Examples of such cults included the worship of Isis (note the fine temple in Pompeii), Mithras (with associated subterranean temples found across the empire, for example the fine example beneath the Basilica of St Clemente in central Rome), and Bacchus. In the case of the latter two, Roman London provides unique insight into the synergy between these various eastern cults, with the Mithraeum sited on western bank of the Walbrook Stream which bisected Roman London later morphing into a temple of Bacchus at some stage in the 4th century AD (Hingley, 2018, 215). Worship of all of these gods (particularly those of the classical pantheon), and also the dates of the traditional festivals of Rome, structured the Roman religious year, with the emperor's birthday and accession date added from the time of the Principate empire.

The thoughts and memoirs of the Roman emperor Marcus Aurelius, which survive to this day as his *Meditations*, provide unique contemporary insight into how the Romans engaged with their deities. Based on his own writings, the emperor turned to the gods as a matter of course when faced with adversity, whether natural in the form of plagues, earthquakes, or storms, or man-made in the form of conflict and political division. His own personal engagement was with the principal gods of the classical pantheon, with him believing he could interact with them through prayer and the guidance of oracles. In so doing, he believed he was transacting agreements with them through his worship in return for their favour. The simplest and most common form of such engagement was through the act of sacrifice, with Potter detailing that (2009, 223):

> People gave what they could, either burning it on an altar if they were trying to reach a God thought to dwell in the heavens, or pouring it on the ground to reach one of the Gods thought to dwell beneath the earth.

We are fortunate to have a very specific example of such divine intervention involving Marcus Aurelius highly visible in Rome today. This is the so-called 'rain miracle' series of panels on the Column of Marcus Aurelius that record a famous incident at the height of the Marcomannic Wars on the Danube in the later 2nd century AD. Here, *legio* XII *Fulminata* and perhaps *legio* I *Adiutrix pia fidelis* had been trapped by a larger force of Germanic Quadi and were on the brink of surrendering because of thirst and heat. A terrible fate then awaited them. However, a sudden thunderstorm provided a deluge that refreshed the legionaries and *auxilia*, while a lightning strike on the Quadi camp sent the Germans fleeing in terror. This was attributed by some at the time to the intervention of either Jupiter, Mercury, or the river god Tiberinus, the deity shown on the panels as a giant otherworldly figure dripping rain from his beard and arms to save the Roman troops.

Marcus Aurelius' engagement with the classical pantheon was stoic in nature, with him believing the will of the gods (particularly Jupiter) was identical with fate. Later in life his writings illustrate this, with an almost benign acceptance of the trials and tribulations he'd already experienced, or was yet to face. Take for example the following from his *Meditations* (5.9):

> Do not be distressed, do not despond or give up in despair, if now and again practice falls short of precept. Return to the attack after each failure, and be thankful if on the whole you acquit yourself in the majority of cases as a man should.

However, religious belief in the Roman world was not just focused on the 'above', but also the 'within', in this case at a more domestic level with *lares familiares*, the household gods. These were domestic spirits of many kinds who, again through transactional worship, took care of the prosperity and welfare of those within a household. In a standard Roman townhouse or rural villa they were worshipped in the *lararium*, an alcove shrine often in a corner of the *atrium*. It is also within such a domestic setting that one can also see another key facet of classical world religious belief, specifically in the context of the 'evil eye'. In an age where there was little understanding of socially transmittable illness, it was commonly believed that one individual could curse or infect another with ill fortune or illness through the simple act of looking at them with harmful intent. This was called the 'evil eye'. To counter this, an individual would deploy their own spiritual countermeasures, often featuring other 'eyes' to deflect the harmful gaze. Prime examples were the peacock feathers that so frequently appear on painted wall plaster in Roman households, and also medusa heads with their multitude of snake eyes. It is no coincidence that such medusas were also one of the most common decorations used on Roman armour and shields.

One aspect of classical worship that the Roman state specifically discouraged was the worship of prophets, defined by Hornblower and Spawforth as mortals who spoke in the name of a god, or interpreted his or her will (1996, 1,258). Given these usually operated outside the context of state-sponsored religion, and certainly the imperial cult, prophets were thought very dangerous and were often referenced as wizards and witches in contemporary literature. Indeed, most Roman emperors from Augustus onwards issued edicts against such unauthorized contact with the divine (Potter, 2009, 223). One result was to set the Roman state on a collision course with the two eastern religions which specifically featured a plethora of prophets, namely Judaism and Christianity, whose adherents were also the most belligerent when encouraged to worship the imperial cult. While Rome's conflicts with the Hebrew faith through three revolts were sanguineous in the extreme, and play a key role in the political and military history of the Principate, here I now concentrate on Christianity, given its importance regarding Vandal North Africa.

The Catholic Church

Today Catholicism is the largest Christian faith, with around 1.3 billion baptized Catholics around the world as of 2018, living in almost 3,500 diocese. In Catholic tradition the church was founded by Jesus Christ, with the Bible's New Testament recording his life story and teachings, his appointment of 12 apostles, and finally his instructions to them to continue his work after his crucifixion at the hands of the Roman state. The latter event is traditionally dated to the early AD 30s, based on the dates in post for two of the main protagonists. These are Pontius Pilate who was the Roman governor in the province of Judaea from AD 27 to AD 36, and Caiaphas who was the Jewish High Priest from AD 18 to AD 37 (Wilson, 1999, 223). The public ministry of the church then began with the coming of the Holy Spirit among the apostles after Christ's crucifixion, this event known as Pentecost. From that point on they and their successors began to spread the message of Christianity across the empire, with Saint Peter eventually becoming the first Bishop of Rome (and so the first Pope).

Of all the empire's eastern cults, Christianity proved the most resilient, even more so than Judaism. Its successful dispersal was helped by the empire's well-defined network of state-maintained roads and maritime connectivity, with Augustus' *pax romana* providing comparative safety when traversing from one region to another. Meanwhile, the nature of Roman society also provided a fertile setting for the new religion to thrive. This was particularly the case among the lower classes, with for example slaves and manumitted freedmen given the promise of salvation in the afterlife. However, certainly to the surprise of the Roman authorities, Christianity also proved increasingly attractive to freemen merchants, artisans, and soldiers, and even with members the aristocracy, no doubt tapping into the more stoical leanings of classical pantheon worship. Further, especially in the east, the common use of Greek as the language of government and commerce also enabled the easy transfer of ideas, including those of a religious nature.

Initially early Christians worshipped alongside Jewish believers, but by the mid-1st century AD a schism occurred (the first of many within the Christian Church) which saw Sunday recognized as the primary day of worship in Christianity. Things progressed rapidly from that point, and by the end of the century over 40 independent Christian communities had been established. These were located as far afield as Rome in the west, Cyrene in eastern Libya, and Edessa in upper Mesopotamia (Dowley, 1997, 74). This wider community was then first called the Catholic Church (*Ecclesia Catholica Romana*) around AD 110 by Saint Ignatius of Antioch in his Letter to the Smyrnaeans.

The early Christian Church was loosely organized, though by the end of the 2nd century AD a common, structured hierarchy allowing at least some commonality of worship had begun to emerge, featuring bishops with authority over the clergy in a given region. As this system developed, bishops from broader geographies then began to gather at regional synods where they shared ideas and resolved policy and doctrinal issues. The advent of these bishops soon led to the emergence of a hierarchy of importance within the principal places of Christian worship in the empire, with Rome, Antioch-on-the-Orontes, Alexandria, and Carthage the most important. However, over time it was the former that eventually emerged as the main arbiter regarding any issues arising from the different interpretations of the Christian cannon among the various synods and bishoprics.

THE ROMANS • 15

Persecution at the hands of the Roman state was a key aspect of early Christian worship, at its most extreme in the form of martyrdom. As detailed earlier, Christianity is a monotheistic religion, requiring its adherents to renounce the worship of any other gods. Given that in the world of Rome this included the imperial cult, Christians were frequently viewed with suspicion when they refused to participate in the worship of the emperor, becoming a common scapegoat when the Roman authorities needed a culprit to blame for any negative occurrence, man-made or otherwise. Significant persecutions occurred in the reigns of Nero, Domitian, Trajan, and Hadrian, from the time of Marcus Aurelius into the mid-3rd century AD, and then later under Valerian and Diocletian (the latter one of the most severe, with major implications for North Africa given it later gave rise to Donatism). However, as Potter says (2009, 226):

> The awkward and often brutal response of the Roman government to the new faith helped publicise its message. Just as bans on magic did not quell interest in magic, so a ban on Christianity, which was only enforced erratically (usually based on the region), did little beyond encouraging people discontented with the world around them to have a look. The rise of Christianity in the course of the first two centuries AD was not the result of weakness in the existing belief system, but rather a result of the fact that it offered a profoundly different vision of the way that people ought to live their lives.

Often faced with the most bestial of fates in the arena, many early Christians renounced their faith, if only in public. Even then, over 50,000 were still murdered, either directly by the state or by others encouraged to do so at its bidding. An extreme example of this can be seen on a visit to the museum in Cherchell (Roman Caesaria) in modern Algeria. Here, amid the fine sculptures that once adorned the halls of the Roman governor's palace, is a beautiful statue of Diana, the goddess of hunting. The visitor will note its arms have been broken, in popular legend by the Christian martyr St Marciana of Caesaria who was a leading noblewoman from North Africa at the end of the 3rd century AD. She converted to Christianity later in life and publicly refused to acknowledge the imperial cult during the persecutions of Diocletian. This came to the attention of the governor, who had her arrested and brought before him. He then presented her with the statue of Diana to acknowledge the deity. Instead she threw it to the floor, breaking off its arms. She was quickly condemned to *damnatio as bestias* and taken to the nearby amphitheatre where she was gored by a bull before a leopard savaged her to death. This was by no means an isolated incident, either. Indeed, such were the depredations inflicted on the Christian community in North Africa during the reign of Diocletian that the event was called the Great Persecution by later Christian writers.

However, great change was on the way in the fortunes of Christianity across the empire as the Dominate progressed. This began with Constantine I's defeat of Maxentius, his rival for the Western throne, at the battle of Milvian Bridge near Rome on 28 October AD 312. The victor attributed his success here in part to the support of the Christian God, converting to the faith afterwards, and from that time Constantine I increasingly supported the Church both vocally and financially. For example, in Rome he built a number of Christian basilicas, the best-known being Old St Peter's constructed in AD 319 atop the former Circus of Nero where St Peter had been crucified in AD 64. Today this is the most revered location in the Catholic Church, given it is the site of the Holy See featuring modern St Peter's and the Vatican City.

More specifically, in the Edict of Milan (Roman Mediolanum) in AD 313 Constantine I and the eastern emperor Licinius established religious tolerance as the legal norm across the empire, effectively ending the persecution of Christians. Constantine I then presided over the Council of Arles (Roman Arelate) in AD 314, the first representative meeting of bishops in the Western Empire (including three British bishops from London, Lincoln, and York). This convoked primarily to deal with schismatic issues related to the emergence of North African-based Donatism (see below for detail).

The growth in the popularity of Christian worship of all denominations at this time is more evident in this region than anywhere else in the empire. There, North African cities feature huge baptisteries built at the beginning of the 4th century AD, designed to facilitate the rapid spread of the religion. Their locations were carefully chosen within the built environment to emphasize the superiority of the new faith over traditional Roman religion. For example, that at Djemila (Roman Cuicul) in the Atlas Mountains in modern Algeria, together with its associated fine Christian basilica, was built on the hillside above the *forum* with its prominent Temple of the Gens Septimia. The latter was the centre of imperial cult worship there, built by Alexander Severus to celebrate the Severan dynasty, with the location of the new Christian precinct sending a very clear message showing the dominance of the new faith.

However, intriguingly, there is also evidence in Djemila that the new religion didn't have everything its own way. There, in a spectacular town house belonging to an unnamed senior imperial official in the Western emperor's court, an extraordinary 10m by 4m corridor mosaic was created in the mid-3rd century AD featuring 73 circular medallions. Each shows an image of a regional animal, or a person of the household going about their daily tasks. Two in particular stand out in their finery, one featuring the patron himself, and the other an ass. The latter gives its name to the house and mosaic today; the House of the Ass, and the Mosaic of the Ass. However, it is the motto that accompanies the image of the ass that is so remarkable, given it says *asinus nica*, meaning 'victory to the ass'. This is clearly a satirical play on the contemporary *christos nika*, meaning 'To Christ, the victory'. The imagery is particularly relevant given the role an ass plays in the story of Jesus' triumphal entry into Jerusalem. So here we have a rich local dignitary, possibly the most important aristocrat in the city, showing in the most overt way his adherence to traditional Roman religion, and rejection of the Christianity sweeping through the region, by equating Christ with an ass. The mosaic is now on display in the fine museum in Djemila, amid room after room of other mosaics from this wealthy city.

Back to my narrative, many have questioned Constantine I's motives for converting to the Christian faith, especially as it was only on his deathbed in AD 337 that he was actually baptized by Bishop Eusebius of Nicomedia. Some have argued there was a realpolitik element to his decision given the growing numbers of Christians in the Roman military. Even then, the act was still in defiance of the beliefs of the vast majority of his subjects (Bury, 1923, 366). However, in his extensive review of the emergence of Christianity in the west, Brown does see a significant faith-based component, saying (2012, 33):

> If Constantine calculated, he did so in supernatural terms in an age that took the choice of supernatural protectors seriously. His conversion to Christianity was an act of supreme willfulness, such as only a charismatic Roman emperor could have undertaken. He put himself under the protection of the Christian God, and in so doing, he deliberately chose a God as big and as new as himself. He chose an all-powerful and transcendent deity who owed nothing to the past. The Christian God and those who worshipped Him had no need of other, smaller Gods. Constantine hoped that this God would protect both himself and his empire as effectively as He seemed to have protected His church and His people the Christians, in times of persecution.

Even more important in the continued growth of Christianity was the First Council of Nicaea in AD 325, convoked by Constantine I in the Bithynian city after he'd become sole emperor in both east and west in AD 324. This Council resulted in the Nicene Creed, the set of core beliefs on which the Catholic Church is based to this day and which states that God and Jesus are one entity. This decision was at the expense of Arianism, the rival Christian belief system (Dowley, 1997, 77, see below for detail).

Then, on 27 February AD 380, the eastern emperor Theodosius I signed a decree in Thessalonica (Roman Thessaloniki) in the presence of the Western emperor Valentinian II that made Christianity the official religion of the Roman state, at the same time proscribing pagan religious worship. The latter had continued alongside Christian worship in the decades following Constantine I's conversion, but was now banned. Theodosius was well positioned to carry out this seismic break with past religious tradition given worship of the traditional Roman gods had long been in decline across the empire as the popularity of Christianity grew, despite the best efforts of the likes of Julian the Apostate. This trend was increasingly evident in all aspects of Roman life, for example the built environment where, as Mattingly explains (2006a, 325):

> Pagan monuments in towns were particularly vulnerable to the changing religious politics of the empire, which moved from the persecution of the Christians to the persecution of pagans within the course of the 4th century AD.

Indeed, the changing nature of the urban environment in the later Dominate phase of empire was directly impacted by the teachings of the Church. In the Principate the wealthy in society had been aggressively encouraged by the state to invest in the construction of grand public buildings in the cities and towns of the empire. This was a very specific part of the early imperial experience, particularly in new provinces. Tacitus provides an excellent example in the AD 70s with regard to Agricola after his first two years of campaigning in Britain, with him saying that (*Agricola*, 21):

> Agricola had to deal with people living in isolation and ignorance, and therefore prone to fight: and his object was to accustom them to a life of peace and quiet by the provision of amenities. He therefore gave private encouragement and official assistance to the building of temples, public squares and good houses. He praised the energetic and scolded the slack. And competition for honour proved as effective as compulsion.

However, by the end of the 4th century AD this had dramatically changed. Now, with the Christian Church the focus was instead on the wealthy using their surplus income to help those less well off, with the juxtaposition between civic generosity and Christian giving to the poor a key tenet of religious teaching (Brown, 2012, 71). Recently found sermons by St Augustine of Hippo from the cathedral library of Erfurt in central Germany provide a unique snapshot of such religious thinking in real time, given he actually preached the sermons in Annaba (Roman Hippo Regius) and elsewhere in North Africa. In one Augustine says (*Erfurt Sermon*, 4.6):

> ...lazy members of our churches are to be challenged to action, seeing that they barely break a single loaf of bread to feed the starving Christ (in the poor), while those who lavish wealth on the theatre leave hardly a loaf of bread for their own sons.

Astonishingly, one can still physically stand in the exact spot where St Augustine delivered this sermon, in the cathedral basilica in the centre of the Christian district of the *Hippo Regius* Archaeological Park in Annaba.

While the success of Christianity at the expense of other religions in the 4th century AD may in part have been due to the state's acceptance that its highly structured nature leant itself to use as a means of state coercion (certainly by less devout emperors, this set against the fractured and regional nature of pagan worship), religious division and debate remained a core part of the development of the Christian faith. This was particularly the case after the end of the Constantinian dynasty, and especially in North Africa. Before that, after Constantine I had presided over the First Council of Nicaea, such rifts had been well managed. Now, with increasing pressures on the borders of the Dominate empire requiring close imperial attention, religious differences began to emerge again. This was particularly the case under Valentinian I who ruled in the west from AD 364 to AD 375. Brown calls him a parsimonious man who, while committed to maintaining the dominance of the church within the empire, was focused on a doomed attempt to maintain the integrity of his imperial frontiers, these breached time and again by invading Germans and Goths (2012, 50). This saw a rise in what have been termed Christian ultra-heretics, often sponsored by wealthy patrons.

As a result, following his AD 380 decree in Thessalonica making Christianity the state religion of the empire, Theodosius I convoked the Council of Constantinople in AD 381 where the Nicene Creed was again approved, once more bringing together all of the mainstream forms of Christian worship under his patronage. It is also around this time that we see the Bible appear for the first time in a form recognisable today.

Later, as the empire moved to stay ahead of revisionist forms of Christian worship, Theodosius II convoked the Council of Ephesus in AD 431 which clarified the nature of Christ as a single union of divine and human nature, before the Council of Chalcedon convoked by Marcian in AD 451 gave its predecessor's determinations the full imperial seal of approval. This set out the definition still used today in the Catholic Church to describe the divine-human person of Christ.

Such was the strength of the church by this time that it was well placed to survive more or less intact the terrible experiences of many in the west as the empire there gradually collapsed under intense external and internal pressure as the 5th century AD progressed. This grim picture of imperial decline is well illustrated in a spiritual context by Augustine's *The City of God*, while slightly later the Gallic Christian author Salvian of Marseille provides even more personal insight. A native of Cologne (Colonia Claudia Ara Agrippinensium) or Trier in northern Gaul, by the AD 420s he found himself a refugee on the Mediterranean coast in the *diocese* of Viennensis. Reflecting on the fate of his fellow Gallo-Romans, he blames the regressive nature of the church in his day for his fate, saying (*Ad Ecclesiam*, 1.1.2):

> That exceptional and outstanding blessedness which once the first community…had enjoyed has passed away…How different the Christian people are now from what they had been! In a new and hitherto unheard-of manner, the Church wanes as it reaches its fullness, slipping back as it advanced.

And yet, broadly across the old *diocese* of the west, including North Africa, the Church continued to thrive and grow, perhaps providing a sense of continuity in an age of upheaval and change.

Three key themes emerge from the above narrative on early church history. The first is Christianity's resilience in the face of repeated attempts by the Roman state to abolish it during the first three centuries of the Christian era, with its steady growth eventually permeating all levels of Roman society. This leads to the second observation, that Christianity's eventual success provided later Dominate emperors with a ready means of exerting societal control through affiliation with, and the financial support of, the Church. Finally, we have the rise to prominence in the early Catholic Church of the Bishops of Rome who by the late 5th century AD had begun to flex their muscles not only in a religious sense but also as key players in the political and economic developments of early post-Roman antiquity (Brown, 2013, 456). This first became evident in the pontificates of Simplicius (AD 468 to AD 483), Gelasius (AD 492 to AD 496), and Symmachus (AD 498 to AD 514).

Crucially, the pre-eminence of the Pope as the leader of the Western Church by the late 5th century AD provided a focus for the religion to thrive even after the final fall of the empire in the west in AD 476. By that time, any pagan elites rising to power in these former territories of the Western Empire were swiftly targeted by the Church for conversion to Christianity, if not already Christian themselves like the Vandals. As with earlier Roman emperors and other leaders, such elites soon realised that alignment with the Church provided a ready means of maintaining authority, spiritual and otherwise, over their new subjects. In this context, the most influential figure in the Western Church by the middle of the 6th century AD was

Pope Gregory I 'The Great', Pontif from AD 540 to AD 604. As Dowley details (1997, 81):

> He set his sights on the northern frontiers of Christendom, and his attempts to gather the pagan tribes of England and Germany signalled the gradual turning of Christianity from a Mediterranean to a European religion. Church leaders encouraged popular forms of Christian piety which appealed to the pagan mind. Miraculous cures associated with shrines and holy relics, and the protection of patron saints became more prevalent.

One can clearly see here the Catholic Church firmly embedded as the core religion not only in the Mediterranean heartland of the former Western Empire but also now across the former north-western territories too, such that even to this day, despite the potent challenges of the Umayyad conquest of much of Spain in the 8th century AD and the reformation in the 16th century AD, it remains a core foundational component of European culture and society. As Moss concluded in his seminal appreciation of the birth of the Middle Ages (1947, 280):

> ...the church retained the fabric of Roman organisation, and the idea of imperial unity...a fortress which guarded within its monastery and castle walls the treasure, spiritual and material, snatched so precariously from the wreck of the ancient world...

Donatist Christianity

While Catholicism ultimately prevailed as the main Christian creed in the Roman and post-Roman world, it did face significant challenges in the form of schisms or internal divisions, particularly in North Africa. In the first instance, this was with the emergence of Donatism, a hardline North African Christian sect whose origins in Carthage were directly linked to Diocletian's Great Persecution there at the end of the 3rd century AD. It spread quickly, proving resilient in the face of vigorous opposition by the mainstream Catholic Church, and continuing in existence until the Arab Conquest in the 7th century AD. It is particularly important in the context of Vandal North Africa given many contemporary commentators, particularly Victor of Vita, equated Donatism with the Arian beliefs of the Germanic newcomers.

Donatism was named after the Berber Christian bishop Donatus Magnus who took a particularly hard line against lapsed clergy in North Africa. These had renounced their faith during Diocletian's persecutions, turning over liturgical books, scriptures, and other Christian goods to avoid exile, torture, or death. They were called *traditors* (meaning in Latin, 'surrenderers') by those who'd maintained their faith in extremis, with many seeking to resume their ministries after the end of the persecutions. However, Donatus argued they could not be reinstated without being re-baptized and re-ordained, and that any rituals they performed until they did so were invalid. This aligned him with the 'rigorist' movement in early Christianity which set a very high bar for the behaviour of adherents to the religion, putting him at odds with mainstream Christian worship in the region, which was much more forgiving. His hard-line stance now set him and his increasing number of followers on course for what became a full schism. This came to a head in AD 311 when a senior regional bishop called Felix of Aptungi, also an alleged *traditor*, consecrated a new bishop of Carthage called Caecilian. The followers of Donatus refused to recognize the new bishop and set up their own rival called Marjorinus, who was soon replaced by Donatus himself.

Donatism continued to grow quickly in North Africa, enticing many with a grievance against the Roman state or an eye for the main chance. Unrest and riots followed in Carthage, all connected to the bishop controversy, with Heather saying that the gangs of seasonal cereal and olive harvesters who congregated there ahead of the regional harvest soon joined in (2011, 162).

This focused the attention of the emperor and church hierarchy back in Rome, with Constantine I now deciding to step in personally. It is worth noting at this point that these events were taking place against the real-time backdrop of Constantine's final campaign against his Western-throne rival, Maxentius, which came to a head with his victory at the battle of Milvian Bridge in AD 312. Given the events that follow only mention Constantine, and it is after the battle that he converted to Christianity and so began to establish official links with the church in Rome, the events now detailed must have taken place afterwards.

Constantine's first act was to publicly give money from the imperial *fiscus* (treasury), already much denuded by Maximian to fund his doomed campaign against Constantine, to Caecilian to pay for repairs to mainstream churches and church property in Carthage that had been damaged in the earlier rioting. The Donatists then appealed to Rome for equal treatment, arguing that their own property had also been damaged.

Constantine now tasked Pope Miltiades to establish a commission in AD 313 with orders to investigate the destructive events in the North African Church. This quickly condemned Donatus and his followers, who then refused to abide by the findings. They demanded a local council be set up to adjudicate the dispute, appealing directly to Constantine to step in. Clearly frustrated, the emperor now ordered the Pope to initiate what became the AD 314 Council of Arles to resolve the Donatist issue. This again ruled against the Donatists, who were warned against any further unrest, the event known today as the 'Constantinian Shift'.

However, the Donatists still refused to give up. The emperor then ordered all protagonists to Rome for an imperial hearing, which once more ruled in favour of Caecilian and the mainstream church in North Africa. The Donatists responded with an aggressive campaign to demonise Constantine who, after several more attempts at reconciliation, issued an edict in AD 317 threatening public execution to anyone who disturbed the imperial peace in the name of Donatism. This was quickly followed by another edict which called for the confiscation of all Donatist church property. Predictably, Donatus refused to obey, with the *vicarius* of Africa then sending troops from the Lambaesis-based *legio* III *Augusta* to Carthage to deal with the situation. Many Donatists were killed, with the clergy rounded up and exiled.

The Donatist movement still proved highly resistant to attempts at suppression, though, especially in the countryside where its churches and clergy were largely undisturbed. Its popularity away from urban centres was helped by the Donatist clergy holding communion in Berber and other regional languages, not just the Latin used in the mainstream church. Further, when the military did move against the Donatists deep in the North African interior, the schismatists were often supported by bands of anti-Roman rebels called *circumcelliones*, the regional equivalent of the *bagaudae* in Gaul.

Eventually, Constantine tired of his clearly failing efforts to unite the church in North Africa. In AD 321, only three years before he won his final victory over Licinius to become sole ruler of the empire, he wrote an open letter to the Catholic bishops in the region with orders to show moderation and seek compromise with the Donatists. For a time, the latter then became the dominant form of Christian worship in the region. This is very evident in the archaeological record, with, for example, a number of fine mosaics on display in the National Museum of Antiquities in Algiers showing the Donatist sympathies of their original owners. Investment in such overtly expensive displays of wealth shows Donatism was by this time a normal part of mainstream society again. However, back in the imperial centre it was still regarded with suspicion and in AD 347 Donatus was exiled to Gaul by the emperor Constans, the Donatist founder dying there in AD 355. By this time Donatism was suffering from internal dissensions of its own, eventually splintering into one branch keen to find accommodation with the Catholic Church and another holding fast to its hardline teachings. The latter was then revitalized during the apostate reign of Julian when the emperor, keen to push back on the power of the Catholic Church as part of his wider campaign to promote the return of paganism, insisted Donatism was treated equally with the mainstream church.

The schismic sect then reappears in rather more dramatic circumstances in the early AD 370s in the context of the rebellion of the Numidian Berber prince Firmus. He was the son of a senior *legate* in the Western army called Nubel, who was also a key figure in the Donatist Christian Church. Nubel had amassed great wealth, and when he died in AD 373 Firmus killed his half–brother, Zammac, accusing him of stealing his inheritance. Unsurprisingly, this quickly attracted the attention of the *vicarius* in charge of Africa. He was a friend of the now dead Zammac, and quickly moved to arrest Firmus. However, the latter knew the *vicarius* was unpopular, with a reputation for protecting the rich cities in the region from raiding Berber tribes only if they paid him a substantial bribe. Those particularly affected included Constantine, Djelima, and Timgad. Firmus, with an eye for the main chance, decided to risk all and led a revolt which lasted two years.

Initially, Firmus proved highly successful given he went to great lengths to ensure the support of the Donatist Church and its aristocratic supporters. However, given the importance of the grain supply from the region to Rome, the emperor Valentinian I soon intervened. He knew how popular Firmus was, and sent his main imperial trouble-shooter to deal with the issue. This was Flavius Julius Theodosius (often called Theodosius the Elder, or *Comes Theodosius*), a remarkable soldier of Spanish birth whose second son later became the emperor Theodosius I. The older Theodosius had earlier made his name defeating the 'Great Conspiracy' insurgency in Britain in AD 367 when styled the *comes Rei Militaris per Britanniarum*.

Arriving at Cherchell on the Mediterranean coast, Theodosius received word that Firmus was ready to compromise and was on the verge of reaching a settlement with the emperor. However, Theodosius' *exploratores* scouts warned him that Firmus was actually plotting to assassinate him. With characteristic speed, Theodosius rounded up the local Donatist magistrates whom he suspected of being in league with Firmus. Under brutal interrogation they confirmed the story was true. Quickly, he then moved to arrest Firmus. Sadly for the *comes*, the rebel was tipped off and fled south to the Aures Mountains on the Saharan fringe, there obtaining support from the local Berber tribes who were strong Donatist supporters.

This presented Theodosius with the prospect of a protracted guerrilla war against these elusive opponents from the Numidian interior, similar to previous insurgencies in the region that had lasted years, including those of

Jugurtha and Tacfarinas centuries earlier. However, Theodosius was a highly experienced commander and mounted a lightning offensive southwards with a fast column of cavalry and specialist light infantry. These drove Firmus over the mountains into the Sahara proper, where the rebel leader then fled from one tribe to another ahead of the Roman pursuit. Finally, the Donatist Isaflenses tribe decided to challenge the Romans in return for a huge bribe from Firmus.

After an inconclusive battle in which the Isaflenses king Igmazen fielded 20,000 men, and during which Firmus tried to convince the Romans to desert Theodosius and turn him over in return for another bribe, the Isaflenses had a change of heart and arrested the usurper. However, Firmus managed to strangle himself to death before the Romans could take him into their custody. His body was then tied to the back of a camel and taken back north by Theodosius to Setif (Roman Sitifis), capital of the province of Mauretania Tabia, and there shown to the local nobility to prove the revolt was finally over (Hughes, 2013, 131).

After the rebellion had been defeated, Valentinian issued new laws against the Donatists when it emerged that supporters of Firmus had carried out a massacre of Catholic-worshipping citizens in the coastal town of Dellys (Roman Rusuccuru). This was an important centre of Nicene worship given it had been the birthplace of the martyr St Marciana, detailed above in the context of the Diocletianic persecutions.

As before, however, Donatism persisted, a perpetual thorn in the side of the Church in Rome. Indeed, Dowley argues that for a time it had the upper hand against Catholicism in North Africa even after Valentinian's intervention (1997, 78). Only a vigorous campaign against the sect led by St Augustine turned the tide back in favour of the Church in Rome. He campaigned aggressively against Donatism from the late 4th century AD, attending and later hosting councils set up to deal with the issue, and also wrote extensively on what he called the Donatist Heresy, as did his followers, including his friend, Bishop Possidius of Calama (modern Guelma) in Numidia Cirtensis. Gradually, Donatism was marginalised, with its last known bishop in Carthage a man called Primian who is last mentioned in AD 400. Such was the aggression shown by Rome against the sect around this time that St Augustine himself stepped in to protest their treatment.

However, Donatism did continue to exist in rural North Africa to the south, often in extreme forms. Writing around AD 451, the Syrian theologian

Theodoret of Cyrrhus describes these later Donatists in his compendium of heresies, saying (*Haereticarum fabularum liber*, 4.5):

> ...they have devised a new and strange type of madness. They call any kind of violent death a martyrdom, and those persons who desire this name make this known early on to their fellow believers. These others then take care of them in every way possible, and also bring every type of food to them as if, indeed, they were feeding and fattening up sacrificial victims. After having been supported in these delicacies as much as possible, they then compel those whom they happen to encounter on the public roads to use their swords to strike them lethal blows.

Notably, this was written after the Vandal conquest of Roman North Africa, an event which gave Donatism an unexpected final boost when the German adherence to Arian Christianity persuaded many Catholic and Donatist communities to work together in common cause against the newcomers. Donatism was still being referenced in North Africa after the Byzantine reconquest there, though disappears entirely with the Arab Conquest as part of the wider scouring of regional culture at that time.

Arian Christianity

Arianism was another major Christian sect that proved even more divisive than Donatism given its empire-wide spread. In particular, its adoption by the various Germanic confederations settling in the west from the 4th century AD, including the Vandals, gave it a particular longevity.

Arianism was founded by an Alexandrian priest, ascetic, and presbyter called Arius. Little is known of his early life except he was born in AD 256. The main point of difference in his teachings with that of Catholicism concerned the nature of Jesus Christ. Here, he developed a complex tautological concept in which he argued that, although Jesus did pre-exist the creation of the universe, he was a God in name only given he had been physically made by God the Father. Thus, in Arius' view, while Jesus was divine, and God sent him to earth for the salvation of mankind, he was not an equal with God himself, to whom he was inferior in every way. This ran counter to mainstream Catholic thinking, which held that both God (the Father) and Jesus (the Son), together with the Holy Spirit, were a single co-equal entity forming the Holy Trinity from the beginning of time.

Arianism proved highly controversial, causing political turmoil and mob violence at a time when Christianity was only just rising in popularity after Constantine I's accession (and remembering this was only just after the final phase of Christian persecutions under Diocletian). It led to the emperor's second major theological intervention (after the earlier AD 314 Council of Arles to deal with Donatism) when in AD 325 he convoked the highly influential First Council of Nicaea which ruled against Arianism, setting in place the Catholic Nicene Creed as the core set of beliefs for the mainstream church based around the Holy Trinity. Here, of the 300 bishops who attended, only two refused to sign the resulting creed. Constantine then issued an edict particularly harsh to Arian believers. This is detailed by the 5th-century AD Greek church historian Socrates Scholasticus, who has the emperor write the following (*Church Histories*, 1.9.30):

> If any writing composed by Arius should be found, it should be handed over to the flames, so that not only will the wickedness of his teaching be obliterated, but nothing will be left even to remind anyone of him. And I hereby make a public order, that if someone should be discovered to have hidden a writing composed by Arius, and not to have immediately brought it forward and destroyed it by fire, his penalty shall be death. As soon as he is discovered in this offence, he shall be submitted for capital punishment.

Despite this, Arianism continued to thrive. Indeed, when Constantine was baptized on his deathbed it was by an Arian bishop, Eusebius of Nicomedia. From that time through to AD 360, no less then 14 different creedal formulas were adopted in ecumenical councils in an effort bring mainstream church worship and Arianism together, with the pagan Ammianus Marcellinus writing that '...the highways were covered with galloping Bishops...' (*The Later Roman Empire*, 15.5.2). Matters were complicated by Constantius II, and later Valens, favouring Arianism, if only for political expediency, while between their reigns Julian the Apostate again took a middle ground (as he had in North Africa with the Donatists), allowing Arianism to flourish. It was Constantius II who came closest to resolving the differences between Catholicism and Arianism with his twin councils at Rimini (Roman Ariminum) in Italy and Seleucia in Turkey which concluded in AD 360. These adopted a compromise he hoped would bring church unity, though inevitably the result pleased nobody.

The tide finally turned against Arianism with the death of Valens at the battle of Adrianople in AD 378. His successor, Theodosius I, a Spaniard, strongly supported the Nicene Creed. On arrival in Constantinople in November AD 379 he immediately favoured the Catholic Church there, which at that time had a smaller following in the eastern capital than its Arian rival. This led to rioting which he put down with great severity. Then in February AD 380 he published an edict in the city which ordered all Roman subjects to profess their faith in the Catholic Church. He followed this with the First Council of Constantinople in AD 381, where all of the assembled bishops from the east accepted the Nicene Creed. Most historians agree it was this event that led to the final demise of Arianism among all but one group: the various Germanic peoples then settling in the Western Empire.

The key figure behind the widespread German conversion from paganism to Arianism was the bishop and missionary Ulfilas. He was a remarkable man whose parents originally lived in the Cappadocian town of Sereflikochisar (Roman Sadagiolthina). There they were abducted as youngsters in AD 264 by marauding Goths and taken as captives north of the Danube when their captors retreated. They later married, with their son Ulfilas born in AD 311, his name a Latinised version of a native original meaning 'Little Wolf'. The boy was literate in Greek, Latin, and Gothic, and was highly intelligent, quickly rising through the ranks of Transdanubian society at a time when relations between the various German confederations there and Rome were improving. Ulfilas was baptised and raised a Christian, and at the age of 30 was sent as part of a Gothic embassy to the imperial court in Constantinople. Heather argues his inclusion in the embassy was the result of a specific invite by the Romans who had already recognised his prominence amongst the nascent Christian community in Transdanubia (2005, 76). Once in Constantinople, in AD 341 he was consecrated as 'bishop for the Christians in Gothica' by the Arian bishop Eusebius of Nicomedia, only five years after the latter had gained fame baptising Constantine I on his deathbed.

This was a time when Arianism was gaining traction in the Eastern Empire after the earlier low point following the First Council of Nicaea. Ulfilas clearly made an impression on Constantius II, who as detailed favoured Arianism, and was tasked with leading a religious mission back to Transdanubia to convert the various Gothic confederations there to Arianism. In this he proved spectacularly successful, no doubt supported by financial incentives from Constantinople, with Constantius II jumping on a new means of neutralising any military threat from north of the Danube while he focused on the Sassanid Persians in the east. Here Ulfilas was canny, targeting the very top of Gothic society. Williams details this approach in his broader analysis of Christianisation among non-Romans at the time, saying (2022, 129):

> The adoption of Christianity was a top-down process: when kings changed their faith, the people were expected to follow suit.

However, although Ulfilas was initially successful, not everything went the way of his new ministry. While living among the Tervingi, something went badly wrong and he was forced to flee back south again to seek sanctuary in imperial territory south of the Danube. On arrival with a large group of Christianised Gothic followers he was met personally by Constantius II, with contemporary writers comparing him to the biblical Moses. The emperor then settled Ulfilas and his followers at Nikyup in modern Bulgaria (Roman Nicopolis ad Istrum), close to the Danube frontier.

It was here the bishop made his greatest contribution to the spread of Christianity within and without the empire, producing the Gothic translation of the Bible. Remarkably, much of this survives to this day as part of the later *Codex Argenteus*, produced for the Ostrogothic king Theoderic the Great. Ulfilas' simple method was to translate word for word the Greek-language Bible then in use in Constantinople, only missing out the Old Testament 'Book of Kings' given his imperial sponsors felt this might encourage the Goths north of the Danube to cause more trouble. Of particular note, this was the first ever literary work written in a German language (Heather, 2005, 78).

Though later in life Ulfilas supported attempts to unify Catholicism and Arianism, even favouring the former before his death in AD 383, his earlier Arian mission with the Goths proved so successful that, when in the 5th century AD many of the confederations and tribes began to settle in the west, many were still Arian. Thus, as the Western Empire collapsed, a large number of the new churches established in the Germanic successor kingdoms were Arian, with the Franks in Gaul the exception given many were still pagan. However, in most places an easy accommodation was reached with the remaining post-Roman population living there. Here, just as with law codes, while the German elites at the top of society followed their own ways with their adherence to Arianism, the rest of society continued as before with their Nicene Creed.

Intriguingly for this work, the only place in the west this was not the case was in Vandal North Africa. There, if one takes the primary sources at face value, the Vandals kings tried for several decades to force their Arian beliefs on their new post-Roman Catholic subjects. This included the dissolution of Nicene monasteries, exiling Trinitarian clergy, and putting great pressure on Catholics to convert to Arianism.

However, one should note here the peculiar nature of Christian worship in North Africa at the point the Vandals arrived, they introducing a third creed of the religion there given the region was still in the midst of the Donatist Schism. Even if the Arian newcomers did, by their very arrival with a new form of Christian worship, unite the Trinitarians and Donatists for a time in opposition, it didn't stop Nicene commentators like Victor of Vita equating Donatism and Arianism as heretical forms of Christian worship. In particular, the Catholics refuted the Arian claim to be a mainstream form of Christianity, while the Arians countered by refusing to call Catholics by that name given the agency it inferred. Instead, they called those following the Nicene Creed *homoousians* (meaning those with a Trinitarian belief) (Shanzer, 2004, 285).

Overall, this is a very confusing picture, with multiple Christian creeds in play at the same time in North Africa, and a new elite in the form of the Vandals taking control of the upper levels of society. Therefore, the utmost care must be taken when using primary sources, especially Victor of Vita with his clearly pro-Catholic viewpoint. Certainly, looking earlier in time, there is little evidence of religious friction between the Arian Vandals and the Catholic population in Spain during the former's travels through Hispaniae. Further, even if the religious situation in North Africa was as fraught as detailed after the Vandal arrival, it had greatly eased towards the end their rule there, just at the point Justinian I turned his attention westwards. These are clearly complex issues, all of which will be examined in detail in Chapter 5.

CHAPTER 2

The Barbarians

Having considered what it was to be Roman, I now turn to the barbarians. As the Romans viewed the Vandals an extreme example of such, this is important given it helps explain why Roman and later historians presented them in such a negative way. We can then strip back the obvious Roman tropes in their narrative of Vandal North Africa to see the Germans there for who they really were. This then allows a reappraisal of post-Roman North Africa, and particularly the contribution made by the Vandals.

The Roman attitude to barbarians was largely based on their own sense of identity, detailed in Chapter 1, and also their experience of conflict with non-Romans. This is particularly important given the viewpoint was used to validate imperial aggression on a vast scale. As Mattingly says (2011, 212):

> In the Roman world, as in more recent colonial societies, proto-racist views about the inferiority of barbarian peoples helped to justify war, subjugation, mass murder, enslavement, and exploitation on an unprecedented scale across vast territories.

By way of example, think of the British governor Publius Ostorius Scapula's sanguineous reaction to the revolt of the Silures in south east Wales in AD 48 as Rome expanded its new province of Britannia, Hadrian's savage response to the third 'Bar Kokhba' Jewish Revolt in the AD 130s, and Septimius Severus' genocide in the lowlands of modern Scotland in his second AD 210 attempt to conquer the far north of Britain (Elliott, 2022, 174).

Here, to help define the barbarians as the Romans knew them, I first consider how the term was used in the classical and late antique worlds. Then, to provide context, I detail how historians use it today. Finally, I then consider four examples of Roman conflict with barbarians in the Republic and Principate phase of empire to show how these events helped shaped their later views.

Who Were the Barbarians

How was the term barbarian used in the classical and late antique worlds? This is important given that, while other cultures ancient and modern have similar words used to denigrate outsiders, the term is actually Western, as I show below. Having discussed its origins, I then set out how various ancient authors used it, before finally considering how modern historians use the term today.

Ancient

The word barbarian originated as βαρ-βαρα, an onomatopoeic ancient Greek term referencing the (to them) incomprehensible 'bar bar babbling' sound made by those speaking a non-Greek language (Newark, 1985, 7). The earliest written form appeared in Mycenaean proto-Greek, where it was scripted as ρα-ρα-ro. The term then later appeared in Homer's *Iliad* as βαρβαρόφωνος in the context of the Carians, a Luwian people from south-western Anatolia fighting as Trojan allies (2.867).

By the beginning of the 6th century BC, barbarian was being used by the Athenians and their Attican allies to deride their various *polis* rivals in the Peloponnese, though it soon came to be used by all Greeks as a term of abuse for the Achaemenid Persians after the onset of the Greco-Persian Wars. In this context, it is most overtly visible today through the work of the Athenian tragedian Aeschylus, in particular his *The Persians* which was first performed in 472 BC. This play, based on his own experiences fighting in the Greek naval victory at Salamis in 480 BC, is threaded with references to the Persians in a negative context. For example, in one line we have a leading protagonist say (433):

> Alas! In truth a vast sea of troubles has burst upon the Persians and their entire barbarian race.

In *The Persians* Aeschylus extended the distinction between Greeks and Persians from the latter's lack of competence in Greek, as detailed the origin of the word barbarian, to an additional absence of moral responsibility. This included a lack of *logos* (the ability to think and speak clearly), and of control regarding cruelty, sex, and food. Writing over a century later, Aristotle then made the difference between the Greeks and barbarous Persians one of the key themes in his *The Politics* (1.1252b). Later in the same century, the Athenian statesman Demosthenes then extended the term of abuse to cover the Macedonians, and particularly their all-conquering king Philip II (Elliott, 2021d, 146).

Barbarian was later adopted by the Romans as the Latin *barbarus* after their conquest of the later Hellenistic kingdoms in the eastern Mediterranean, they using it to describe all of those living outside the borders of land under Roman control. Given the Romans often portrayed such non-Romans with beards in their literature and artwork, it is from *barbarus* we have the Latin name for beard, *barba* (Newark, 1985, 7). Meanwhile, by the mid-1st century BC the Roman statesman and scholar Cicero was using barbarian to derogatively describe those living in the mountainous interior of Sardinia, this having such an impact at the time that the region is still called Barbagia today (*Speech in Defence of Marcus Aemius Scauro*, 2.7). Meanwhile, writing shortly afterwards, the Greek-speaking historian Diodorus Siculus picked up Aeschylus' commentary on the lack of control among the barbarians, with his focus specifically on alcohol. In his *Library of History* he says (5.26.3):

> Great drinkers are the Gauls. They drink wine at full strength: and when drunk either pass out or act crazy. Small wonder the Italian merchants rate them as their most valued customers, plying the drink upriver by the boatload and overland by the cartload. And great is their reward, for the price of one amphora is one slave.

Barbarian was first used by the Romans to describe the Germans at the end of the 1st century BC. By this time, *barbaricum* was in regular use to detail the vast tracts of dense forest north of the Rhine and Danube. Later, St Paul employed barbarian to describe non-Greek speakers in the New Testament (*1 Corinthians*, 14.11), while a century later Lucian of Samosata used barbarian to satirically describe himself given that, as a native of Commagene in northern Syria, his family had only been 'Roman' for a few decades (*Works*, 5.1).

Into the late antique world of the Vandals in North Africa, barbarian was still being used there by those who considered themselves Roman to describe any they thought outsiders. For example, Procopius calls the Moors barbarians when they attempted to apprehend Sergius, an early Byzantine governor of Tripolitania within the newly reconquered Exarchate of Africa (*The Vandalic War*, 4.21). Meanwhile, all of our primary sources for the period repeatedly call the Vandals barbarians, a fact used on numerous occasions by Justinian I to justify his North African campaigns.

Modern

The word barbarian is still widely used today by modern historians who offer their own interpretation of the primary data and, more often than not, go out of their way to provide context. The vector from the classical and late antique worlds to the modern for its enduring use was the renaissance period, when the term continued in use in a derogatory context. For example, in *The Prince* Niccolò Machiavelli uses 'barbarian invasions' to describe the intervention in Italy by non-Italian monarchs, including Louis XII of France and Ferdinand II of Aragon, this in a chapter tellingly entitled 'Exhortation to Liberate Italy from the Barbarians' (1961, 133).

Today, Hornblower and Spawforth in their *Oxford Classical Dictionary* provide a useful modern definition. Here, they specifically reference the Greek origins of the word, and the 'us' and 'them' nature it overtly alludes to, saying (1996, 233):

> Social groups frequently assert their cohesiveness by emphasizing the differences between themselves and 'outsiders'. Individuals belong to a range of groups, and which they choose to emphasize will depend on particular historical situations. While we associate classical culture primarily with emphasis on citizenship, classical Greek literature also assigns considerable importance to defining a common Greek identity and creating the figure of the barbarian in contrast.

Meanwhile, in his earlier analysis of the relationship between the Greeks, Romans, and (as they saw them) barbarians, Newark also remarks on how ancient literary tradition still informs our view on outsiders today. He says (1985, 7):

> The general image we now have of the barbarians is still very much one derived from Greek and Roman historians. Barbarians are seen as the antithesis of civilization. Destroyers. For this reason, it is always said, our advanced societies must always be on their guard against barbarian elements or lapses into barbarism.

This theme was later picked up by Williams, who focused on the lack of any narrative surviving from the classical and late antique worlds from the barbarian (and particularly German) perspective, this important here given it is an underpinning theme in this book. Focusing on the Romans, he says (1998, 2):

> While the Roman Empire bequeathed words by the hundred thousand, those outside its European borders left none. Nor have barbarian oral traditions survived from this time. So classical authors became the spokesmen for the barbarian by default; and it could be rightly said that they have hijacked our way of seeing his world.

Further, as Williams argues, not only are the Roman and post-Roman sources heavily biased against the barbarians, but they are often only interested in them as worthy opponents for the Romans to overcome. Thus we only ever hear of their martial prowess, and very rarely of their other key behaviours. This has led to a paucity of wide-ranging primary source references, which is certainly the case with the Vandals. MacDowall points out that when considering their ravaging of Gaul as they travelled through this key Roman territory on their way to Spain, '…the sum total of what contemporary chroniclers have to say amounts to no more than a few hundred words' (2016, 3).

Heather also picks up on this theme when considering how the behaviour of barbarians in the classical and late antique world was reported at the time, and once more how this influences the way they are considered today. He says (2005, 49):

> Barbarians were expected to behave in certain ways and embody a particular range of negative characteristics, and Roman commentators went out of their way to prove this was so.

In his later work on the wars of Justinian I, Heather also alights on written Roman law (see Chapter 1 for detail) as a decisive cultural characteristic separating the Romans from the barbarians, particularly from the time of the Dominate. Citing primary source references, he says (2018, 23):

> One Roman author famously has the Visigothic king Athaulf say that he had given up on the idea of replacing the Roman Empire with a Gothic one precisely because his followers couldn't obey written laws. The best option he could come up with was to use Gothic military might to support Rome.

A final point to make here is that very few communities of barbarians, as the Greeks and Romans saw them, were homogenous as we understand the word today. For example, when speaking of the first Gothic maritime raids along the southern Roman shores of the Black Sea in the mid-3rd century AD, and later the eastern Mediterranean, Goldsworthy says (2009, 120):

> The barbarians who swept across the Black Sea were said to have learned how to make boats and then sail them from the survivors of cities they had overrun. It is clear that many army deserters and runaway slaves joined the raiding bands, while others set up as bandits on their own.

Given the vast distances travelled by the Vandals on their epic migration through Gaul and Spain on their way to North Africa, that would certainly have been the case with them too.

Rome Against the Barbarians: Four Case Studies

Prior to the Vandal-era German and Gothic incursions across the Rhine and Danube, four events through six centuries shaped the Roman psyche regarding how they considered the barbarians of the north. All were negative, and in the extreme. These were the Gallic invasion of Latium in 387 BC, the Cimbrian War from 113 BC to 101 BC, the Varian Disaster in the Teutoburg Forest in AD 9, and the Marcomannic Wars in the later 2nd century AD.

Brennus and the Senones Gauls

Early Republican Roman foreign policy was often far from successful. Much of the 5th century BC was spent struggling against external threats from near and far. In the first instance Rome fought the Latin War with its Latin League neighbours from 498 to 493 BC. Here, even though Rome was victorious in the main engagement at the battle of Regallus in 496 BC, the Senate had to acknowledge its Latin neighbours as equals in the subsequent Cassian Treaty.

At the time, the Etruscan city-states to the north in Etruria were the dominant power more broadly across the region. However, as their authority waned, a new threat to Rome and the Latin League emerged. These were the hills tribes of the Apennines, particularly the Aequi, Sabini, Umbri, and Volsci, who found themselves increasingly squeezed out of their own lands and onto the plains of Latium by the expansion of the Samnites to the south and east. In the mid-5th century BC these tribes burst into southern Italy and, driving all before them, conquered Campania, Apulia, and Lucania. The Latin towns led the fightback, with the Aequi defeated in 431 BC and the Volsci then driven back into the Apennines in 429 BC. The Latin League then consolidated their control over central-western Italy, leading to comparative peace for a short time.

However, this was not to last as the Etruscans now re-asserted their grip on the region. This again led to conflict with Rome, whose army began an epic eight-year siege of the key Etruscan city of Veii in 404 BC. This finally fell in 396 BC, the high point for Roman foreign policy in the first half of the 4th century BC. This was because a true nemesis now appeared to challenge the Romans, the Senones Gauls from northern Italy. Here, Gallic tribes from central Europe had been settling in the Po Valley for some time, challenging the Etruscans there who had earlier established Bologna (later Roman Bononia) as their principal city. Soon the riches to the south proved too strong a draw for the Gauls and, after capturing Bologna, they burst through Etruria, with a Gallic army of 30,000 under the chieftain Brennus suddenly arriving on the borders of Latium.

The Romans took the lead in defending the region, deploying an army of 25,000. This comprised four complete Tullian-style legions, with the Senate expecting a swift victory. However, in a shocking outcome, the Roman army was annihilated at the battle of Allia on 18 July 387 BC. Livy says a key issue here was Roman underestimation of their new opponents; he adds that despite the earlier Gallic defeat of the Etruscans, the Roman army '…was not any larger than in a normal campaign…' (*The History of Rome*, 5.37).

In particular, the Romans were surprised by the height of the Gallic warriors and their fighting technique, which involved a ferocious charge armed with long slashing swords and spears. This overwhelmed the elite Roman warriors who at this time were equipped as traditional Greek-style hoplites, as had been the Etruscans earlier (Elliott, 2020b, 54).

The battle site at the confluence of the River Tiber and the Allia stream was only 14km from Rome, which was now undefended, and Brennus lost no time in seeking new plunder. Indeed, his army marched so quickly that Livy says '...Rome was thunderstruck by the swiftness at which they moved...' (*The History of Rome*, 5.37). When the Gauls arrived, the famous sack of the city soon began, spreading terror through the region, and although the Romans quickly paid Brennus vast amounts of gold to leave, the event changed Rome's sense of communal security forever. As Kneale says (2017, 25):

> The Gauls left a permanent mark on the Romans' worldview, giving them a new sense of fear. Romans had an enduring and increasingly irrational conviction that the Gauls would return one day and finish the job by destroying the city. When Gallic raiders returned to Latium, which they did at least twice, the Romans responded by declaring a state of emergency, a 'tumultus Gallicus', under which all exemptions from military service were suspended and officials could recruit soldiers by restraint.

Further, each time the Romans were later threatened by a Gallic army, they performed a grisly new ritual to encourage divine intervention. This involved burying alive a Gallic man and woman and a Greek man and woman in the *Forum Boarium* (cattle market) of the city. The event was last practiced in 114 BC when a Gallic tribe defeated a Roman army in Macedonia. However, by that time a new and even deadlier threat was about to emerge to challenge the might of Rome, this time from the far north of Germany.

The Cimbrian War

The Cimbri were a fierce Germanic people who originated in the Jutland Peninsula of modern Denmark. In 113 BC they migrated south into Gaul, along with some neighbouring tribes, including the Teutons and Ambrones. Once there they fought a series of wars with the Gauls, including the Taurisci in Noricum (modern Austria and part of Slovenia) who were allies of Rome. In response, the Senate sent an army to their aid under the command of the consul Gnaeus Papirus Carbo. His first action on arrival in theatre was to demand the Cimbri retreat. Though the Cimbri complied, it was actually part of a trap, with the Romans setting an ambush for them. However, the

Germans found out and attacked the Romans first at the battle of Noreia. Carbo's treachery here then backfired spectacularly, the Romans suffering a catastrophic defeat. They were only saved from complete destruction by a storm, with Carbo and the few survivors lucky to escape.

This battle marked the beginning of the Cimbrian War, a conflict that lasted until 101 BC and stretched the Romans to the limits of their military endurance. After the victory at Noreia the Cimbri could have attacked Italy directly, but instead chose to march westwards to invade the new Roman province of Transalpine Gaul in 109 BC. This was a direct challenge to the Romans who sent an army under Marcus Junius Silanus to intercept the Germans. Sadly for Silanus, the legions were comprehensively defeated again, setting a pattern to be repeated over the next few years. They were soon defeated once more, this time at the hands of the Gallic Tigurini tribe who were allies of the Cimbri. The name of this battle is unrecorded, though shortly afterwards the Romans again engaged the Tigurini at the battle of Burdigala (modern Bordeaux), with the same result: total defeat, with the consul Lucius Cassius Longinus Ravalla killed leading his men to their doom.

Worse was to follow in 105 BC when the Romans determined to settle matters with the Cimbri once and for all. Here the new consul Gnaeus Mallius Maximus gathered an enormous force of 80,000 legionaries and allies. The army was so huge that part had to be commanded by Quintus Servilius Caepio, who was his fellow consul, and also the governor of Cisalpine Gaul in northern Italy. The campaign began badly when the two consuls, who disliked each other intensely, fell out and set off in two separate columns. Both arrived at the River Rhône near modern Orange at the same time, though in a completely uncoordinated way. Distrusting each other, the two consuls then camped on opposite sides of the river, thus dividing their forces in the face of the enemy. Caepio then attacked the nearby Cimbri and their Teuton and Ambrones allies on his own, trying to steal the glory for himself. However, his legions were soon crushed by the fierce German warriors. Maximus and his troops saw this unfold across the river and quickly became demoralised. The Germans then crossed the waterway, engaged them, and quickly defeated them, too. Many Roman survivors tried to flee but were slaughtered, with the legions and their allies losing over 60,000 men, the largest number since Cannae against Hannibal in 216 BC. Only Maximus, Caepio, and a few horsemen escaped this disastrous battle, later called the battle of Arausio, with the Rhône choked with dead legionaries for days afterwards.

Panic now gripped Rome, with a new phrase coming into use to describe the mood of the people, the *terror cimbricus*. However, as so often, true Roman grit showed through. This time it was in the form of the great political and military leader Marius. Born in 157 BC, though not into an aristocratic family, through sheer hard work and ambition he had risen to become a *quaestor* in 123 BC, tribune of the plebs in 119 BC, and *praetor* in 115 BC. Although no great administrator, Marius proved time and again to be a supreme soldier. His first command was in Spain, he earning fame there by defeating a bandit uprising and then ensuring Rome's silver-mining interests in the region were set on a firm footing. Then in 109 BC he led the Roman campaign in Numidia in North Africa where he ultimately defeated the rebel king Jugurtha, additionally becoming consul in 107 BC while still there.

After the devastating defeat of the legions at the battle of Arausio, the Senate turned to Marius for the salvation of Rome, with all expecting a German invasion of the Italian peninsula at any moment. Elected consul once more in 104 BC, even though he was still in Numidia concluding matters there, he soon journeyed back to Rome for his triumph. Here he took up the new consulship immediately by entering the Senate after his victory parade while still wearing his *triumphator's* robes. Though this didn't impress the conservative Senate, the people of Rome loved it.

Marius then gathered an army to counter any Cimbri invasion. He cannily based this in southern Gaul where he waited, training new legions and being elected consul yet again in 103 BC and 102 BC. In the latter year he finally confronted the Cimbri's allies at the battle of Aquae Sextiae in Aix-en-Provence where he destroyed a combined force of Teutons and Ambrones. Here he inflicted over 90,000 casualties, capturing a further 20,000, including the Teuton king Teutobod.

Marius was elected consul once more in 101 BC, and in the same year was able to tackle the Cimbri directly. The enormous tribe had begun to move south, for the first time penetrating the Alpine passes and entering Cisalpine Gaul. A Roman force there of 20,000 legionaries and allies withdrew behind the Po River. This allowed the Cimbri to devastate the fertile countryside to its north, but crucially gave Marius time to arrive with his legions from southern Gaul, his army now totalling 32,000 men. He then led the combined Roman army of over 50,000 (including the 20,000 troops already in Cisalpine Gaul) to a huge victory at the battle of Vercellae, which took place near the confluence of the Po and the Sesia river. The defeat of the Cimbri was total, they losing over 160,000 men, with another 60,000 captured. Soon, the slave markets of Rome were overflowing with Germans.

Marius was again the hero of the hour, and for a time restored stability to the Republic. However that quickly evaporated, with 70 years of vicious civil war following. That saw Octavian, last man standing among the late Republican warlords, become Rome's first emperor as Augustus in 27 BC. Sadly though, another disaster at the hands of the barbarians soon awaited, this time in the dark forests of northern and eastern Germany.

The Varian Disaster

After years of civil war savagery, Augustus' first aim as the first Roman emperor was to provide stability across the now vast territories incorporated into the Roman world. However, even though his new *pax romana* promised a newfound peace within the embryonic empire's borders, Augustus' foreign policy remained expansionist in nature. This was a classically Augustan smoke-and-mirrors strategy, designed to deflect popular attention away from domestic issues which he was terrified could ignite civil war at any time. Instead, he shrewdly directed the public's gaze towards what seemed a never-ending process of Romanisation (the controversial term useful here) as the empire grew.

As a priority, Augustus first completed the pacification of northern Spain, bringing the Cantabrian Wars there to a successful end by 19 BC. His legions and auxiliaries then campaigned in North Africa to consolidate his newly named province of Africa Proconsularis. Next, he targeted the Danube frontier, bringing huge tracts of new territory under imperial control. However, his most high-profile campaign was the attempt to expand Rome's northern footprint beyond the Rhine frontier established by Julius Caesar in his conquest of Gaul in the 50s BC. Here Augustus settled on the idea of occupying the lands between the rivers Rhine and Elbe after abandoning three high-profile incursions to Britain in 34 BC while still Octavian, and then in 27 BC and 25 BC when emperor (Elliott, 2021b, 68). His initial aim in Germania, as the Romans now styled the territory north and east of the Rhine, was to create a buffer zone to prevent the increasingly frequent raids by predating German tribes from the far side of the river. This proved highly successful, with new territory soon coming under full imperial control. Augustus now saw the opportunity to go further than his initial plan, and looked to create a new province beyond the Rhine. The man he chose to consolidate his gains as a first step there was Publius Quinctilius Varus, the husband of his great-niece Claudia Pulchra. Varus' exact title here is unclear, some arguing he was appointed the full *legatus augusti pro praetor* governor of what would become the new province, though that may have been premature even for the ever-optimistic Augustus. Varus was a highly experienced administrator, though crucially far less proficient as a military leader. The picture painted by the contemporary Roman historian, soldier, and Senator Velleius Paterculus is one of blandness. He says he was (*Roman History*, 2.117):

> A man of gentle character and quiet habits, rather inert in both mind and body, more familiar with leisurely life in the camp than with service on campaign.

Varus was soon busy establishing *Romanitas* beyond the Rhine. However, at exactly the wrong moment Augustus' attention was diverted away. This was towards Illyricum in the western Balkans, where in AD 6 a huge rebellion broke out in territory only recently incorporated into the empire. This completely undermined Augustus' northern ambitions, given this key region linked the Rhine and Danube frontiers (Cornell and Matthews, 1982, 60). Augustus now intervened in Illyricum in person, leaving Varus to his own devices. So began a series of missteps that were to lead to disaster.

Initially Varus' posting went well, with a thriving cross-border trade developing that saw the German tribes beyond the frontier supplying wood, cattle, food, iron, and slaves in exchange for Roman currency and luxury goods. As time went on, many pledged their allegiance to Rome, with large numbers of German warriors joining the ranks of the Roman military. The overwhelming military force Varus had inherited, with 13 legions in theatre, clearly helped him here. However, when in AD 6 imperial attention suddenly turned to Illyricum, the big loser was Varus, for two reasons. First, he immediately lost eight legions that quickly redeployed to the Balkans, leaving him with just three on the frontier, plus two as a theatre reserve. The three which remained on the *limes* were *legio* XVII, *legio* XVIII, and *legio* XIX, these variously given the cognomens *Gallica* and *Germanica* at one time or another. All were originally Caesarian foundings disbanded after the dictator's death and then refounded by Octavian to fight in the final round of Republican civil wars (Pollard and Berry, 2015, 55). Second, he was overlooked to take command of the new military operation in Illyricum. Augustus knew Varus was an administrator and not a soldier, better suited to his task on the Rhine, with Goldsworthy adding this showed Augustus believed him '...capable rather than gifted...' (2014, 447).

Soon Varus was in trouble. Despite the severe cuts to his military capability, he continued establishing *Romanitas* in the fully pacified regions of Germania at full pace. This included the introduction of Roman law and the imposition of new taxes. However, the latter infuriated the native Germans who were unused to Roman ways. Soon even the tribal leaders who had signed peace treaties with Rome began to push back. Some now cannily made up fictitious lawsuits against each other to occupy Varus and his administrators, while ignoring his tax collectors. This lulled the Romans into a false sense of security, with the German leaders heaping praise on Varus every time he settled one of their 'disputes'. However, in reality they were playing for time, gathering resources for a rebellion against Roman rule. And here they had a deadly surprise ready, one of staggering magnitude. This was Arminius, son of the Cherusci tribal leader Segimer, ostensibly a key Roman ally. The former was already an experienced Roman officer, having led auxiliary units in battle after his father had been forced to send him to Rome as a boy. Now apparently 'Romanised', Arminius had recently joined the staff of Varus on the Rhine frontier as a tribune, setting the scene for one of the greatest betrayals in military history.

By this time Varus had finally realised the German tribal leaders were stalling his planned process of bringing Roman rule to Germania. Therefore, in early AD 9 he introduced martial law to deal with any Germans who refused to accept Roman law or pay their new taxes. Varus had a reputation as a harsh disciplinarian, and before long summary executions were taking place, with families enslaved for sale in the slave markets of Trier (Roman Augusta Treverorum) and Mainz (Roman Mogantium), and German property seized and destroyed.

Unsurprisingly, what had begun as German obstinacy now turned into something much darker, with relations totally breaking down with the Romans. It is at this point Arminius began his betrayal of Varus, though historiography is an issue given we have no detail of his specific motivation. It is worth remembering he'd spent most of his adult life among the Romans, and as far as they were concerned was fully Roman. Goldsworthy suggests he was driven by '…anger at his own and other tribes' loss of independence…' (2014, 449), though I would go further. This was a dramatic, life-altering decision for one so used to the luxuries of 'civilised' living. Perhaps some extreme slight occurred against Arminius' close family, as later happened with Boudicca in Britain. Sadly, the likelihood is we will never know exactly what happened, but we can be sure of one thing. The result was a terrible disaster for Augustus and the Romans.

In the first instance, Arminius began to secretly forge an anti-Roman alliance among the most fractious German tribes, including his native Cherusci, the Chatti, Marsi, and Bructeri. Warming to his task while still serving on Varus' command team, he then looked to bring the Romans to battle on his own terms. That meant an ambush. Here, he proved a skilful diplomat as well as warrior. At the beginning of August, he convinced some of the leading tribal groupings to stage a minor rebellion, on a scale just large enough to oblige Varus to respond in force given the Roman leader knew he would lose face if it wasn't quickly stamped out. Varus received news of the revolt while travelling from the river Weser to his winter headquarters at Mainz, and quickly set about planning a short campaign. The last thing he wanted was a delay to his plans for Romanising Germania, with Augustus expecting his new province to come into being shortly.

We now have the curious tale of Varus being warned of Arminius' treachery. Tacitus says that another Cheruscan nobleman called Segestes, leader of the tribe's pro-Roman faction, told Varus the night before the Roman forces departed that they were being led into a trap (*The Annals*, 9.16). Segestes then went further, suggesting Varus apprehend Arminius along with some other Germanic leaders he identified as the perpetrators of the insurrection. Tacitus adds that Segestes was Arminius' father-in-law, the latter having married the former's daughter, Thusnelda, against her father's wishes. For some reason, perhaps because of the bad blood between Arminius and Segestes, Varus ignored the warning and foolishly left Arminius to his own devices. The German quickly left the Roman camp under the pretext of drumming up native support in advance of the Romans launching their campaign. Sadly for the Varus, once Arminius was free from prying eyes he quickly took command of those Cherusci warriors loyal to him, and shortly afterwards of the whole German army.

Having dismissed Segestes' warning, the unwary Varus was ready and set off. It was now the beginning of September in AD 9, late in the campaigning season, and he expected a short campaign with little opposition once his troops confronted the German rebels. His army comprised the three legions on the frontier, together with six *cohorts* of auxiliary foot troops and three *alae* of auxiliary cavalry. Given an early imperial legion numbered (at full strength) 5,500 men, an auxiliary foot *cohort* either 480 troops in a *quingenary* unit or 800 in a *milliary* unit, and an auxiliary cavalry *ala* 512 in a *quingenary* unit or 768 in a *milliary* unit, this gave Varus a total force of between 20,916 and 30,900 men. Either way this was a sizable army, the latter the same scale as that used by Agricola in his AD 83 Mons Graupius campaign in modern Scotland. Though nowhere near the size of the vast armies used in earlier Roman campaigns in Germany, Varus still believed his force easily up to the task at hand given he chose not to call up his two theatre reserve legions. These were the highly experienced *legio* I *Germanica* and *legio* V *Alaudae*, both based at Trier under the command of his own nephew, Lucius Asprenas (Pollard and Berry, 2012, 57).

At first, and despite bad weather, Varus made good progress. Given the size of his army, any German tribes they came across quickly submitted. Soon his vast column, which Goldsworthy suggests may have stretched 16km long (2014, 451), was snaking well to the northeast of modern Osnabrück in Lower Saxony, heading for what Varus thought was the epicentre of the rebellion. No doubt continually fed false information by the Cherusci scouts supplied by Arminius, Varus led his men deeper and deeper into the German forested interior. However, as the end of September approached and the decisive engagement he'd been expecting failed to materialise, Varus came to the conclusion that his mission was accomplished. Keen to continue establishing his new province, he ordered the Roman column to slowly turn around and head back to the Rhine. However, Arminius was watching. The rebel leader had been busy planning his assault, and now Varus' guard was down he determined the time right to spring his trap.

Before I set out my own view on how the battle unfolded from this point, I now consider three key issues to set the scene and provide context. First, the nature of the engagement, second its exact location, and third the size of the German army involved.

In terms of the type of encounter, each primary source differs with regard to the finer detail. This is not surprising given all had different motivations in how they depicted Varus' shocking defeat. Further, some are broadly contemporary, while others were written long after the event. I begin with the earliest, the account of Paterculus, who knew both Varus and Arminius. He describes a classic large-scale ambush in the field, saying (*Roman History*, 2.119):

> Varus was surrounded and attacked, with no opportunity as he had wished to give the soldiers a chance of either fighting or of extricating themselves, except against heavy odds. Hemmed in by forests and marshes and ambuscades, his army was exterminated almost to a man by the very enemy whom it had earlier always slaughtered like cattle, and whose life or death had depended solely upon the wrath or the pity of the Romans.

Next, writing in the early 2nd century AD, Tacitus is briefer given his focus on the later punitive campaigns of Tiberius and Germanicus. He says only that (*Annals*, I.55):

> …Varus succumbed to his fate and the sword of Arminius rather than listen to the warnings of his father-in-law Segestes to have him arrested.

Meanwhile, the contemporary North African-born poet, orator, and historian Julius Florus says Varus was actually engaged in diplomacy with the German confederations and tribes when attacked, possibly while still in camp. Specifically, he says (*Epitome of Roman History*, 30.1):

> At a moment when, such was his confidence, he was actually summoning the German leaders to appear before his tribunal, they rose and attacked him from all sides. His camp was seized and three legions were overwhelmed.

Also writing at this time, Suetonius covers the Varian Disaster (or as he styles it, the *clades variana*) in his chapters on Augustus and Tiberius. In the first instance, he says (*The Twelve Caesars, Augustus, 23*):

> Augustus suffered two severe and ignominious defeats, those of Lollius and Varus. Of these the former was more humiliating than serious, but the latter was almost fatal, since three legions were cut to pieces with their general, his lieutenants, and all the auxiliaries. When the news of this came, he ordered that watch be kept by night throughout the city, to prevent an outbreak of violence and protest, and prolonged the terms of the governors of the provinces, that the allies might be held to their allegiance by experienced men with whom they were acquainted. He also vowed great games to Jupiter Optimus Maximus, hoping the condition of the commonwealth would improve, a thing which had been done in the Cimbrian War.

Meanwhile, in his chapter on Tiberius, Suetonius adds that defeat of the Illyrian revolt at around the same time as the Varian Disaster proved timely given it stopped a likely alliance between the victorious Germans on the Rhine and the various German tribes on the Danube frontier (*The Twelve Caesars, Tiberius, 17*, see below regarding the response of the Marcomanni after Varus' defeat).

Finally, when writing in the early 3rd century AD, Cassius Dio presents the Roman defeat as a classic large-scale trap in the field, saying that while the Romans were returning to the Rhine frontier and were struggling with the weather conditions, Arminius struck. He says (*Roman History, 56.20*):

> The barbarians suddenly surrounded the Romans on all sides at once, coming through the densest thickets, as they were acquainted with the paths. At first they hurled their volleys from a distance; then, as no one defended himself and many were wounded, they approached closer to them.

The key point to note in all of these narratives is the broad agreement that Varus' force was ambushed by Arminius on a large scale, and as we will see, more than once.

Next, regarding the location of the main engagement, until recently this was very difficult to determine given we have so little historical detail. Early theories emerged in the late 15th century AD with the rediscovery of key classical texts, including new chapters of Tacitus' *The Germania* and *The Annals*. In particular, the latter records a region called the saltus Teutoburgiensis. This was the first mention of the Teutoburg Forest, which Tacitus said was a huge, wooded region in Germania. Early antiquarians quickly identified this as the land between the upper reaches of the Ems and Lippe rivers. However, by the early 19th century AD academic opinion had changed, with the vast forest now located along a huge, wooded ridge called the Osning Forest near

Bielefeld in North Rhine-Westphalia. Soon, this had been officially renamed the Teutoburg Forest, a name it retains to this day.

With the location of the forest identified, academic attention then turned to where within it the actual main Varian Disaster engagement took place. By the mid-1960s four broad theories were in circulation. These were that it occurred in the Weser Hills, in the eastern half of the Teutoburg Forest near the Weser itself, in the southern Teutoburg Forest near Beckum in the northern part of North Rhine-Westphalia, and finally southeast of the Westphalian lowlands.

However, by the late 20th century AD archaeology began to play a key role in finally locating the specific Teutoburg Forest battle site. Here, finds of Augustan coins and lead Roman slingshots at Kalkriese Hill between the villages of Venne and Engter near Osnabrück led to an intensive investigation. Soon, large quantities of early 1st century AD Roman and German battlefield debris were found, these numbering over 6,000 artefacts to date. Most recently, an almost complete set of early *lorica segmentata* banded iron armour was excavated there.

Subsequent archaeological research after the initial finds at Kalkriese Hill has revealed that the battlefield archaeology in the region is actually spread along a 24km long, 1.6km wide corridor running south from the deepest Roman penetration back towards Kalkriese Hill, this being Varus' most likely route back to the Rhine frontier, as we will see. Further, likely German field defences have also been discovered at Kalkriese Hill. The whole region is also beset with deep ravines and rough terrain, a key aspect of contemporary descriptions of the battle. Together, all of this historical, archaeological, analogous, and anecdotal evidence has led to Kalkriese Hill becoming the most popular speculative location for the main Teutoburg Forest engagement.

In terms of the German force engaged in the battle, Pollard and Berry say Arminius' army initially comprised a large gathering of nobles and warriors from his own Cherusci tribe, and also from the Bructeri and Marsi (2012, 56). Contingents from other German tribes later joined after his initial ambush, when its success attracted other Germans after fame and loot, as I detail below. His force may also have featured deserting Germanic recruits from Roman auxiliary units in the region, as later occurred en masse during the Batavian Revolt in AD 69/70. Such troops would have been better equipped than most Germans fighting in their native manner. Regarding numbers for Arminius' force, this is difficult to determine. Initially, his army may have only been 15,000 strong, far smaller than Varus' huge army. This was later bolstered by other Germans joining once victory seemed certain.

Having set the scene for the battle and provided key context, I argue below it comprised three phases over two days and one night. First, Arminius' initial ambush deep in the forested interior. Second, Varus' night-time attempt to extricate his army. Third, Arminius' final ambush at Kalkriese Hill, which I determine was the main encounter.

Back to the chronological narrative, Arminius had already observed Varus turning his huge column back towards the Rhine frontier, and carefully chose a location for his initial ambush that would funnel the Romans into a pre-planned killing zone. He deployed his Cherusci, Bructeri, and Marsi warriors in ambuscade positions, and waited for the Romans to march past. As the head of the lengthy Roman column almost cleared his trap late in the morning, Arminius struck at the front and sides en masse, the Germans launching themselves on the unsuspecting Romans from deep within the forest with savage ferocity. This initial ambush shocked Varus and his troops, with many panicking in the bad weather and difficult terrain. Soon the Roman column disarticulated into large but isolated units along their line of march. In some places, where the Germans managed to achieve local numerical superiority, they overwhelmed the Romans and their camp followers, with the first of many massacres taking place. In other areas, large groups of Romans maintained coherence, standing their ground and fighting off the German onrush. However, Varus then made a crucial error by ordering the main baggage train burnt. Though intended to lighten his men's load, allowing them to march more quickly out of the danger zone, the move actually caused morale to plummet given it signalled the true jeopardy they were in.

Varus now ordered his surviving units to break out into open country. This was towards the Wiehen Hills near modern Ostercappeln. As the day went on, his Romans were harried all the way by parties of Germans darting out of the murky undergrowth to pick off weaker units. Soon, as late afternoon approached, Roman casualties began to mount again. Goldsworthy says that by this point only an exceptional commander would have been able to extricate the Romans from their desperate predicament (2014, 452). Varus was certainly not that.

Meanwhile, Arminius knew total victory was within his grasp, and as word spread of his amazing success, other warriors from neighbouring tribes now began to join him. Cassius Dio adds detail here, saying that by this point (*Roman History*, 56.21):

> ...the German forces had greatly increased, as many of those who had at first wavered joined them, largely in the hope of plunder, and thus they could more easily encircle and strike down the Romans, whose ranks were now thinned, many having perished in the earlier fighting.

Still, many Romans survived the day, in places in sufficient numbers to maintain their increasingly isolated formations and begin the process of building marching camps. However, before they could complete the task, Varus ordered a drastic change of strategy. With no idea how many Germans were surrounding him as night fell, he convinced himself a desperate march in the darkness was their only hope of reaching safety. The canny Arminius had anticipated this and knew exactly where the Romans would travel – along a wide, sandy expanse of open terrain that led directly to the foot of Kalkriese Hill. There the Germans prepared their final, huge ambush.

As the Romans approached in the dark, their way lit by damp torches, the route began to narrow. Finally, they were funnelled onto a 100m wide sand bar, with dense woodland and swamps closing in on either side. Given the weight of numbers to their rear, those at the front had no choice but to continue. As they did, they were increasingly attacked from all sides, with small groups of legionaries, *auxilia*, and camp followers dragged screaming into the pitch-black night. Florus graphically describes their fate, saying (*Epitome of Roman History*, 2.30):

> The Germans put out the eyes of some men and cut off the hands of others. They cut off the tongue of one man and sewed up his mouth, and one of the barbarians, holding the tongue in his hands, exclaimed 'That stopped your hissing, you viper.'

Finally, as a rainy dawn broke on the second day, the head of the Roman column came to a shuddering halt when, out of the gloom, it reached a freshly built series of German fortifications on Kalkriese Hill. These comprised deep trenches with palisaded earthen walls, now swarming with German warriors. As terror and confusion rippled down the Roman line of march, Arminius now launched his final mass ambush. Those Romans to the rear were soon overpowered, but those near the front made a final desperate attempt to storm the German defences. The frenzy here is still evident in today's landscape, with the still visible German defences scattered with a huge amount of Roman battlefield archaeology. Given much of this has been found on the far side of the earthen walls, many Romans managed to fight their way over in their desperation, only to be slaughtered on the far side. Animal remains have also been found, including one mule skeleton with a broken neck where it had fallen down the far side, and another with the remains of grass stuffed into its bell to muffle the sound during the earlier night march. As Varus had already ordered the baggage train to be destroyed earlier in the engagement, these may have been carrying Roman wounded.

Sadly for Varus, despite the heroism of these surviving troops, the Roman attempt to force their way through Arminius' barrier failed. At that point command and control finally broke down in the Roman ranks. Varus' second in command, the *legate* Numonius Vala, fled with the remaining auxiliary cavalry, but was soon hunted down by Germans and killed (Paterculus, *Roman History*, 2.119). Two other senior officers also soon fell, the *prefect* Eggius dying while leading a last stand with his bodyguard, while another called Ceionius took his own life after being captured. Cassius Dio describes a brutal endgame, with any surviving Romans butchered or having taken their own lives. The last surviving members of Varus' command team chose the last option, including their commander, with Dio saying (*Roman History*, 16.21):

> Varus, therefore, and all the more prominent officers, fearing that they should either be captured alive or be killed by their bitterest foes (for they had already been wounded), made bold to do a thing that was terrible yet unavoidable: they took their own lives.

The battle was over. Varus was dead, and his army was entirely destroyed. Roman losses numbered in the tens of thousands, including all of the legionaries and most of the auxiliaries. Tacitus says that any captive Roman officers were gruesomely sacrificed as part of the German tribal ceremonies celebrating the victory, graphically adding some were cooked in pots, their bleached bones then used in religious rituals (*The Annals*, 1.61). Meanwhile, any other Roman captives who survived German brutality were quickly enslaved, disappearing into the German interior never to be seen again.

Crucially for morale back in Rome, Varus' army also lost hundreds of battle standards. These included the *aquila* (eagle) standards of the three legions, which only left the chapel of the standards in a legionary fortress when the entire legion was marching to battle. The loss of one was viewed as shameful. The loss of three was beyond the understanding of many Romans, with Augustus decreeing their numbers – XVII, XVIII, and XIX – suffer *damnatio memoriae* and be officially struck from the Senatorial record.

In Rome the blame game began straight away, with Varus in the frame immediately. This wasn't undeserved, given he had arrogantly ignored Segestes' warning of Arminius' treachery and then led his army on a doomed march into a heart of darkness he clearly didn't understand. Augustus undoubtedly blamed him, with Suetonius graphically describing the emperor's response which, based on this narrative, caused a psychotic episode (*The Twelve Caesars*, Augustus, 23):

> Augustus was so greatly affected that for several months in succession he cut neither his beard nor his hair, and sometimes he would dash his head against a door, crying: 'Quintilius Varus, give me back my legions!' And he observed the day of the disaster each year as one of sorrow and mourning.

Varus certainly paid a terrible price for his catastrophic failure, even post-mortem. Paterculus morbidly describes the fate of his remains, discovered by the Germans after his suicide (*Roman History*, 2.119):

> The body of Varus, partially burned, was mangled by the enemy in their barbarity; his head was cut off and taken to Maroboduus [king of the Marcomanni on the Danube frontier] and was sent by him to Augustus; but in spite of the disaster it was honoured by burial in the tomb of his family.

Arminius clearly hoped the arrival of Varus' severed head would encourage the Marcomanni to join their assault on the Roman frontier. However, the shrewd Maroboduus knew the Romans would never let such a defeat stand.

Based on the contemporary written record, this was Arminius' only misstep. The focus on the failures and shortcomings of Varus in modern commentary (and on Augustus' decision to appoint him in the first place) often masks how skilful a campaign Arminius fought. Teutoburg Forest was as much a German victory as a Roman defeat, and in its aftermath Arminius joined the pantheon of literary foes the Romans thought worthy enemies, with Tacitus calling him '…beyond doubt the liberator of Germany…' (*The Annals*, 2.88).

However, despite Rome's shocking loss to Arminius, the Rhine frontier was soon stabilized, and this time by a real warrior. This was the future emperor Tiberius, with retribution for the Germans swiftly following as he and then Germanicus launched huge legionary spearheads north into Germania. By that time though, the damage to the Roman psyche had already been done, and never again would they plan to settle there. From that time the northern frontier in the west would be set firmly by the *limes Germanicus*. Indeed, it was east along the Danubian frontier where Rome next had cause to fear the barbarians.

The Marcomannic Wars

The Marcomannic Wars fought along the Danube from the later AD 160s featured a series of conflicts that tested the Roman–Danubian frontier there to breaking point, and often broke it. It was here on the northern *limes* that in AD 170 the Roman lynchpin fortress at Carnuntum was destroyed, with its garrison wiped out in open battle. This shattering defeat, which occurred when the attention of the emperor Marcus Aurelius was elsewhere in the region, allowed thousands of Marcomanni and Quadi warriors to stream across the border into imperial territory. Soon they were in Italy, the first Germanic invasion there for 300 years, with panic ensuing in Rome on a scale to match the *terror cimbricus*.

Rome's principal opponents in these wars were the Germanic Marcomanni, Juthungi, and Quadi, and their Sarmatian Iazyges allies. They were all being driven hard against Rome's northern Danubian frontiers by the westward expansion of the Visigoths and Ostrogoths. These German peoples to their east were themselves being driven westwards by the early expansion of the Huns.

The Marcomanni were descended from the Suebi, the huge German confederation which had fought Julius Caesar in his Gallic conquests in the 50s BC. By the mid-AD 160s they had migrated away from the borders of Gallo-Roman territory to settle in what is now modern Bohemia. Meanwhile, the Juthungi were also Suebian by origin, they now residing near their original homelands in modern Bavaria. Finally, the Quadi (again originally Suebian) lived further east in modern Moravia. Additionally, by this time the fearsome Iazyges Sarmatians had settled near the Danubian *limes* in what is now modern Hungary and northern Serbia, travelling there from the Pontic Steppe over the previous century.

The Marcomannic Wars began in AD 166. Here, 6,000 Germanic Lombard and Lacringi warriors forced their way over the Danubian *limes* into Pannonia Superior (Heather, 2009, 96). Although they were soon defeated by *cohorts* from *legio* I *Adiutrix pia fidelis* under the command of a *legate* called Candidus, supported by the auxiliary cavalry *ala Ulpia Contariorum* unit under the Senator Marcus Macrinius Avitus Catonius Vindex, their initial success did not go unnoticed by the other German tribes along the northern frontier, setting a trend lasting for the next 14 years.

After these initial breaches of the frontier, the Romans first tried the tactic they had traditionally used when trying to keep the German tribes quiet: bribing their elites with huge amounts of portable wealth. Shortly after Marcus Iallius Bassus, governor of Pannonia Superior (a noted literary figure and also an adopted member of Marcus Aurelius' family), then started negotiations with the 11 most aggressive tribes to set in place a long-lasting truce along the Rhine and Danube. This was soon agreed with the help of the Marcomanni overking Ballomar, after which any Germans remaining on the south side of the Danube withdrew back to their home territories.

However, sadly for the Romans, although they thought this a permanent peace deal, the Germans didn't. Soon trouble was again mounting along the frontier, and later in AD 166 this was tested again when the Sarmatian Iazyges, together with their Germanic Vandal allies (this the first time the Vandals are mentioned in conflict with Rome, with full contextual detail in Chapter 3), invaded the redoubt province of Dacia north of the Danube. Here the frontier defences failed completely, with the provincial governor Calpurnius Proculus killed when leading a hastily assembled army to its doom in an attempt to stem the incoming tide of invaders. The Iazyges and Vandals then penetrated deep into the provincial interior, with the emperor forced in extremis to redeploy the veteran *legio* IV *Macedonia* from Moesia Inferior in order to drive the invaders out of Dacia. An uneasy peace then settled in the region, though again this wasn't to last.

Back in Rome, the two co-emperors Marcus Aurelius and Lucius Verus viewed the ongoing threat north of the Danube as serious. Taking advice from their leading military advisors, they quickly determined to carry out a major punitive expedition against the Iazyges and Vandals. It is unclear whether they intended to physically conquer new territory north of the Danube in this campaign, though it seems unlikely given the abandonment of any similar ambitions north of the Rhine after Varus' disastrous defeat in AD 9. More likely their ambition was a punitive expedition on a grand scale. Whichever it was, sadly for them it was not to be as in AD 167 a serious pandemic broke out across the Mediterranean and Levant which put their plans on hold for that year. Today this is called the Antonine Plague, an event so serious the emperors were forced to recruit bandits, gladiators, and Germans to fill the depleted ranks of the Roman military (*Historia Augusta*, Marcus Aurelius, 21.6).

By AD 168 things had stabilized in Rome. The emperors now headed north to *Aquileia* on the north-eastern Adriatic Coast, establishing their forward headquarters there. They then dispatched orders to all of the military units along the Danubian frontier to provide troops to help create an enormous army to campaign across the Danube, planning to lead this in person. Their new force included two newly raised legions, *legio* II *Italica* and *legio* III *Italica*. The emperors first targeted marauding bands of Marcomanni, Quadi, and Victohali tribesmen who'd taken advantage of the disruption caused by the plague in AD 167 to attack Pannonia Superior. However, as the Romans approached the important legionary fortress of Carnuntum (also headquarters of the *Classis Flavia Pannonica*), the Germans swiftly withdrew, providing assurances of future good conduct. Marcus Aurelius and Lucius Verus then returned to Aquileia to overwinter, leaving their army ready for further campaigning in AD 169. However, the death of Lucius Verus in January that year put back military operations once more, with Marcus Aurelius having to return to Rome to supervise Verus' funeral.

Now sole emperor, Marcus Aurelius returned to the offensive that autumn. His first target was the Iazyges, though the war at first went badly for the Romans. This was because the Sarmatians struck first, attacking the important Roman gold mines at Alburnum in Dacia. Marcus Aurelius then ordered his friend Claudius Fronto, the governor of Moesia Inferior, to gather a local force there and intercept the Iazyges. However, in the ensuing encounter, the governor was killed and his force destroyed. Meanwhile, with the emperor's attention focused on this crisis, several German tribes along the Danube decided to use this as an opportunity to raid deep into Roman territory. In the east, these included the Dacian Costoboci, who struck Thracia with savage ferocity from their Carpathian Mountain homelands. They rampaged through the province, soon reaching Greece proper. There, near Athens, they destroyed the ancient Temple of the Eleusinian Mysteries.

Sadly for Marcus Aurelius, however, this wasn't his biggest problem. This was because, across the Danube, the Marcomanni overking Ballomar now seized his chance and launched an invasion deep into Pannonia Superior. Gathering his own warriors, and Quadi allies too, he first headed directly for Carnuntum where he forced a decisive meeting engagement with the Romans in AD 170. Here the Romans suffered a great defeat, one of the biggest of the Marcomannic Wars as a whole, with *legio* XIV *Gemina Martia Victrix* and 14,000 auxiliaries almost destroyed. Ballomar's army then split in two. One column headed west to ravage the province of Noricum, while the other continued south where it sacked the city of Oderzo (Roman Opitergium) in north east Italy and then besieged *Aquileia*. This sent shock waves through the Roman world of a kind not experienced since the Cimbrian Wars. Marcus Aurelius, still on the Danube to the north, quickly ordered the *Praetorian Prefect* Titus Furius Victorinus to hastily gather an army to repel the Germans, but he was promptly defeated and killed, the third senior Roman leader to die since the troubles had begun.

Marcus Aurelius was now faced with a very serious situation. He therefore turned to the up-and-coming trouble-shooter Pertinax, later briefly emperor in AD 193, to take the fight to the enemy. First, he promoted Pertinax to the post of procurator in both Dacia and Moesia Superior, the general then immediately setting his command team to work reordering the economy of Dacia. This had been so severely damaged by the earlier incursion of the Iazyges that the finances there were in total disarray. However, soon taxes from the region's industry, agriculture, and population began to once more flow into the imperial *fiscus* (treasury), allowing new troops to be raised and frontier fortifications to be strengthened.

Then, in spring of AD 171, the emperor was at last ready to strike back. First, he swiftly redeployed the legions from the northern frontier to the imperial interior to challenge the raiding Germans, the latter by this time running out of provisions. He then appointed the highly experienced Tiberius

Claudius Pompeianus as commander in chief, who immediately recruited Pertinax as his chief aide. Pertinax served with Pompeianus for only a short time while the Romans made preparations to go back on the offensive. He was then elevated again, this time to become an adlected Senator, allowing him to take command of *legio* I *Adiutrix pia fidelis* in Pannonia Superior as part of Pompeianus' wider military reorganization on the Danubian frontier. This widespread activity included increasing the size of the *Classis Flavia Moesica* on the lower Danube, and also the building of a new series of defence-in-depth fortifications in northern Italy called the *praetentura Italiae et Alpium*.

Pompeianus then divided his force into spearheads of legions and auxiliaries, outmanoeuvring the Germans and quickly relieving Aquileia. The routed Marcomanni and Quadi then fled back north across the Danube, suffering heavy casualties in the process. Meanwhile, another column of Roman troops, under Pertinax, struck out for the second German force that was still ravaging Noricum. More success for the Romans followed; this second German force was also driven beyond the Danube with heavy loss of life. The emperor then publicly praised both Pompeianus and Pertinax for their sterling service bringing order back to the Danubian *limes*.

However, Marcus Aurelius knew his forces were still in no position to go on the offensive across the Danube against the Germans in their homelands. Therefore, he chose to consolidate his forces along the northern *limes*, rebuilding and reinforcing the defences there again, especially where they had been earlier overrun. Intense diplomatic activity followed as the emperor attempted to win over as many German and Sarmatian leaders as possible before he went back on the counterattack. Specifically, peace treaties were signed with the Quadi and the Iazyges, and also with the Silingi and Hasdingi Vandals. All then became, at least ostensibly, Roman allies, they agreeing to provide warriors for his future campaigns (all fully detailed in Chapter 3).

By spring AD 172 the Romans were finally ready to go on the offensive. Marcus Aurelius then launched a massive assault across the Danube from Pannonia Superior and Noricum, his target the Marcomanni and any German and Sarmatian tribes who were still allied with them. This proved highly successful, with the weight of numbers quickly working in Rome's favour. Ballomar's loose confederation was shattered, with the Marcomanni quickly suing for peace and the emperor taking the title 'Germanicus', with coins also minted featuring the phrase 'Germania Capta'. Pertinax, by now leading *legio* I *Italica*, was again in the vanguard. However, another *legate* gained the greatest fame, this being Marcus Valerius Maximianus, who while leading the Pannonia

Inferior-based *legio* II *Adiutrix pia fidelis*, killed the chieftain of the German Naristi tribe in single combat. As a reward, the emperor granted the *legate* the chieftain's fine stallion.

The Romans campaigned north of the Danube again in AD 173, this time against the Quadi who had predictably broken their earlier treaty. Once more, Roman victory followed swiftly, though this campaign is perhaps best known for the 'rain miracle' incident which is recorded on the Column of Marcus Aurelius in Rome. Here *legio* XII *Fulminata*, and perhaps Pertinax with *legio* I *Adiutrix pia fidelis*, had been encircled by a large force of Quadi. They were on the brink of surrendering because of thirst and heat at the height of summer, when a sudden thunderstorm provided a deluge that refreshed the Roman troops, while a lightning strike on the Quadi camp sent the Germans bolting away in terror.

The next Roman campaign in the conflict was on the Rhine frontier. Here, the future emperor Didius Julianus (who briefly succeeded Pertinax in the 'Year of the Five Emperors') was the governor of Gallia Belgica, a post he had held since AD 170. This province, which had once been home to some of Julius Caesar's most determined Gallic opponents when he conquered Gaul in the 50s BC, stood just south of the northern border provinces of Germania Inferior and Germania Superior. In AD 173, the region suffered a major incursion from the Germanic Chauci over the Rhine. Taking advantage of the Roman focus on their troubles along the Danubian *limes*, they smashed through the defences along the lower Rhine, penetrating deep into the rich farmlands of modern Flanders. The legions and auxiliaries in the two German provinces struggled to contain this threat, with Didius Julianus forced to raise a new force of local recruits, these probably veterans settled in the regional *coloniae*. He then led them to great effect, and soon the Germans were forced back over the Rhine. The governor then began a programme of re-fortification along the English Channel coast of his province, before returning victorious to Rome to celebrate a triumph with the emperor.

With the Rhine frontier stabilized, in early AD 174, Marcus Aurelius was now ready to go on the offensive again. He crossed the Danube with another huge force, targeting any of the Quadi tribes still holding out against the Romans. There, over the winter, a number of tribes had deposed the pro-Roman king Furtius, replacing him with an arch rival called Ariogaesus. However, the emperor refused to recognize him, forcing him to stand down and then sending him to Alexandria where he lived out the rest of his life in exile. By the end of AD 174 the whole of the Quadi confederation were subjugated, their leading nobles sending hostages to Rome and Quadi warriors recruited into the ranks of the Roman auxiliaries, with Roman garrisons additionally being installed in new forts throughout their territory.

Marcus Aurelius had one more piece of unfinished business along the Danubian frontier, this to punish the Sarmatian Iazyges for the death of his friend Fronto in AD 169. Thus, in AD 175 he once more gathered a mighty army, launching a new assault from Pannonia Inferior and Dacia deep into their homelands. He called this his *expeditio sarmatica*, targeting the plain of the River Tizsa in modern Hungary where he won a series of victories. After this, the leading Iazyges king Zanticus surrendered, with a peace treaty agreed. Any surviving captured Roman prisoners were then returned, with the Iazyges agreeing to supply Rome with 8,000 *contos* (lance) armed cavalry. Marcus Aurelius then took the title 'Sarmaticus', and once more minted coins to celebrate victory. This ended the First Marcomannic War.

Here we have remarkable first-person insight into the true jeopardy facing the empire in this lengthy conflict through the words of the Marcus Aurelius himself, this in the form of his philosophical musings written down in Greek when on campaign, which he styled *To Himself*. These survive to this day as his *Meditations*. Given the unpredictable nature of the first conflict in the Marcomannic Wars, I think one observation is particularly prescient (5.9):

> Do not be distressed, do not despond or give up in despair, if now and again practice falls short of precept. Return to the attack after each failure, and be thankful if on the whole you acquit yourself in the majority of cases as a man should.

However, even though he had secured a peace with the Germans, the emperor's resolve was soon tested yet again. This was because in early AD 177 the Quadi again reneged on their peace agreement and attacked the Danubian frontier. Predictably, the Marcomanni soon followed, and so began the Second Marcomannic War. This new conflict quickly spread along the upper Danube, and soon the Germans had penetrated across the *limes* and began raiding imperial territory. The emperor reacted swiftly, calling this new campaign the *secunda expeditio germanica*. With his legions and auxiliaries again led by Marcus Valerius Maximianus, Marcus Aurelius arrived at Carnuntum on the lower Danube in August AD 178. There the Romans forced a meeting engagement with the Marcomanni, comprehensively defeating them. The Romans then targeted the Quadi, these almost wiped out at the battle of Laugaricio in modern Slovakia. The few German survivors were then chased back beyond the Danube, where the Praetorian Prefect Tarruntenus Paternus led a punitive campaign against them in the Quadi homelands, which he ravaged.

Campaigning along the Danube ended dramatically though on 17 March AD 180 when Marcus Aurelius died of natural causes in Vienna (Roman Vindobona), aged 58. He was succeeded by his son Commodus, who had no interest in continuing his father's campaigns in the north. Instead, he was keen to return to Rome to secure his position. Commodus quickly established new peace treaties with all of his German and Sarmatian opponents, this against the advice of his senior military commanders. His terms included the Marcomanni and Quadi providing 20,000 warriors to serve in the Roman military, these distributed to auxiliary units throughout the empire. Those who remained were partially disarmed, and then forbidden from attacking their Iazyges and Vandal neighbours without permission from Rome. Finally, the Germans were additionally forbidden from settling along a narrow strip on the northern bank of the Danube, and also the various large islands along the river's length. The new emperor then left for Rome in early September AD 180, he celebrating a solo triumph there on 22 October. This ended the Second Marcomannic War, with the so called 'Peace of Commodus'.

Sadly for Commodus, trouble north of the Danube continued and soon the Iazyges and the Germanic Buri, whose homeland was to the north of the Marcomanni and Quadi near the headwaters of the Vistula river, rebelled once more. Again the emperor ordered his legions and auxiliaries north of the Danube, with victories quickly following, to be celebrated by Maximianus once more, and also the leading Senators Pescennius Niger and Clodius Albinus, both to play key roles in the 'Year of the Five Emperors'. When a lengthy peace finally descended on the northern frontier in AD 182 Commodus then himself celebrated by taking the title 'Germanicus Maximus'. This finally ended the most challenging series of conflicts faced by the empire for over a century, and one that, given the settlement of many Germans within the empire afterwards, began a process which was to change the very nature of imperial identity.

Having considered Rome's experiences, all negative in the extreme, fighting barbarians in the Gallic war of 387 BC, the *terror cimbricus*, the *clades variana*, and the Marcomannic Wars, we can now turn to the story of the Vandals, fully understanding how their depiction by historians of the classical and late antique worlds was shaped.

CHAPTER 3

Vandal Origins

The Vandals were a Germanic people who, through ill repute, are still associated to this day with antisocial behaviour of the worst kind. Modern historians often comment on this when narrating their story, with for example MacDowall saying (2016, 1):

> The very name conjures up violent images of wanton destruction. It is a label given to those that deliberately destroy or damage property.

Taking a similar line, Matyszak adds (2022, 241):

> If asked for an archetypal tribe that rampaged around the late Roman empire like a barbarian wrecking ball, the Vandals would be many people's first choice.

But do the Vandals deserve this reputation? In this book I later argue not, and in so doing re-interpret the story of post-Roman North Africa. First, however, I begin their tale in this chapter at the point they first appear in the historical and archaeological record.

To start, I provide a detailed physical description of *barbaricum*, as the Romans styled the lands north and east of the Rhine and Danube. This includes an analysis of the border region with the Roman world there, then a geographic description of *barbaricum* as the Romans knew it, before detailing the impact of climate and climate change on the region in the classical and late antique worlds. I then consider the German and Gothic peoples referenced in this book, including an analysis of their origins and their early religious beliefs. Finally, I focus on the Vandals themselves, examining their story from their first appearance to the point they crossed the Rhine in mid-winter AD 406 as part of an enormous diaspora alongside Alans and Suebi, never to return to their homeland in the east.

Note that while we do have primary source material to use regarding the early story of the Vandals, as detailed it is always written from a Roman or post-Roman perspective. Further, historians ever since have interpreted this literary data in their own way, often with a specific purpose in mind. However, what you read here is my own narrative, in which I provide a firm timeline to enable the reader to engage with their unlikely story, all based on my personal interpretation of the primary sources and archaeological data, and aided by my recent visits to North Africa.

Barbaricum

By the 1st century BC the word *barbaricum* was being specifically used in the Roman world to describe the enormous region north and east of the Rhine and Danube, particularly after the frontier was fixed firmly in place along the two continental river lines by Augustus after the Varian Disaster and his more successful campaigns to the east. This was a vast area, and a true heart of darkness for the Romans who were more used to their civilised (as they saw it) Mediterranean world with its warmer climate. However, Roman interests did remain to the north and east in a variety of ways, as I detail below.

The Border Region

Any frontier is a place where power, commerce, and ideas intermix, and that was certainly the case along the northern Roman *limes*. In the first instance, the military presence there was very noticeable for much of the Principate given the legions and auxiliaries were specifically based along the empire's borders rather than deeper within imperial territory (Pollard and Berry, 2012, 34). Indeed, this martial presence actually extended beyond the frontier, with Goldsworthy explaining that (2009, 105):

> ...neither the Rhine nor the Danube was a strict limit to Roman territory, for a strong military presence was maintained on the far banks.

By way of example, each major river crossing featured a fortress on the far bank to ensure control of the crossing point. Carroll highlights a prime example, the bridgehead fortress of *Divitia* built by Constantine I on the eastern bank of the Rhine directly across from the city of Cologne to protect the key bridge there (2009, 251). James says this fortification's sophisticated military design and technology rivalled anything in later medieval Europe, emphasizing the importance of its bridgehead role (2011, 241).

Further, the Romans frequently ventured well beyond the Rhine and Danube in force when carrying out punitive expeditions, sometimes in penetrations deep into *barbaricum*. Examples include those detailed in Chapter 2 in the

Marcomannic Wars, and those of Maximinus Thrax when campaigning against the Alamanni in AD 235. The latter was an immense undertaking, the then new emperor driving his legionary spearheads an astonishing 600km beyond the Rhine according to Herodian (*History of the Roman Empire*, 7.2.7). Though likely an exaggeration, this still indicates a far-reaching campaign. Further, Roman *exploratores* scouts ranged even further north and east of the frontier, in much the same way modern special forces might (Elliott, 2023, 61). Here a key task, in addition to strategic level reconnaissance, was to prevent the coalescence of critical mass by any enemy tribes gathering to challenge the Romans along the *limes* to the south and west.

Roman engagement north and east of the Rhine and Danube was not only restricted to military activity, with large-scale two-way trade taking place in normal circumstances, particularly from the time of Augustus. This featured elite goods heading north and east from the Roman world, often specifically targeting the Germanic tribal elites the Romans were seeking to favour. As Goldsworthy explains (2009, 107):

> It was much easier for the Romans to deal with a few kings or chieftains than large numbers of individualistic tribesmen.

In return, raw materials and slaves headed south and west. In particular, vast amounts of timber from the forests of Germany found their way into the empire, helping the rapid spread of urbanisation in the frontier region, and also the fortification process along the *limes*. Williams, in his detailed analysis of Rome's relationship with its neighbours, the barbarians, calls this border region 'near *barbaricum*', and argues the commercial zone there extended hundreds of kilometres into the forested interior (1998, 11).

Additionally, significant territory north and east of the twin river-line frontier was also occasionally taken under full imperial control. Prime examples included the Agri Decumantes region linking the Rhine and Danube between the provinces of Germania Superior and Raetia (this the region where Maximinus Thrax campaigned against the Alamanni), and the salient province of Dacia north of the Danube, famously conquered in two brutal campaigns by Trajan.

However, one shouldn't be distracted here. There is no doubt that from the reign of Augustus, if not earlier, the Romans considered the line of the Rhine and Danube a hardened, fortified border. As far as the Romans were concerned, whatever the martial or commercial opportunities in *barbaricum*, to the south and west of the frontier was civilisation, and to the north and east barbarians. Normal and ordered society on the one hand, rank savagery on the other.

Land of the Barbarians

I now consider how the Romans understood *barbaricum* geographically. Here, terminology can be confusing given the different ways various regions in Europe and Asia have been described over time. This is especially the case in the modern era when historians and geographers have often pandered to the political elites of their day. Therefore, I have developed my own geographic template based on the most up-to-date research, which I think will help the reader better navigate the travels of the Germans and Goths, and particularly the Vandals.

The German and Gothic peoples of the classical and late antique worlds originally resided in part of a vast region called the Great North European Plain. This comprises a huge swathe of territory above the Mediterranean world and Middle East, stretching from the lowlands of south-eastern England to the Ural Mountains in modern Russia.

In the Principate phase of the Roman Empire, at its western edge were the provinces of Britannia, Gallia Belgica, and Germania Inferior. Moving east across the Rhine, next came Germania (also called Magna Germania by the Romans), this stretching through modern Germany and Poland to Belarus, and including southern Scandinavia. Finally came Scythia, this covering an enormous stretch of trans-continental territory that, in modern geographic terms, passes through the Urals to include what we today call the Central Eurasian Steppe. Scythia was a region Herodotus had earlier claimed was inhabited by griffons and a race of one-eyed men called the Arimaspi (*The Histories*, 4.13.1). More importantly for this work, it was also home to the Huns, whose westward travels from the mid-Principate period triggered the cascade of Germanic and Gothic migrations that form the backdrop to the story of the Vandals. Specifically, *barbaricum* as the Romans understood it was Germania and Scythia, although in truth they had little knowledge of the latter.

Throughout the broad sweep of the Great North European Plain there is a unity of geological structure, creating dense clay soils which require heavy ploughs to be agriculturally productive (Heather, 2009, 4). However, given its continental stretch, distinct variations in climate lead to marked differences in the farming potential across the region, even today. In the west, temperate forests predominate, this the land most sought after given its suitability for intensive agriculture. However, once in Germania dense coniferous forests increasingly predominate. Finally, moving even further east into Scythia, the general lack of summer rainfall makes farming increasingly difficult, particularly beyond the river Don. There, in the temperate grasslands and savannahs, a nomadic lifestyle predominated in the classical and late-antique worlds, with the Huns a prime example (Goldsworthy, 2009). The western region of Scythia, which ranges from Belarus to the Urals and sits above the Black Sea, is often referred to as the Pontic Steppe, and I will use that term here given it helps differentiate between western and eastern Scythia.

Finally, to the south of the Pontic Steppe is the Iranian Plateau, a geographic region defined by great folding mountain belts resulting from the collision of the Arabian and Eurasian tectonic plates. This extends from the west of modern Iran to the north east of the Indian subcontinent. It was an important region in the classical and late antique worlds given it was home to the Parthians and Persians.

Climate and Climate Change

Climate across the Great North European Plain varies greatly from west to east, both today and in the Roman world. In the western regions through to Germany, Atlantic weather systems predominate, leading to mild summers with plenty of rain, and cooler and damper winters. In the east, continental weather systems are increasingly dominant, with hotter summers and colder winters, and less rainfall throughout (Heather, 2009, 4). As noted above, this makes agriculture increasingly difficult as one travels east.

Changes in the climate are always occurring, some major and some minor, and for a variety of reasons. Lengthier periods are often called climate change, shorter periods climate stress. To avoid confusion, here I will use the former. Such changes have led to variations in continental weather patterns at various times during our period of interest. We are fortunate that long-term oak tree-ring data from France and Germany, and the analysis of ice cores from Greenland and Antarctica, have allowed us to track these changes, most of which can be shown to be causative factors in historical events (Lambshead, 2022, 63).

First, a rapid fall in temperature and precipitation began around 400 BC, with a peak drop of 2°C by 350 BC. This corresponded with the southerly migration of many Gallic tribes from central Europe and northern Italy, including Brennus' Senones Gauls in their Allia campaign. Then, from the middle of the century, temperature and rainfall quickly recovered to its earlier levels, remaining stable for the next 250 years. This was the period when the Roman Republic rapidly expanded to control first Italy, then the western Mediterranean, and finally the eastern Mediterranean.

The next period of major climate deterioration started at the beginning of the 1st century BC, peaking around 50 BC. This was a particularly steep downturn, especially in temperature. In the Roman world this corresponded with the rapid spiral of civil war violence that eventually saw the Republic come to an end in 27 BC.

However, again the climate recovered to its earlier levels, and for the next 200 years the Roman world expanded to nearly its maximum extent. However, a sharp drop in temperature began around AD 160. This was caused by changes in the North Atlantic Oscillation (NAO), the index that describes changes in the strength of two recurring pressure patterns in the atmosphere over the North Atlantic, these a low-pressure system near Iceland and a high-pressure system near the Azores.

Rapid changes in climate are often associated with major public health events given the stress they place on societal resilience, and that is definitively the case here, with the Antonine Plague breaking out in AD 165 which lasted 15 years. It was this pandemic, thought to be a virulent form of smallpox, that forced Marcus Aurelius and Lucius Verus to cancel their planned AD 167 campaign in *barbaricum* north of the Danube during the Marcomannic Wars.

In the decades that followed, the climate returned to previous levels again, though after AD 200 precipitation levels began to fall once more, with temperature following by the middle of the century. This coincided with the 'Crisis of the 3rd Century', the period at the end of the Principate when the Roman Empire came close to imploding. Here, another major pandemic occurred, once more coinciding with a big change in climate. This was called the Plague of Cyprian, which claimed 5,000 lives a day in Rome at its height (Stathakopoulos, 2007, 95). Recent research suggests it was either a form of bubonic plague, or a particularly lethal strain of measles (Breeze and Hodgson, 2020, 32). Lambshead argues this lengthy period of climate deterioration bottomed out in the early 4th century AD, when rainfall levels began to recover again, later followed by temperature (2022, 65).

The final major climate change event in our period of interest began in early AD 536, only two years after the Byzantine reconquest of Vandal North Africa. This featured a severe and protracted episode of climactic cooling caused by a series of volcanic eruptions on the western coast of North America, part of the tectonic 'Ring of Fire' around much of the Pacific rim. This event sent huge amounts of sulphate aerosols into the upper atmosphere, leading to a volcanic winter of such severity it was noted by many primary sources at the time. For example, Procopius says (*The Vandalic War*, 4.14):

> During this year a most dread portent took place. For the sun gave forth its light without brightness... and it seemed exceedingly like the sun in eclipse, for the beams it shed were not clear.

Modern estimates indicate European summer temperatures in AD 536 fell by up to 2.5°C, a dramatic fall in such a short space of time. Moreover, the impact of the eruptions was not short lived. For example, writing two years later while serving in the court of the Ostrogothic king Theodoric the Great, Cassiodorus reports that the sun remained weak, with no shadows visible on the ground at noon. Further, he adds that the moon was '…empty of spleandour…', and most tellingly that the seasons were jumbled together, with the land gripped by famine (*The Variae*, 25.1).

The lingering impact of the AD 536 volcanic eruptions on European weather patterns was then exacerbated by further major eruptions, of unknown location but once again thought to be in the North American region of the 'Ring of Fire'. These occurred in AD 540, 574, and 626. Such was the effect of these multiple eruptions on the global climate that it was two decades before temperature and precipitation levels returned to earlier levels of stability. The dramatic impact on the lives of millions has led to the period being called the Late Antique Little Ice Age. Further, once more it coincided with a major pandemic, this the Plague of Justinian, another bubonic plague event.

Note that North Africa was less impacted than Eurasia by these various climate change events given the dominance there of African and equatorial weather systems, though even here the dramatic impact on climate caused by the Pacific volcano eruptions proved a challenge.

Germans and Goths

The Germanic peoples of north and eastern Europe were a major opponent of the later Roman Republic, and then the empire throughout the entirety of its existence. After their initial encounters, the Romans early on identified them as a distinct ethnic group when compared to the Gauls. Further, they also distinguished between the economic potential of the two peoples (or certainly their territories). While early in the Principate the empire did have ambitions to establish imperial control in Germania, this was quickly abandoned after the Varian Disaster, the imperial centre deciding the price of conquest was not worth the financial return.

Origins

The Germans originated in the westward Indo-European migrations from the Pontic Steppe, and by 3,300 BC had split off from the main migratory group, heading northwest towards the coastline of the Baltic Sea through what the

Romans would later call Germania. There they settled in its northernmost reaches.

Writing at the end of the 1st century BC, Strabo provides contemporary insight into how the Romans viewed the Germans, saying (7.1.3):

> Now the parts beyond the Rhenus (Rhine), immediately after the country of the Gauls, slope towards the east and are occupied by the Germans, who, though they vary slightly from the Celtic stock in that they are wilder, taller, and have yellower hair, are in all other respects similar, for in build, habits, and modes of life they are such as I have said the Gauls are. And I also think that it was for this reason that the Romans assigned to them the name *Germani*, as though they wished to indicate thereby that they were 'genuine' Gauls, for in the language of the Romans *Germani* means genuine.

This last point, referencing the Germans as 'genuine' Gauls, is most likely a literary device by Strabo reflecting what he believed was their superior martial prowess following the conquest of Gaul by Caesar in the 50s BC, and the comparative ease with which the Gallic provinces were later incorporated into the empire.

Tacitus says there were three broad groupings of early Germans who all believed they were descended from the earth-born German god Tuisto (*The Germania*, 2.4). In this creation myth, his son Manno then had three sons of his own who became the founders of these three original groupings. The first were the Ingaevones, the second the Istvaeones, and the third were the Herminones. Tacitus says that all subsequent German confederations and tribes evolved from these three groups over the following centuries. Confusingly for this work, Tacitus goes on in *The Germania* to report hearsay that Mannus may have also had other sons who founded additional Germanic tribal groupings, including the Vandilii (2.7). However, he then rules this out.

Soon the German tribes began a new wave of migrations south through Germania, carving out new territories between the Pripet Marshes in Belarus and the Rhine. There they slowly consolidated until they eventually coalesced into the confederations we know well today, with Pliny the Elder listing the five of his day in his *Natural History* (4.28). These are the Vandilii (our first confirmed mention of them historically, if one discounts Tacitus), the Varini, the Charini, the Gutones (the Goths, later to separate into the western Visigoths and eastern Ostrogoths), and the Burgundians. Adding to the confusion here, Pliny says the latter were actually a sub-grouping of the Vandilii, which may be true given their later close co-operation with the Silingi Vandals (MacDowall, 2016, 5). Broadly, it was these confederations that caused so much trouble for the later Roman Empire, particularly after the Hunnic expansion westward from the Central Eurasian Steppe which drove the Germans increasingly against the Roman *limes* on the Rhine and Danube.

The Romans were unimpressed by the lands of the Germans, with Tacitus saying (*The Germania*, 2.1):

> Who would leave Asia or Africa or Italy and seek out Germania, with its unlovely scenery and bitter climate, dreary to inhabit and even behold.

This is damning commentary indeed, with Tacitus adding in the same passage that Germania bristled with dense, impenetrable forests and festering marshes. Other classical and late antique writers had the same opinion. For example, Caesar says the Germans were unable to plough the heavy clay soils of Germania and were essentially pastoralists, with the bulk of their foodstuffs derived from their flocks and herds, and from hunting (*The Conquest of Gaul*, 4.1.4). Such foods included meat, cheese, and milk. This is clearly a huge oversimplification, reflecting a lack of detailed knowledge of the lands beyond the Rhine and Danube on the part of the Romans. Even Tacitus, overtly damning of the Germans in his wider narrative, admits the lands to the immediate north of the Roman frontier were fertile when tilled well, with grain, root crops, and vegetables grown (*The Germania*, 2.1).

Setting aside obvious Roman propaganda and ignorance, the true picture painted here of agriculture in Germania is one of diversity, with arable farming and pastoralism practiced side-by-side nearer the Rhine and Danube, and pastoralism increasingly predominant as one moved further north and east, away from contact with the empire. This reflects the osmosis of wealth and ideas crossing the frontier from the imperial centre to *barbaricum*, a common occurrence throughout the empire. Goldsworthy adds that in the frontier zone there is also clear archaeological evidence that German towns and villages there thrived, often for centuries, despite periodical destruction by the Romans (2009, 105).

Early German society was largely feudal in nature. At the top, some confederations and tribes had kings, though not all. Indeed, in Caesar's day many Germanic groups he encountered elected their leaders from the broader aristocracy and were notably egalitarian. This lessened over time, perhaps through contact with Rome, and by the time the Vandals began their migration through the Western Empire all major Germanic and Gothic groupings were ruled by hereditary dynasties. Each ruler maintained a cadre of professional warriors who were always under arms and ready to fight as required at a moment's notice. Tacitus refers to them as the leader's *comitatus*, and says that (*The Germania*, 14.1):

> When they go into battle, it is a disgrace for the chief to be surpassed in valour, a disgrace
> for his followers not to equal the valour of the chief. And it is an infamy and a reproach for
> life to have survived the chief, and returned from the field. To defend, to protect him, to
> ascribe one's own brave deeds to his renown, is the height of loyalty.

The rest of male German and Gothic society, excepting slaves, comprised soldier farmers who fought when called upon by their rulers, these completing the line of battle in major actions. Here, the call to arms in time of war was not universal, with Caesar describing the innovative way the Suebi he fought were still able to farm while many were away fighting (*The Conquest of Gaul*, 4.1.1):

> Each of their cantons provide annually a thousand armed men for service in foreign wars.
> The rest are left at home to support those in the army as well as themselves, and the next
> year take their turn of military service, while the others stay at home. Thus pastoralism and
> agriculture, and military activity, continue without interruption.

In terms of material culture, the German Iron Age began around 800 BC, slightly later than in Gaul to the south. However, most household goods continued to be made from wood, leather, and ceramic, with most metallic objects still made from copper and bronze, even in Caesar's day. Military equipment, particularly long slashing swords, daggers, and spearheads, were the most likely to be made with iron (see below). Regarding economic activity, Caesar says the German tribes closest to Gaul were the most advanced. In particular, he highlights the Ubii, who he says were '…a considerable and prosperous nation…' (*The Conquest of Gaul*, 4.1). Though Caesar does not mention coin use, Tacitus does, saying that by the end of the 1st century AD those Germans living nearest the northern *limes* had adopted various kinds of coinage from the Romans, particularly gold and silver currencies (*The Germania*, 5.17). He adds that those Germans living in the forested interior, well away from the frontier, still traded through bartering (*The Germania*, 5.1). Meanwhile, German pottery was mostly handmade, with wheel-turned pottery rare even in late antiquity. Any found in quantity in the German archaeological record is usually associated with Roman mercantile activity.

Finally in terms of material culture, Caesar says that the Suebi he encountered in his 57 BC campaign wore little clothing, though one should note these were warriors. He says (*The Conquest of Gaul*, 4.1.2):

> They inure themselves, in spite of the very cold climate in which they live, to wear not
> clothing but skins, and these so scanty that a large part of the body is uncovered, and so
> bathe in the rivers.

Where we do have more detailed contemporary descriptions of male German clothing, they describe smocks being worn with or without sleeves, short breeches, leg bandages around the knees and shins, and leather footwear fastened with laces. When needed, a cloak would also be worn. Early on, most garments were made from leather or hide, though later patterned materials made from wool, twill, bast (the fibre from the skin of a plant), and felt were also used, with linen being added by the time the Gothic confederations emerged. We have little detail of how German women dressed in this early period, with primary sources usually focusing on men.

Early German armies were very similar to those of the Gauls who fought Caesar, though they lacked chariots. Their cavalry fought in much the same way, though German horses tended to be smaller, with Caesar saying the Germans made up for this through daily exercise of the mounts, this designed to improve their stamina (*The Conquest of Gaul*, 4.1). He adds that German cavalry often fought dismounted, with the horses standing '...perfectly still...' while battle raged around them. Further, a particular innovation of early German armies was the deployment of light troops among the ranks of their own cavalry when they did fight mounted. Armed with javelins and shields, these swarmed around the flanks of opposing troops, hamstringing their mounts if they were cavalry.

Early German infantry often fought in a wedge formation rather than a standard shield wall. Most warriors wore little armour, though they carried a shield, usually of square design. Their principal weapons were javelins which they carried in quantity, with the aim to shower an opposing formation with volleys prior to contact. In most German armies the most common type was the *framea*, with Tacitus providing a detailed description of this weapon. He says (*The Germania*, 6.1):

> The *frameas* they carry have short and narrow heads, but are so sharp and easy to handle that the same weapon serves at need for close or distance fighting.

Some German tribes also deployed troops armed with long thrusting spears in their front ranks, for example Arminius' Cherusci and the Batavians, while the Marcomanni were well known for using the *bebrae* heavy throwing spear. The main side arm was a long dagger, for example the Saxon *seax*, though a few warriors also carried an iron slashing sword if they could afford it. German troops of all periods were known for their blood chilling war cry called the *barritus*. This started in a low rumbling voice and rose to a high-pitched, chilling scream immediately prior to a charge. It proved so effective it was later copied by the Romans themselves, especially after Germans started joining the ranks of the legions and *auxilia*.

Later German armies evolved in different ways based on regional circumstances. For example, the Ostrogoths in the east had a much higher proportion of cavalry given their proximity to the Sarmatian and Turkic tribes of the Pontic Steppe. These mounted Gothic warriors often wore armour and a helmet and carried a large, round shield. Their main weapon was the light spear (not the lance of the Sarmatians), of which a number were carried, and a long sword. Their preferred tactic was an impetuous charge to contact. Most foot troops in later Ostrogoth armies were lightly armoured bowmen.

By way of contrast, Visigothic, Frankish, Burgundian, and most other late German armies were still predominantly heavy infantry based, fighting in a manner similar to that of their forebears. Many were well known to contemporary writers for the use of specific weapon types. These included the *francisca* (throwing axe) and *angon* (armour-piercing javelin) used by the Franks.

Interestingly, the Vandals began their travels through the Western Empire fighting in the latter fashion, with heavy infantry predominant. However, at some stage on their journey south they adopted a style of fighting based on heavy cavalry, similar to that of the Ostrogoths. The vector of cultural transfer here may have been the Alans who accompanied the Vandals for much of their journey. This transition is discussed in detail in Chapter 5.

Note that all German and Gothic armies, once resident within the Western Empire after the collapse of imperial control there, made use of the existing Roman troops they inherited, particularly *limitanei* in border garrisons. In this book I will present fresh evidence showing this process in action in Vandal North Africa.

As a final point, while the overwhelming bulk of warriors fought by the Romans along the northern *limes* were Germans and Goths, not all were. For example, the Dacians, Carpi, and Getae resided in the Carpathian Mountains and Danubian flood plains west of the Black Sea. These peoples all spoke Dacian and were closely related to the Thracians. The neighbouring Bastarnae may also have been Dacian, though some argue they were German.

Meanwhile, the Sarmatians inhabited the Pontic Steppe and were a series of Iranian peoples who migrated west through southern Germania from the 4th century BC onwards. The Romans first encountered them when they invaded Moesia in Nero's reign in the 1st century AD. They then fought alongside the Dacians as allies against Trajan in his two conquest campaigns in Dacia in the early 2nd century AD, and were next allies of the various German confederations and tribes fighting Rome during the Marcomannic

Wars in the later 2nd century AD. Their territory was finally overrun by the Huns in the AD 370s.

The principal Sarmatian tribes included the Siracae, Iazyges, and Rhoxalani, with the vast majority of their troops mounted lancers carrying a 3.5m *kontos* (lance). This was held two-handed, braced across the thighs, allowing them to charge to contact at breakneck speed, even against disciplined foot. Many were also armed with a bow. Those who wore armour were clad in coats of horn scales or chainmail, as depicted on the base of Trajan's Column.

Germanic Religion

In truth, we know very little about pre-Christian German religion. What we do know is through the prism of others, in this case three groups in particular. First, as usual classical and late antique Greek and Roman historians. Second, histories written centuries after for post-migration German elites in former Roman territories, the best-known example being the *Anglo-Saxon Chronicle*. Finally, high medieval Norse sagas, primarily from Iceland. All three, as we read them today, have been heavily influenced by subsequent Christian commentary, while modern popular culture has also distorted how we engage with ancient German religion, whether in movies, television, or literature. That said, it is still useful to set out what we do know, if only to provide context for the later conversion to Christianity of various Germanic and Gothic confederations and tribes, including the Vandals.

Broadly, early German religion had more in common with the polytheistic transactional religions of the classical Mediterranean than it did with the Levantine congregational variety. German deities were closely linked with the natural world, either skyward, earthbound, or below. Methods of worship reflected this, with fire and smoke, flora and fauna, or libations and the deposit of precious goods the focus of sacred rites. Here, classical and late antique sources go out of their way to emphasise the commonality of sacrifice in all of these activities, particularly human. Prime examples can be seen in my earlier Chapter 2 description of the fate of Roman captives after the Varian Disaster, with the fact that much of the Roman senior leadership team, including Varus himself, chose to commit suicide showing they were fully aware of the fate that awaited them if captured alive. However, Tacitus does reference one key point of difference between Mediterranean and early German religion, this regarding the physical spaces where the act of worship actually took place. In the Mediterranean this was often in a bespoke temple, the house of the god who was usually represented with a monumental statue inside, and with the altar outside. When talking of German religion, though, he says (*The Germania*, 9.1):

> The Germans do not deem it consistent with divine majesty to imprison their gods within walls or represent them with anything like human features. They consecrate woods and groves, and they call them by the name of the gods the hidden presence represents.

In terms of the specific deities worshipped by the early Germans, earlier I set out how Tacitus explained the three early Germanic tribal groupings were all descended from the deity Tuisto through his grandsons (*The Germania*, 2.4). Tacitus later goes on to add further detail about early German religion, saying (*The Germania*, 9.1):

> As for the gods, the Germans worship Mercury above all, and consider it proper to win his favour on certain days even by human sacrifices; Hercules and Mars they appease with the beasts normally allowed. Some of the Suevi sacrifice also to Isis.

In the same passage he also references Castor and Pollux in the context of the German pantheon. Clearly, the early Germans didn't worship classical world deities. Rather, what we are seeing here is Roman cultural appropriation of Germanic religion in the context of Tacitus' *interpretatio romana* detailed in Chapter 1. This was a frequent occurrence in both Republic and empire, though we are then left to guess which German deities Tacitus is referring to. Many believe Mercury here represents Wōden (Odin in Norse mythology), Hercules Thunor (the Norse Thor), and Mars Tīw (the Norse Týr). Intriguingly, these deities still exist in our everyday lives as days of the week, with Wednesday for Wōden, Thursday for Thor, and Tuesday for Tīw (Williams, 2022, 182).

To find historical references to these and other German deities is more difficult than it sounds. Indeed, we must move forward substantially in time to the post-Roman world. Here they begin to appear in inscriptions, literary works, and king and genealogy lists, often retrospectively. Take, for example, Wōden. This key German deity, often referenced as the All Father in the German pantheon, was associated with wisdom and warfare. Yet surprisingly given his importance, the name doesn't appear in writing until the 6th century AD. This is in the form of a runic inscription scratched on the back of a brooch found in Nordendorf in Bavaria (Williams, 2022, 122). By that time this region was part of the post-Roman Merovingian kingdom, with the Franks there notably late converting to Christianity.

Wōden also appears in a variety of literary works, perhaps centuries after he was last worshipped. The best-known example is the *Anglo-Saxon Chronicle*, a collection of Old English annals which narrate the history of

The usurper Constantine III, whose bid for power in the north-western theatre encouraged the Vandals over the Pyrenees. (Wikimedia Commons)

Justinian I, the great early Byzantine emperor who ordered Belisarius to reconquer Vandal North Africa. (David Hatcher)

Honorius, ineffectual emperor in the west as the Vandals travelled through Gaul and Spain. (Wikimedia Commons)

The traditional view of the Vandals – Gaiseric's sacking of Rome AD 455. (Wikimedia Commons)

Vandal warrior around AD 500 in North Africa. By this time Vandal armies comprised mostly shock cavalry. (Wikimedia Commons)

Late Roman field army troops on the Arch of Constantine, Rome. Those fighting the Vandals in the later 4th and early 5th centuries would have been similarly equipped. (Author's collection)

The Colosseum and *Forum Romanum* in Rome, key targets for the Vandals when they sacked Rome in AD 455. (Author's collection)

The Aurelian Walls in Rome. One of the finest defensive wall circuits in the Roman world, it failed to save the city from the Vandals in AD 455. (Author's collection)

Roman legionary *testudo* in action against Germanic warriors in the Marcomannic Wars in the later 2nd century AD. Column of Marcus Aurelius, Rome. (Author's collection)

Roman theatre and Odeon, Lyon. The Vandal capture of the key city of Lugdunum opened the way for their onward journey to the Mediterranean coast. (Author's collection)

What the Romans really thought of barbarians. With this sculpture, originally a mausoleum decoration though later used as a fountain head in Corbridge, northern Britain, it is very clear who is who. Classic Roman propaganda, telling the locals to behave, or else. (Author's collection)

Christianity initially found it difficult to compete with classical Roman religion. Here Venus is pulled in a *quadriga* chariot by four elephants, from a workshop in Pompeii. (Author's collection)

The baptistry in Djemila in the Atlas Mountains, Algeria. Christianity swept through Roman North Africa at great speed and on an industrial scale. (Author's collection)

Arena beast hunt mosaic, Djemila in the Atlas Mountains. The Vandals readily took to the Roman amphitheatre and hunting in North Africa. (Author's collection)

Centre piece of the Mosaic of the Ass from a fine town house in Djemila. The motto says *asinus nica*, meaning 'victory to the ass'. A satirical play on the contemporary *christos nika*, meaning 'To Christ, the victory'. The owner clearly was not a fan of the rapid spread of Christianity through the region. (Author's collection)

The author in front of the mausoleum of Lollius Urbicus, the Numidian Berber imperial trouble-shooter in the 2nd century AD who, as British governor, established the line of the Antonine Wall. Roman North Africa was home to some of the empire's greatest administrators and warriors. (Author's collection)

The Severan forum in Djemila, with the snow-clad Atlas Mountains in the background. Centre right, the Temple of Gens Septimia. (Author's collection)

Vandal Heaven. The lush coastal plain near modern Annaba, Roman Hippo Regius. Perfect countryside for Vandal horse warriors as Gaiseric secured his first capital there in North Africa. (Author's collection)

Hunting beasts in the countryside to supply the Roman arena, an industrial scale operation in Roman and Vandal North Africa. Annaba, Roman Hippo Regius. (Author's collection)

More Vandal Heaven. The Atlas Mountains in late spring. Green everywhere. (Author's collection)

Byzantine fort at Madauros in the Atlas Mountains. Built from reused Roman building stone, right on top of the Roman *forum*. (Author's collection)

The rear of the same fort, featuring the reused Severan theatre in Madauros in its entirety. (Author's collection)

The Aures Mountains viewed from the Saharan fringe. The view of Roman *limitanei* (border troops) guarding the southern *limes*. (Author's collection)

Monumental water basin and spring complex, Khemissa in Algeria. Built adjacent to the exceptionally well-preserved theatre in this key town, it featured a colonnaded courtyard and central temple. (Author's collection)

Byzantine watchtower, built from reused Roman stone, Madauros. Keeping an eye on the locals. (Author's collection)

Khemissa, Roman Thubursicum Numidarum in the Atlas Mountains. A key city on the trunk road from Hippo Regius to the Saharan fringe. (Author's collection)

The astonishing Mausoleum of Madghacen near Batna in modern Algeria, in the high plains north of the Aures range. (Author's collection)

Timgad, Roman Colonia Marciana Ulpia Traiana Thamugadi on the fringes of the Aures mountains. Home to the retired legionaries of *legio* III *Augusta*. (Author's collection)

Public toilet with a view. *Forum* lavatory in Timgad, with the Aures Mountains in the distance. Beyond them is the Sahara Desert. (Author's collection)

View of the high plains and Aures Mountains from atop the public theatre, Timgad. (Author's collection)

Capitoline temple, Timgad. Monumental temple to Jupiter, Juno, and Minerva built on a high podium in the south-west of the city. (Author's collection)

Arch of Trajan, Timgad. The city was sacked by local Berbers after the Justinian reconquest, and later featured a Byzantine fort. (Author's collection)

Groma in the centre of the Roman legionary fortress at Lambaesis, home of *legio* III *Augusta*. (Author's collection)

Entrance to the amphitheatre in Lambaesis, with the Aures Mountains in the background. (Author's collection)

The enormous rotundral Royal Mausoleum of Mauretania in Algeria, high above the modern coastal route between Algiers and Cherchell. Burial place of Juba II and his queen, Cleopatra Selene II. (Author's collection)

View from the Royal Mausoleum of Mauretania across the coastal plain to the Atlas Mountains in late spring. Again, green everywhere, some of the most fertile land in the Mediterranean. (Author's collection)

Carthaginian gravestone, Guelma (Roman Calama), in modern Algeria. Note the war elephant. (Author's collection)

Roman theatre in Djemila, with the Atlas Mountains as the backdrop. (Author's collection)

Constantine, the city in the clouds in the Atlas Mountains, key regional capital in the classical and late antique periods. (Author's collection)

the Germans elites who migrated to Britain in the post-Roman period, and their descendants. The original was created late in the 9th century AD in Wessex during the reign of Alfred the Great. In the chronicle Wōden is referenced as the dynastic founder of the West Saxons, though interestingly the emphasis here is on his human rather than god-like form, no doubt reflecting the Christian beliefs of the writer. Further, this is by no means an isolated example, given Wōden is listed as the dynastic founder of all German migrant dynasties in Britain (apart from the East Saxons who claimed descent from the deity Seaxnēat).

Intriguingly, Wōden also appears in king lists associated with non-German Brittonic kingdoms. One example can be found in the Anglian collection, a series of early medieval regnal lists and genealogies which survive in four manuscripts. Two reside in the British Library, one in Corpus Christi College in Cambridge, and one in the library of Rochester Cathedral. Here, in the list of the later kings of Lindsey, the post-Roman kingdom centred on Lincoln (Lindum Colonia) in north Lincolnshire, Wōden has been inserted mid-list as one of its rulers. This is most unusual given most of the other listed kings, both earlier and later, are Brittonic. This reflects Lindsey originally being a Romano-British *civitas* that survived well beyond the official Roman withdrawal from Britain. Perhaps here we have a snapshot in time showing a new dominance on the part of the Germanic incomers over their British neighbours after a century or more living around, but not within, Brittonic Lindsey. Whether through trade, marriage, or war, here clearly the Germans had taken control, if only for a short period before Brittonic rule returned. German control later resumed though, with Lindsey eventually subsumed into the kingdom of Northumbria in the 7th century AD.

We also have direct evidence of pagan conversion to Christianity in the context of Wōden. Again this features the Saxons, this time in their north German homelands where they were noted for their adherence to old religious beliefs, even in the face of the aggressive Christianisation taking place across north-western Europe in the 8th century AD. The evidence features a set of vows which survived in a monastery in Mainz, these later taken to the Vatican Library where they remain today. The vows were originally called the *Abrenuntiatio Diaboli* ('renunciation of the Devil') and are known today as the Old Saxon Baptismal Vow. They contain the exact words a Saxon convert was required to say before baptism, with the first three lines covering who the individual should renounce in their new Christian life. Specifically, these were Wōden and the other principal deities of the German pantheon (Williams, 2022, 181).

Finally, to find the most detail about early German religion we must jump forward in time again, and to the farthest fringes of the medieval Christian world. There, in the wonderful literature of Norse Iceland, Wōden was now being referenced as Odin. In the 13th century AD, an Icelandic historian and poet called Snorri Sturluson wrote an epic poem called the *Völuspá* whose narrator was an age-old seeress raised by primeval giants. In his poem, Sturleson embedded a much older collection of verse called the *Elder* (or *Poetic*) *Edda*. This included a version of the mythical German creation story which for the first time he wrote down.

In the myth, before creation was *Ginnungagap*, a void bursting with magical force. Within it three gods were created, the most senior Odin. Between them they created the sea, from which they then raised up the earth. Then, as the sun shone down on the newly created barren rock, green herbage began to grow. Later, the three gods found two lifeless tree trunks while walking along a seashore which they called Askr and Embla. They endowed these with reason, a fair countenance, breath, and hair, creating the first man and woman.

To be clear, this is only one Nordic creation myth among many. However, given it was the first to be written down, it gained the most traction in medieval and renaissance Europe. Thus, given his prominence in the story, Odin (and so Wōden) became the best known of the Germanic gods, which remains the case today.

The Vandals

Some etymologists believe the name Vandal was derived from an early form of the modern German word *Wandel*, meaning change in the sense of physically wandering. Though there is no direct evidence to support this, if true it is highly accurate based on the story of their extensive travels, which I begin in this chapter (Matyszak, 2022, 241). First I consider their language, and then their material culture, before narrating their early journeys through Germania through to the dramatic mid-winter Rhine crossing in AD 406. Finally, I detail Vandal service in the Roman army given this began during this phase of their travels.

Vandal Language

The Vandals spoke a language called Vandalic. This is mentioned a few times in contemporary literature and legal documents, the last dating to the 6th century AD. Although there is no definitive evidence regarding its origins, Vandalic was most likely a branch of Gothic, the extinct Eastern Germanic language spoken by the various Gothic confederations. Procopius provides our best evidence of a link here, saying that the Goths, Vandals, and Gepids (another eastern Germanic confederation) all spoke a single language, Gothic (*The Vandalic War*, 1.2).

As a Germanic language, Gothic (and so Vandalic) was a sub-group of the Indo-European language family which comprises nearly all of the major linguistic sub-groups spoken in Europe today, and their predecessors, with the exception of Finno-Ugaric and Basque. In addition to Germanic, the other major Indo-European groups are Italic (including the Romance languages derived from Roman Vulgar Latin, as discussed in Chapter 1), Celtic, Balto-Slavic, and a number of other original languages, including Greek (Williams, 2022, 335).

Little is known of Vandalic except a few personal names and short phrases. The most important surviving remnant is thought to be the modern regional name for southern Spain, Andalusia. This is derived from the Arabic word Al-Andalus, the Moors who later conquered southern Spain adopting it from the then incumbent Visigoths, who in turn had adopted it from the Vandals after the latter had travelled through Spain on their way to settle in North Africa. Meanwhile, we also have the Vandalic name for one of the most common incantations or prayers in the Christian liturgy, the '*Kyrie, eleison*'. Meaning 'Lord have mercy', its Vandalic translation *Froia arme* has been preserved in contemporary literature (Berndt, 2016, 62). Other likely Vandalic words which have survived in ancient Latin and Greek texts include *Baudus* (master), *drincan* (drink), *eils* (hello), *matzia* (to eat), *scapia* (to make or create), and *Vandalirice* (king of the Vandals). Finally, we can also trace the impact on Vandalic language of their extensive travels through the Roman world by the evolution of Vandal aristocratic names, with many later featuring Latin suffixes or elements. Examples include Mauritta and Bictoricus.

Vandal Material Culture

The Vandals were long settled in north-eastern Germania by the time they first made contact with the Roman world after their earlier travels from the Pontic Steppe. Specifically, the region they occupied ranged from the middle and upper stretches of the river Vistula to, heading west, Silesia, all in modern Poland. Archaeologists call their bespoke material culture here the Przeworsk culture (Pohl, 2004, 33). Some etymologists have also argued that the range of territory controlled by the Vandals resident there also stretched north to incorporate southern Sweden, given a region there is today called Vendel (Vaendil in Old Norse), and also the Jutland Peninsula in modern

Denmark given its northernmost tip is called Vendsyssel (Wendila in Old Norse). However, to date no archaeological data has been found to support these hypotheses.

Przeworsk culture takes its name from the Polish town of Przeworsk, the location where the first artifacts associated with it were found. Archaeological excavations have shown that at this time the Vandals lived in small, unprotected villages with a few dozen residents at most. Their houses were rectangular and semi-sunken in the ground, with log and turf walls and thatched roofs, each covering an area of up to 22m². Vandal settlements also featured timber-lined wells.

Early Vandal settlements were classically agrarian, with crop rotation used to grow arable crops and pastures to graze cattle. Later, perhaps after contact with Rome, iron ploughshares were introduced, significantly increasing land productivity.

Przeworsk culture is best known today for its large collective cemeteries, where the Vandal elites from multiple locations were buried in one place. Most of the burials are cremations, with the human remains placed in urns, many part engraved to create a distinctive bulge. Within the burials, most of the grave goods were bent or broken before interment, this interpreted as a sign of closure. Later, after contact with Rome, inhumation burials begin to feature, often with Gallic and occasionally Roman grave goods.

Przeworsk culture continued to flourish in the region after the departure of the Vandals and is found therein associated with the Huns as they subsequently travelled through. It was later finally replaced by the Prague-Korchak culture.

Early Travels

As detailed above, our first specific mention of the Vandilii is by Pliny the Elder in his *Natural History* as one of the five German confederations in the AD 70s (4.28). Next we have Tacitus and his discounting in *The Germania* of the contemporary hearsay that Manno, in addition to having earlier founded the Ingaevones, Istvaeones, and Herminones, also founded the Vandilii at the same time (2.7). However, of note here, Tacitus does say their name is 'genuine and ancient', and clearly when he wrote this work at the end of the 1st century AD the name Vandilii was well-known to both him and his audience.

Interestingly, the Alexandria-based Claudius Ptolemy does not name the Vandilii in his *Geography*, written later around AD 150, though he does mention the Burgundians (2.11) who Pliny had earlier said were a sub-grouping of the Vandilii (*Natural History*, 4.28). However, in the region the Vandals were inhabiting at the time, Ptolemy does mention a people called the Lugii. Pohl convincingly argues these may have been the Vandilii (2004, 32), his hypothesis based on references by Tacitus (*The Annales*, 12.20) and later by Cassius Dio (*Roman History*, 68.1).

We next get our first reference to an historical event which included the Vandals. This is retrospectively through the *History of the Lombards*, a late 8th century AD account of this Germanic people, comprising six books written by Paul the Deacon, an Italian-based Benedictine scholar. He recounts an ancient Lombard legend where they defeated the Vandals in battle, the latter fighting under two kings he calls Ambri and Assi (MacDowall, 2016, 6). Though some question whether this engagement actually took place, those who think it did date it to the mid-2nd century AD, just before the Vandals began the next phase of their migration.

This started soon afterwards, amid the swirl of regional movement by the various Germanic confederations and tribes in Germania. Here a split took place, with the Silingi Vandals remaining in Poland (some argue this is where the modern name Silesia comes from), but with the Hasdingi Vandals heading south. From this point, the latter are the sole focus of the primary sources until much later in the story of Germanic migrations.

The Hasdingi moved at speed, with the archaeological record tracking them crossing the Carpathian Mountains, and by AD 160 at the latest they had settled along the upper reaches of the river Tisza in modern Hungary. This is a major tributary of the middle Danube, which on its lower reaches bounded the Roman province of Dacia to the west. It is at this point contemporary writers begin using the term Vandali rather than Vandilii, while at the same time the term Goth also replaces Gutones.

The Hasdingi's new neighbours there were the Germanic Marcomanni and Quadi, long resident in the region. They also now found themselves increasingly engaged with the Roman world across the Danubian *limes*, at first through trade, though soon the Marcomannic Wars broke out, with some believing their arrival was the causal event given the pressure it put on local resources. Whatever the reason behind the conflict, though the Hasdingi weren't originally involved, the opportunity for plunder proved too great a prospect and soon conflict broke out between the Vandals and Rome for the first time.

We know this retrospectively through the peace treaty signed by Marcus Aurelius in AD 182 with the Quadi and Iazyges Sarmatians and the Hasdingi after the successful Transdanubian campaigns of his leading general Pompeianus. Here Cassius Dio speaks of the '…Astingi, whose leaders were Raus and Raptus…' (*Roman History*, 71.12). Interestingly, he then indicates a new phase of Hasdingi migration, with some heading east from the Tisza valley to ask the Roman governor of Dacia, Sextus Cornelius Clemens, whether they could settle on imperial territory within the province's borders under his protection '…in the hope of being accepted as allies and thereby receiving money and land…' (*Roman History*, 71.12). Although the governor seems to have initially refused, he did allow these Hasdingi to leave their wives and children there. The warriors then left in search of other new land to settle, this in the territory of the Dacian Costoboci to the north who they defeated in battle. However, the nearby Lacringi then attacked the newly victorious Hasdingi in fear they would be the next victims of the Vandals. The Hasdingi were badly defeated, though saved from a massacre by Clemens who led a large Roman force to their rescue from Dacia. The Hasdingi now became allies of the Romans under their protection, with some warriors now allowed to settle in Dacia alongside their wives and children after seeking permission from Marcus Aurelius. Most likely, here we are seeing these Vandals recruited directly by Rome as early *foederates*, with those Hasdingi who remained outside imperial territory in the Tisza valley being paid to act as a buffer against any further German or Sarmatian aggression there.

The Vandals next appear in the mid-3rd century AD, by which time Hunnic expansion westward through the Pontic Steppe had reached eastern Germania. This squeezed the German and Gothic confederations there together even more tightly, putting further pressure on Rome's Rhine and Danubian frontiers. The outcome was renewed conflict between the various Germanic and Gothic groupings, and also with Rome itself, which was struggling with the tribulations of the 'Crisis of the 3rd Century'. In particular, a series of deep Gothic incursions over the Danube devastated the Balkans, with Athens brutally sacked. For the most part, the Hasdingi Vandals in the Tisza valley and Dacia stayed aloof from this regional friction, though we have reports some Hasdingi joined a large Gothic raid into Moesia Superior. This was a key Danubian frontier province comprising, today, eastern Serbia, Kosovo, north-eastern Albania, and the northern parts of North Macedonia. However, this only lasted a short while, and for the most part the Hasdingi stayed out of this bitter series of conflicts.

Next, and still within the 'Crisis of the 3rd Century', another group of Hasdingi under two kings are reported to have joined a large-scale Sarmatian raid west into Pannonia in late AD 270 by the contemporary Athenian historian Publius Herrenius Dexippus. This is detailed in his *History of Rome's Wars with the Goths*, much of which survives in various compendiums written by later classical and late antique historians. At this point Pannonia had long been divided into two provinces, these Pannonia Superior and Inferior. Given the latter was the easternmost, it is likely it is there that this campaign took place.

Here, the timing was again opportunistic. The Roman emperor Claudius Gothicus had recently defeated a huge Gothic army at the battle of Naissus in AD 269 near Niš in modern Serbia. However, soon after in January AD 270 he promptly died of plague at the height of the Plague of Cyprian, which was ravaging the empire at the time. Succession to the imperial throne was for a time confused, with Gothicus' brother, Marcus Aurelius Claudius Quintillus, initially proclaimed emperor in Italy. It is at this point the Sarmatians and Hasdingi launched their raid into Pannonia.

However, Gothicus' leading general, Aurelian, remained in post on the Danubian front. There, his own troops now proclaimed him the emperor. There could only be one winner, the seasoned veteran Aurelian, and soon those troops supporting Quintillus in Italy deserted him for the general in the north. Quintillus had committed suicide by May. From that point Aurelian proved one of the great warrior emperors of the late Principate. He soon turned his attention to the Sarmatians and Hasdingi in Pannonia, defeating them in short order. Aurelian now shrewdly asked his army for their views on how to punish the invaders (Kean and Frey, 2005, 155). They agreed to a peace treaty with them, but only on harsh terms. This included the Romans keeping the large number of prisoners captured in the campaign, and forcing the Sarmatians and Hasdingi to supply 2,000 further cavalry for service in the Roman military. The latter were soon in action when a few groups of Sarmatians, retreating to their home territories, reneged on their deal with Rome. They were quickly rounded up and massacred by Rome's new Sarmatian and Hasdingi recruits. At this point, Aurelian then took the title *Sarmaticus*. MacDowall argues this confirms the Hasdingi were the junior partners in the raid (2016, 10). Then, in AD 274 after four more years campaigning against other Germanic opponents in the north, defeating the Palmyran Empire in the east and the Gallic empire in the west, Aurelian finally held a triumph in Rome to celebrate his many victories. There, among the royalty, usurpers, and noble prisoners on display, were the surviving Sarmatians and Hasdingi captives from the AD 270 conflict.

Attention now shifts to the Silingi branch of the Vandals, still resident back in their Polish homeland. There, the migratory pressures caused by the westward expansion of the Huns were also being felt, and soon they found themselves squeezed tight against the Roman *limes* along the Rhine and upper Danube. The Constantinople-based Greek historian Zosimus, writing retrospectively in the early 6th centuries AD but basing his work on a contemporary original by Dexippus, says they joined with the Burgundians (as we have seen, possibly a sub-group of the Vandals) to invade Raetia. This was in the reign of the emperor Probus, at the very end of the Principate as the 'Crisis of the 3rd Century' came to an end. Specifically, Zosimus details that in AD 278 the emperor moved to counter this new barbarian incursion, forcing a meeting engagement near Augsburg (Roman Augusta Vindelicorum), which Zosimus describes in detail (*New History*, 1.68.1):

> Probus made war on the Burgundi and Silingi. But, seeing his forces were too weak, he tried to divide the enemy force and engage only part. He was lucky because he found the enemy armies on the far bank [of the River Lech, a tributary of the Danube] and challenged them to attack his army. This incensed them and many crossed over, fighting until most were killed or captured by the Romans. Those that remained sued for peace, offering to give up their captives and plunder. This Probus acceded to.

However all was not well, for Zosimus then adds (*New History*, 1.68.1):

> But they did not restore all they had taken when they retreated, and Probus was enraged. He fell on them as they were retiring, killed many, and took prisoner their general Igillus. All of them that were taken alive were sent to Britain, where they settled, and subsequently provided good service to the emperor when any insurrection broke out.

Here we see a pragmatic, cash-strapped emperor making good use of his resources, forcing his newly captured Burgundians or Silingi (or both) to serve as *foederates* in a faraway land.

The Vandals are next mentioned fighting alongside the Gepids against the Thervingi and Taifali in a panegyric given in honour of the western emperor Maximian in AD 291, these most likely the Hasdingi. Jordanes then details an early 4th century AD attack on the Hasdingi by the Goths under their king Geberic in his *Getica*, written centuries later for a Gothic audience, (22.113). One should note here that Jordanes is a highly biased narrator, with MacDowall explaining he never misses a chance to promote the Goths and diminish the Vandals (2016, 6). Notably, Jordanes says the enmity between the two Germanic groupings had its origins centuries earlier when the Goths '...subdued their neighbours, the Vandals...' (*Getica*, 4.26). Also of interest, Jordanes says the Hasdingi he details in this 4th century AD conflict were still living in the Tisza region, rather than those who later migrated eastwards to Dacia. He also details their immediate neighbours were the Gepids, Goths, Marcomanni, and Hermanduri, the latter a German tribe who resided on the Danube frontier itself. The impression given here suggests that all were living increasingly cheek by jowl, slowly being squeezed against the northern Roman *limes* by the steady advance of the Huns.

The Vandals lost this conflict, with their king, Visimar, killed. Soon after, this branch of the Hasdingi migrated west away from the Tisza valley to the borders of the new Dominate *diocese* of Pannoniae. There, around AD 330 Constantine I granted them rights to live on the *limes* (*Getica*, 4.26). It is unclear if this was within or without imperial territory, though clearly the agreement worked because these Hasdingi (no doubt joined by those resident in Dacia, long abandoned as imperial territory) remained there for the next 60 years.

However, as the end of the century approached, dramatic change was on the way for the Vandals. By that time, Rome's eastern army under Valens had been destroyed by Fritigern's combined Gothic army at the game-changing battle of Adrianople in AD 378, with the eastern emperor himself losing his life. Although a peace settlement was soon reached, this left vast numbers of barbarians (as the Romans saw them) within imperial territory, whom the empire was powerless to eject.

Further, by the later 4th century AD the westward migration of the Huns had become a major, existential problem for the Romans. It was their conquest of modern Hungary that had driven Fritigern's Goths hard against the Danube frontier in the first place, and by the late AD 390s the southern branch of these ferocious mounted warriors had crossed the Danubian *limes* in huge numbers, overrunning Thrace in Europe and large parts of Syria in the east.

The Huns proved a formidable foe for the Romans because they were only intent on large-scale pillage rather than settlement on imperial territory. Further, in assimilating the various peoples conquered in their widespread campaigns outside and inside the empire, they acquired huge numbers of experienced warriors, with the Alans the first to submit to Hunnic overlordship (Pohl, 2004, 35). These Iranian-speaking horse warriors were recent arrivals in the region, with many still residing 3,500km from the Rhine in their Pontic Steppe homeland as late as the AD 370s (Heather, 2005, 195). Their armies comprised a highly effective combination of armoured charging lancers and skirmishing horse archers. An early-migrating contingent were present in Fritigern's army at Adrianople shortly after, and later they were to play a key role in the story of the Vandals. Meanwhile, others assimilated by the Huns in this way included former Roman military personnel, giving the Huns the ability to besiege Roman cities and towns. This was the first time barbarians had been able to do this, dramatically changing the dynamic of Roman resistance to such incursions. Shocked, the Romans fell back time and again before this first wave of invading Huns. Eventually, they had to buy them off.

This was the first of many Hunnic incursions into the empire as large raiding groups, some army sized, repeatedly smashed their way through the German confederations and tribes north of the *limes* to reach imperial territory. This caused enormous societal dislocation among the Germans, who were driven ever westwards. As winter approached in AD 401 the Vandal Hasdingi tried to escape the Hunnic onslaught by forcing their way into the Dominate province of Raetia Secunda on the upper Danube, this the northernmost part of the *diocese* of Italia and a key lynchpin territory linking the Danubian *limes* in the east with those on the Rhine to the west. There is a real sense of desperation here, the Hasdingi perhaps trying to emulate Fritigern's earlier success in forcing access to imperial territory. However, they failed, and in short order were driven back across the frontier again, though now for the first time in over a century the Hasdingi and Silingi Vandals found themselves in close proximity. Soon they reunited to form one vast Vandal confederation. Still desperate to escape the predations of the Huns, they now sat poised above the heartlands of the continental empire, with Gaul to the west and Italy to the south. They were soon on the move again; with the natural barrier of the Alps screening Italy, they progressed west through the Agri Decumantes gap, the spur of land separating Raetia Secunda in the east and Germania Prima in the west (and long abandoned as imperial territory). Before long they were on the Rhine frontier in Frankish territory, where on a freezing New Year's Eve in AD 406 a major weather event was set to change their destiny forever, and that of Roman Empire.

Vandals in Roman Service

By the time the Hasdingi and Silingi were on the Rhine their warriors had served the Roman Empire for centuries. First, this was as *foederate* mercenaries under their own leaders or Roman officers. Probus' deployment to Britain of those captives from his AD 275 campaign against the Burgundians and Hasdingi is a prime example. However, by the early 4th century AD they were increasingly recruited directly into the mainstream Roman military, either as individual recruits or collectively into entire units. In that regard, many elite *auxilia palatina* regiments of the Dominate were recruited entirely from indigenous communities, good examples including the Batavi, Heruli, and Regae who fought with Julian in the battle of Strasbourg (Roman Argentoratum) in AD 357. Later, we have specific evidence of a unit being recruited direct from the Vandals into the mainstream Roman military. This is the *ala* VIII *Vandilorum*, detailed in the late 4th century AD/early 5th century AD *Notitia Dignitatum* list of military offices across the later Roman Empire. The entry shows this unit based in Egypt helping defend the southern *limes* there. Interestingly, *ala* indicates this is a mounted unit at a time when most Vandal warriors are still thought to have fought on foot, perhaps showing the transition from the latter to the former had already begun by this point.

However, it is at the most senior level we have the best example of a Vandal serving in the Roman military. This is the famous *magister militum* (high-ranking military officer) Flavius Stilicho, who became chief minister to the emperor Honorius in the west. Heather calls him (2005, 216):

> …a particularly successful product of the late Roman career path that saw non-Romans rise through the military to political prominence.

Stilicho's father was a native Vandal who joined the Roman army in the mid-4th century AD and swiftly rose through the ranks to become a senior cavalry officer under Valens, the eastern emperor later to die at Adrianople. Stilicho's father, having risen to high rank, married a Roman noblewoman, with their son born in AD 360. He was destined for a career in the military from birth, given the earlier administrative reforms of Diocletian. These stipulated that eldest sons were obliged to follow their father's profession, and so the young Stilicho soon followed his father into the army (MacDowall, 2016, 13). There he joined the Western emperor's *protectores domestici*, an elite unit originally founded at court as the *protectores divinis lateris* by Constantine I to provide a cadre of senior military officers for deployment across the empire. By the mid-4th century AD this had transformed into something quite different, a select formation carrying out special operations which reported direct to the emperor. In recent research I argue they were almost, though not quite, akin to modern special forces (Elliott, 2023, 94).

Stilicho is first recorded serving on an embassy to the Sassanid Persian king Shāpūr III in AD 383. After returning to Italy, he then married his wife, Serena, a favourite niece of the emperor Theodosius I, the last emperor to rule both the Eastern and Western Empires. He was then appointed *comes* of the *protectores domestici* in AD 385, a very senior position at court which also gave him oversight of the *agentes in rebus* and *notarii*. These were the official outward and inward facing intelligence organisations of the later empire which, like the *protectores domestici*, reported directly to the emperor. Here Stilicho served the emperor well, and in AD 393 he was promoted again to become, at the same time, the *magister equitum* and *magister peditum*. These were the most senior cavalry and infantry command positions in the Western Empire outside of *magister militum*, meaning he accompanied the emperor whenever the latter was on campaign. He was still Theodosius' senior counsel when, in January AD 395, the long-serving emperor died. Fortune now favoured Stilicho because the deceased emperor's heirs, Honorius (in the west) and Arcadius (in the east), were young. While the latter was just old enough at 17 to take his throne alone, the former was only 10. In his will Theodosius therefore named Stilicho as Honorius' guardian. That put him in a position of immense personal power across the entire empire in the west. As Goldsworthy says (2009, 290):

> Even when emperors were strong, their senior officials and commanders routinely and ruthlessly struggled for power, promotion and influence. When emperors were weak or young there was even less restraint in this never-ending contest for dominance.

Soon the young emperor had promoted Stilicho to *magister militum*, the most senior military official in the west. He was quickly in action, in the late AD 390s dealing with a major incursion of Scots, Attecotti, and Picts across the western and northern frontiers in Britain. The defences there had been depleted by numerous usurpation attempts in the 4th century AD (particularly that of Magnus Maximus in the AD 380s), leaving only the *limitanei* border troops in place, with only a few field army troops to support them. This left Britanniae vulnerable to this new onslaught, with Stilicho forced to intervene in AD 398. Gildas later described this event, saying (*De Excidio et Conquestu Britanniae*, 16–17):

> When all at once, like starved and ravening wolves that leap with hungry jaws into the sheepfold when the shepherd is away, the old enemy burst across the frontier. They slaughtered everything … [and] again the Britons sent ambassadors to Rome… The Romans, moved as much as men can be by such accounts of horror, swiftly sent their cavalry by land and their sailors by sea. Like eagles, they plunged the talons of their sword-points into the shoulders of their enemies.

Either in person, or more likely directing from Milan (then the Western capital), it was the *magister militum* who led the imperial response. He certainly took credit for it, with the court poet Claudian saying in a panegyric (*Works, De Consulatu Stilichonis*, 261ff):

> Then, wrapped in the skin of a Caledonian beast, her cheeks tattooed, her sky-blue garments like the waves of Oceanus falling round her feet, Britannia spoke: 'My neighbours would have killed me, but Stilicho protected me – for the Scot roused all Ireland against me and the sea foamed under their hostile oars. Now, thanks to Stilicho, I need not fear the Scottic javelin nor tremble at the Pict.'

Shortly after this, Stilicho's daughter, Maria, was married to Honorius, with the *magister militum* then becoming consul in AD 400.

Stilicho was next in action in AD 401, leading the defence of Italy after the Visigoths invaded under Alaric. Here Milan itself was threatened, with the *magister militum* withdrawing more troops from Britain and also the Rhine frontier to help the defence of the imperial capital. Battle was finally joined at

Pollenzo (Roman Pollentia) in north-eastern Italy on Easter Sunday AD 402, where Stilicho won the day and captured the Visigothic camp. Alaric then agreed to leave Italy and head east in return for the Romans handing over their Visigothic prisoners. However, on the way he soon reneged and in AD 403 besieged Verona. Stilicho was once more the hero of the hour, defeating the Visigoths in battle there, who now left Italy for Dalmatia on the Adriatic coast (Cornell and Matthews, 1982, 208).

Stilicho again defended Italy in AD 405 when the Ostrogoths under Radagaisus invaded. Once more he was successful, with the Ostrogoth leader executed on 23 August AD 406. The delighted Honorius then erected a triumphal arch in Rome to celebrate the victory. Stilicho next planned to tackle the Visigoths once and for all, planning a major campaign to defeat them in Dalmatia. However, this was put on hold by the mass crossing of the frozen Rhine by the Vandals, Alans, and Suebi on New Year's Eve AD 406 (see Chapter 4 for full detail), and by the usurpation of Constantine III in Britain. The latter was the event which finally triggered this far-north-western *diocese* falling out of imperial control for the final time. Alaric then took advantage of both events and led his army north to the province of Noricum, sitting poised above north-eastern Italy. From there he demanded 1,800kg of gold, claiming it was compensation for the trouble Stilicho had earlier caused him. The *magister militum*, his attention on Constantine III who was by this time in Gaul, persuaded the Roman Senate to pay, though at great cost to his own prestige there with the patricians who had never forgotten his Vandal origins.

By this time the empress Maria had died, leaving Stilicho also vulnerable with the emperor. However, in early AD 408 he persuaded Honorius to marry another of his daughters, called Thermantia. His influence continued to decline though, and when Arcadius died in Constantinople later the same year court officials began spreading rumours the *magister militum* was planning to place his son, Eucherius, on the eastern throne. This led to the revolt of many of the Roman troops in northern Italy, with Stilicho forced to flee to Ravenna, the north-eastern city on the Adriatic coast which Honorius was restyling as his new imperial capital given its highly defensible position. There the emperor ordered Stilicho to be imprisoned, with the *magister militum* and Eucherius promptly executed on 22 August. Thus came to an end the unlikely tale of the Vandal who rose to the very top of Roman society, only to suffer fatally for his barbarian origins at the last.

CHAPTER 4

Vandal Migration

To this point, the story of the Vandals has been largely set in *barbaricum*. There, the German peoples were now facing suffocating levels of external pressure caused by the western migration of the Huns. This had driven them hard against the imperial frontiers along the Rhine and Danube. Against this grim backdrop, the reunited Hasdingi and Silingi found themselves on the eastern bank of the former. An extreme weather event then opened a route for them into the Western Empire when the Rhine froze on New Year's Eve AD 406. Thus began an astonishing migration as, accompanied by their Alan and Suebi neighbours, they spent the next 23 years predating their way through first Roman Gaul, and then Spain. Ultimately, this set the Vandal king, Gaiseric, up to seize the greatest imperial prize of them all, Roman North Africa. In this chapter I tell the story of their travels through Europe, before turning to Africa in Chapter 5.

Note this narrative is my own carefully reconstructed chronology based on the detailed cross referencing of primary sources and archaeological data, the latter for the first time offering a degree of granularity previously lacking. Therefore, here the reader will find a brand-new appraisal of their travels through Gaul and Spain. Also note that given the frequency with which the Vandals, Alans, and Suebi are referenced, for narrative elegance I also refer to them as barbarians and invaders, noting in advance the loaded Roman perspective of both terms as earlier discussed.

In the Bleak Midwinter

The various Roman provinces, and later *diocese*, ranging south and west of the Rhine and Danube have been referenced frequently in this work. Now, with the Vandals, Alans, and Suebi poised to cross the Rhine, a deeper geographic

understanding is required. Therefore, here I first set out the political organization of the region in both the Principate and Dominate.

Next, I fully detail the crossing event itself. This includes a discussion
on who exactly made the passage, why it took place, what provided the
opportunity at that specific moment in time, how firm the New Year's Eve
AD 406 date is, and what the numbers involved were. I then consider where
the actual crossing points on the Rhine were, and the nature of the initial
frontier breach. Finally, I move on to the subsequent destruction of much of
Roman Gaul by ravaging bands of Vandals, Alans, and Suebi prior to their
crossing the Pyrenees into the Iberian Peninsula in AD 409.

The Northern Frontier

The rich Roman provinces in northern Europe had already been broadly
established by the time Augustus died in AD 14, excepting far off Britannia and
Dacia, these later additions under Claudius and Trajan respectively. Each was
interlinked with the rest of the empire by the superb imperial administration
established by the first emperor.

In terms of the Rhine frontier, real Roman interest there had actually begun
much further south as early as the mid-2nd century BC through mercantile
engagement with the Greek colony of Marseille (Greek and Roman Massilia).
There, a treaty was signed to protect the town from Iberians to the west and
Gauls to the north. Further Roman interest there led to the creation of a new
province in 122 BC along the Mediterranean coast called Transalpine Gaul
(also called *Provincia Nostra*, translating as 'our province'), this later being
renamed Gallia Narbonensis after its regional capital of Narbonne (Roman
Narbo) was founded in 118 BC.

The province then became the springboard for Julius Caesar's conquest of
Gaul when he became its governor in 58 BC, along with Cisalpine Gaul. In
pursuit of glory and wealth, Caesar lost no time in campaigning north and
by the end of the decade had reduced the Gallic kingdoms there to Roman
vassalage.

From that time they became new Roman provinces, these later revised
by Augustus in 22 BC, and once more towards the end of his reign as more
territory was added to the north and east of the region. By the later 2nd
century AD, as the Principate empire reached the height of Roman power,
there were nine provinces there. These were:

- Germania Inferior in the Rhine Delta and lower Rhine valley.
- Germania Superior in the upper Rhine valley.
- Gallia Belgica, broadly the area of modern Belgium.

- Gallia Lugdunensis, a broad strip through modern central France ranging from Brittany in the west to the provincial capital of Lyon (Roman Lugdunum) in the east.
- Gallia Aquitania along the Bay of Biscay.
- Gallia Narbonensis in modern Provence, a Senatorial province.
- Three small provinces bordering Gallia Narbonensis and Italy, from north to south Alpes Graiae et Poeninae, Alpes Cottiae, and Alpes Maritimae.

This large region featured distinct cultural and economic differences across its wide geography. The far north and east were more militarised given the provinces there featured the *limes Germanicus* separating the world of Rome from *barbaricum* to the north and east. Further south, the northern Gallic provinces were nicknamed Gallia Comata, meaning 'long haired Gaul'. This territory featured fine-quality agricultural land heavily exploited for arable and fruit crops, including the fine quality wines associated with the region to this day. It was also the home to a dense network of *fabricae* state-run manufactories around Autun (Roman Augustodunum) in the Bourgogne-Franche-Comté region of modern France. These produced much of the equipment for the Roman military in Britain, Germany, and Gaul. As the Principate progressed, this region of non-Mediterranean Gaul also developed a reputation for social conservatism in its arts and culture, and was home to a substantial commercial class whose goods were traded across the empire. Pre-eminent among these were the Samian ware ceramic works at La Graufensque near Millau, Lezoux, and Clermont-Ferrand. These made high-quality table wares using a glossy red surface slip which was popular across the empire. By way of contrast the far south of Gaul at the time was far more urbanized, reflecting the longevity of large-scale stone-built settlements there dating back to the early period of Greek expansion in the western Mediterranean.

The key cities in Germany and Gaul all played a major role in the later Vandal and other German incursions south through imperial territory, the former when on their way to Spain. In addition to Lyon, they included:

- Cologne, provincial capital of Germania Inferior.
- Mainz, a major legionary fortress and provincial capital of Germania Superior.
- Reims (Roman Durocotorum), early provincial capital of Gallia Belgica.
- Trier, later provincial capital of Gallia Belgica.
- Narbonne, provincial capital of Narbonensis.
- Marseille, the key Mediterranean port city.

The Rhine frontier featured a dense chain of fortifications to maintain the northern *limes* that ran for over 570km from the Rhine Delta to the Danube. The key bases were the legionary fortresses, with sites at:

- Nijmegen (Roman Noviomagus).
- Xanten (Roman Vetera).
- Neuss (Roman Novaesium).
- Cologne, already detailed.
- Mainz, already detailed.

A further 55 other forts of various sizes and over 1,000 watchtowers completed the defensive frontier here. The *limes Germanicus* was divided into three sections, these being:

- The Lower Germanic *limes* extending from the North Sea coast to the Rheinbrohl municipality in the Rhineland Palatinate of modern Germany.
- The Upper Germanic *limes* from Rheinbrohl to Lorch am Rhein near Darmstadt in Hesse.
- The Rhaetian *limes*.

By the late 2nd century AD the *limes* of the first two sections were home to some of the crack legions of the Roman Empire. These included *legio* VIII *Augusta* and *legio* XXII *Primigenia pia fidelis* in Germania Inferior, and *legio* I *Flavia Minervia pia fidelis* and *legio* XXX *Ulpia Victrix* in Germania Superior. The military establishment here also featured the usual complement of auxiliaries, and the *Classis Germanica* regional fleet. This large navy was responsible for patrolling the Rhine from deep within the continental interior at its confluence with the Vinxtbach stream in the modern Rhineland Palatinate through to the Zuiderzee and the North Sea coastlines in the Rhine Delta area. It also had responsibility for the Rhine's many tributaries, and was later tasked with patrolling the rivers Meuse and Scheldt. Together the legions, auxiliaries, and fleet faced off against multiple Germanic, and later Gothic, threats to the north. This included the Vandals.

Heading east, the Danubian *limes* completed the northern frontier. Though peripheral to the southerly migration of the Vandals through Gaul and Spain, the region played a key role earlier in their history. More importantly, events south of the Danube at the time of their migration also had a big impact further west. I therefore detail the Danube frontier here for context.

The river Danube is a huge continental waterway, rising in southern Germany and flowing southeastward 2,850km before draining into the Black Sea. The mighty river was a crucial imperial frontier, with eight rich provinces to its south and one to the north at the height of the Principate empire in the late 2nd century AD. West to east, these were:

- Raetia, the province linking the Rhine and Danube.
- Noricum.
- Pannonia Superior.
- Pannonia Inferior.
- Dalmatia.
- Moesia Superior.
- Dacia, the redoubt province standing proud of the Danube, established by Trajan after his final conquest campaign there in AD 106. It was finally abandoned by Aurelian in AD 275.
- Moesia Inferior.
- Thracia.

The Danubian region in the Roman period was complex in terms of wealth and culture, with Cornell and Matthews explaining that (1982, 140):

> The Danubian provinces, taken together, spanned the whole range of Roman civilization, from the settled Celtic tribes of the west and the urbanized seaboard of Dalmatia to the ancient Greek cities of the Black Sea coast. The Thracian regions east of the pass of Succi were Greek-speaking and their cities had Greek names. Meanwhile the 'Latinisation' of Dacia is still actively attested by modern Romanian.

The key cities of the region included:

- Augsberg (Roman Augusta Vindelicorum), provincial capital of Raetia.
- Wels (Roman Ovilava), provincial capital of Noricum.
- Vienna.
- Carnuntum, provincial capital of Pannonia Superior.
- Split (Roman Aspalathos) on the Adriatic coast where Diocletian later built his palace when he retired.
- Budapest (Roman Aquincum), provincial capital of Pannonia Inferior.
- Kostolac (Roman Viminacium), provincial capital of Moesia Superior.
- Ulpia Traiana Sarmizegetusa, provincial capital of Dacia.
- Konstantsa (Roman Tomis), provincial capital of Moesia Inferior.
- Perinthus, provincial capital of Thracia.

As with the Rhine, the Danubian provinces were defined by the northern *limes* there which ran for much of the river's length. Cornell and Matthews call these the backbone of the empire, with the lengthy fortifications divided into four sections (1982, 140):

- The Rhaetian *limes*, here only the section on the Danube.
- The Noric *limes* in Noricum.
- The Pannonian *limes* in Pannonia Superior and Inferior.
- The Moesian *limes* in Moesia Superior and Inferior, running downriver to the Black Sea. From AD 106 after Trajan's Dacian conquests until the province was abandoned by Aurelian this section actually ran far to the north, encompassing the whole Dacian salient and comprising much of modern Romania.

For much of the Principate the Danubian *limes* were home to some of the most experienced legions in the empire. They were based in a string of legionary fortresses along the frontier, ranging from Vienna in the west to Troesmis in the east. By the late 2nd century AD the legions here included *legio* III *Italica concurs* in Raetia, *legio* II *Italica* in Noricum, *legio* XIV *Gemina Martia Victrix*, *legio* I *Adiutrix pia fidelis* and later *legio* X *Gemina* in Pannonia Superior, *legio* II *Adiutrix pia fidelis* in Pannonia Inferior, *legio* IV *Flavia felix* and *legio* VII *Claudia pia fidelis* in Moesia Superior, *legio* XIII *Gemina pia fidelis* in Dacia, and *legio* I *Italica*, *legio* V *Macedonia*, and *legio* XI *Claudia pia fidelis* in Moesia Inferior. As with the Rhine frontier, they were joined by an equivalent number of auxiliaries, while the two regional fleets here were the *Classis Flavia Pannonica* on the upper Danube and the *Classis Flavia Moesica* on the lower Danube. The latter also had responsibility for the Black Sea, controlling access from there to the Mediterranean.

While this provincial structure along the Rhine and Danube proved sufficient to successfully administer the region through most of the Principate phase of empire, the 'Crisis of the 3rd Century' changed this situation dramatically. Such were the multiple shocks then experienced by all levels of Roman society that Diocletian, emperor from AD 284, was forced to take drastic action in order to drag the empire out of the maelstrom it now found itself in.

Once emperor he quickly realised the political structures of the Principate were no longer fit for purpose, and as detailed earlier, from this point we refer to the empire as the Dominate. Diocletian specifically reformed the empire in three ways, in what later became known as the Diocletianic Reformation:

- First, he instituted the tetrarchic system of political control that divided power across his vast empire between first two and then four (two senior and styled augustus, and two junior and styled caesar) brother-emperors. Note he retained overall control.
- Second, he completely reordered the provincial structure of the Principate in order to secure much firmer control of the tax base of the empire. Key to this was the creation of a new system of *diocese*, these much larger units of economic control, to replace the older provinces. Each *diocese* was then broken down into a number of new, much smaller provinces.
- Third, by adding extra layers of public administration to support the above, he greatly increased the coercive power of the Roman state. This allowed a fully systemised taxation regime to be introduced on all economic production called the *annona militaris*.

With the introduction of the new system of *diocese*, the administrative structure of the imperial heartlands in Germany, Gaul, and south of the Danube was completely changed. Each of these much larger units of organisation was now controlled by a *vicarius* (sometimes called an *exarch* in the Greek speaking Danubian region), this a senior official appointed directly by the emperor who combined the power of the earlier provincial governors and procurators. The *vicarii* were usually based in the most significant city or town in the *diocese*. Meanwhile those appointed to run the new, smaller provinces within each *diocese* retained the title governor, though now had far less authority within the rigid new administrative structure of the empire.

Diocletian originally created 12 *dioceses*, with those in Germany, Gaul, and south of the Danube (together with their respective, smaller provinces) detailed in the table below (Cornell and Mathews, 1982, 172):

Diocese	Province
Galliae (the Rhine frontier and northern Gaul)	Germania Prima
	Germania Secunda
	Belgica Prima
	Belgica Secunda
	Lugdunensis Prima
	Lugdunensis Secunda

Diocese	Province
Viennensis (southern Gaul)	Aquitanica Prima Aquitanica Secunda Novem Populi Narbonensis Prima Narbonensis Secunda Viennensis (which gave the *diocese* its name)
Pannoniae	Noricum Ripense Noricum Mediterraneum Pannonia Prima Pannonia Secunda Valeria Salvia Dalmatia
Moesiae (now including the former Principate provinces in the Balkans)	Moesia Prima Dacia (not the abandoned Principate redoubt province north of the Danube, but a new one south of the river) Praevalitana Dardania Epirus Nova Epirus Vetus Macedonia Thessalia Achaea
Thraciae	Moesia Secunda Scythia Thracia Haemimontius Rhodope Europa

A further reform of the Dominate empire's geographic organization occurred under Constantine I. This saw the large *diocese* themselves set within four even larger units of administration with the creation of *prefectures* which effectively quartered the empire, roughly tracing the *tetrarchic* system of imperial rule set up by Diocletian. These were, in the north and west the *Praefectura praetorio Galliarum* and the *Praefectura praetorio Italiae*, then along the Danube frontier and in the Balkans the *Praefectura praetorio Illyrici*, and finally in the east (including Egypt) the *Praefectura praetorio Orientis*. The first two were under the ultimate control of the Western emperor, the latter two the eastern emperor. It is the former two, along with their constituent *diocese*, that provided the administrative backdrop to the transformation of the imperial heartlands in the west from the Roman to the post-Roman world.

The Vandals Cross the Rhine

By the beginning of the 5th century AD the *limes Germanicus* had long been under severe pressure from Germans and Goths eager to predate Roman territory in Gaul. The preceding century had seen the frontier breached a number of times, for example in the AD 350s by the Alamanni and Franks fought by Julian the Apostate. The difficulty the *caesar* faced here expelling them from Gaul should not be underestimated and was only achieved through excellent leadership at a strategic and tactical level, culminating in his victory at Strasbourg in AD 357.

Then, at the beginning of the 5th century AD, an existential threat emerged in the west. This was Alaric and his Visigoths who invaded Italy in AD 401, as detailed in Chapter 3. Though Stilicho defeated the invaders at Pollenzo in April AD 402, it set in place a pattern to be repeated time and again as the northern *limes* were now regularly over-run. More often than not, the system of defence in depth featuring *limitanei* border troops and *comitatenses* field armies deployed deeper in imperial territory failed.

Our best recorded example is the massed mid-winter crossing of the Rhine by the now reunited Hasdingi and Silingi Vandals on New Year's Eve AD 406. Here they were joined by their Alan and Suebi neighbours. The former were a large contingent of the Iranian-speaking mounted steppe warriors who had escaped capitulation to the Huns, while the latter was the name given to the huge Germanic confederation that included the Marcomanni, Juthingi, Quadi, and other tribes. Which branch of the Suebi was engaged here is unclear, though they were led by a king called Hermeric. Drinkwater has argued that the initial gathering of barbarians on the east bank of the Rhine also included remnants of Radagaisus' recently defeated Ostrogoths (1998, 269). This would make sense given that, aside from the 12,000 survivors recruited by Stilicho into the Roman army as *foederates*, there is no evidence what happened to the remainder, who must have numbered in their tens of thousands. Logic suggests they would have either joined Alaric's Visigoths, still in the Balkans, or the Vandals to the north. Sadly there is no direct evidence for either.

Jerome also says in a letter written in Bethlehem in AD 409 that the Vandals, Alans, and Suebi were joined by other peoples including Sarmatians, Gepids, Heruls, Saxons, and Burgundians, though again there is no evidence for this. Most think it a trope on his part to list as many barbarians as possible (*Lettres, Epistle to Ageruchia*, 123.16).

The Vandal Rhine crossing was an event so significant it is unusually well referenced by contemporary authors. It continues to be much discussed today. In terms of why the crossing took place when it did, Gregory of Tours argues in his *History of the Franks* that the cause was a mass raid by the Franks on the Vandals, who were by then resident on the former's territory on the eastern bank of the Rhine. His source was a now-lost account by the 5th century AD Roman historian Renatus Profuterus Frigeridus, today called the 'Frigeridus fragment'. In this narrative the Hasdingi Vandal king Godegisel was killed in the raid along with 20,000 Vandal warriors, with the Alans under their king Respendial and Suebi under Hermeric then coming to their rescue (*History of the Franks*, 2.9). This would explain the close proximity of the three people when the Rhine crossing took place. However, the key point to note here is that the combined forces of both the Hasdingi and Silingi Vandals had been defeated, and they had to rely on neighbours to save them. Further, they were clearly not welcome guests of the Franks, with more predation likely to follow if they remained on Frankish territory. Pohl suggests an additional complexity here, arguing the Franks were actually operating under orders from the Romans, who paid them a huge bribe to disperse the Vandal threat before the *limes* could be threatened (2004, 36). Whether the Romans were involved or not, the Vandal situation was now clearly desperate, with MacDowall saying this explains why they and their Alan and Suebi neighbours risked crossing a major continental waterway at the height of mid-winter into hostile territory (2016, 37).

Opportunity for the Vandals, Alans, and Suebi to cross the Rhine on New Year's Eve AD 406 was threefold. First, today some argue the weather at the time was so cold the Rhine froze. This idea was first suggested as a possibility by Edward Gibbon in the later 18th century AD in his *The History of the Decline and Fall of the Roman Empire*, and has since gained widespread support. This is surprising given there are no contemporary accounts to support it. Further, as detailed in Chapter 3, there is no record of a long-term climate change event at the time, with Lambshead saying that northern Europe was '…enjoying a reasonably stable climate…' at the time (2022, 65).

We are therefore left to consider how likely it is the Rhine would freeze in 'normal' weather circumstances. In the 20th century AD the Rhine froze over a significant length of its course on two occasions, these in the winters of 1929/30 and 1962/63. In the former event, it froze as far upstream as the Nibelungen bridge at Worms (Roman Borbetomagus) in the modern German state of Rhineland-Palatinate. Meanwhile, in the latter it froze even further upstream in a clearly extreme weather event. This was the coldest winter of the 20th century AD in Germany, with temperatures reaching −24°C, and with snow beginning to fall in early November 1962 and staying on the ground until March 1963.

This gives a twice a century likelihood of the Rhine freezing based on this modern, 'normal' weather scenario. However, we then need to consider two additional modern factors which impact whether the river will freeze of not. First, the modern Rhine is far more polluted than in the Roman period, and has been so throughout the industrial age. This pollution raises the freezing temperature of the water, meaning that in the Roman period there was more of a chance it would freeze in the same weather conditions. Second, today's river is canalised for the majority of its length, meaning it is now narrower and deeper than the river of late antiquity. This leads to a faster flow today, again making it less likely to freeze than in the Roman period.

A final consideration here is modern scientific analysis based on measuring solar activity at the beginning of the 5th century AD. This shows that while the climate was indeed broadly stable across the region, as Lambshead suggests, and had been so for decades, in this specific snapshot in time there were several very short but severe climate stress events. In simple terms, this means there were a number of very sharp drops in winter temperature.

Here, one is then left to make an anecdotal decision on whether the Rhine could have frozen in mid-winter AD 406, with no historical but some scientific data to inform the choice. In my view, given the vast numbers of Vandals, Alans, and Suebi who did cross the river in what was clearly a short period of time, I think it more likely than not the river was indeed frozen. This is therefore the narrative I will continue to use.

Second, the Vandals and their allies had detailed intelligence about the depleted state of the *limes Germanicus* at the time. It was common knowledge that Stilicho had removed military units from the Rhine frontier to help defend Italy from Alaric in AD 401, with this campaign still ongoing in AD 403 even after the Visigothic defeat at Pollenzo a year earlier. Then in AD 405 he was in action again, defending Italy against Radagaisus' Ostrogoths. Therefore, it seems likely the troops removed in AD 401 had yet to return. Notably, they included not only *comitatenses* (field army troops) but also *limitanei* (border troops) reformed into *pseudocomitatenses* (line-of-battle units), showing the initial level of jeopardy Italy faced during Alaric's first incursion. Following Pohl's hypothesis, this potentially also explains why the Romans may have paid the Franks to intervene against the Vandals north of the frontier. From Stilicho's perspective, given he lacked the manpower to defend the *limes Germanicus* at that particular moment in time, hiring a rival German confederation (and one already antagonistic to the Vandals given the latter were now resident in their territory) may have been his only alternative.

However, to make matters worse for the Romans, by this time (as detailed in Chapter 3) Vandals had long been serving in the Roman military. On their retirement many returned to their tribes, in so doing passing through the Roman *limes*. They would take with them detailed intelligence about the state of the imperial defences further south, which in some places seem to have been non-existent. To the Vandals, Alans, and Suebi, hard pressed by the Franks, this was clearly a once in a lifetime opportunity to force their way over the frontier into the rich lands of Roman Gaul.

Additionally, the usual Roman response when short of numbers along the frontiers was to hire *foederates* to replace the regular troops. In retrospect, it is clear some Germans and Goths hired to help defend the *limes Germanicus* were untrustworthy and were feeding information to those on the eastern bank, perhaps even playing an active role in allowing the Vandals, Alans, and Suebi to cross the Rhine. By way of analogy we can look here to Britain in the context of a major event in AD 376 which Ammianus Marcellinus styles the *barbarica conspiratio*, and today we call the 'Great Conspiracy' (*The Later Roman Empire*, 27.8.5). Here the late Roman historian and *protector domesticii* details how *comes* Theodosius won a hard-fought campaign to repulse a mass incursion by Germans crossing the North Sea, Picts and Attecotti from the region of modern Scotland, and Irish. At the time the *diocese* had become over-reliant on irregular *exploratores* (border scouts) to protect the frontier region north of Hadrian's Wall (Elliott, 2023, 113). Marcellinus calls them *areani*, and given Theodosius disbanded them after defeating the conspiracy, the inference is they had earlier assisted the Picts and Attecotti to cross the border.

Third, and stating the obvious, is the simple fact the imperial court's attention was diverted away from the northern frontier. This was not just in the context of troop numbers, but in its focus more broadly. I have already detailed how Stilicho's attention at the beginning of the 5th century AD was solely on the defence of Italy, first from Alaric and later Radagaisus. Additionally, Britanniae also remained a troubled *diocese* given Stilicho had to intervene there in AD 398, and within a year of the Rhine crossing the usurpations of Marcus, Gratian, and Constantine III took place (see below).

Finally, as AD 406 came to an end, Stilicho was increasingly looking towards the Balkans, this leading to the series of missteps that ended with his execution in August AD 408. In short, and using modern parlance, on New Year's Eve AD 406 the Romans had taken their eye off the ball on the Rhine frontier.

The traditional date given for the Rhine crossing is 31 December AD 406, this based on the timeline of Prosper of Aquitaine in his *Prosperi Tironis Epitoma Chronicon* where he says (*Arcadio VI et Probo, Wandali et Halani Gallias Trajecto Rheno Ingress*, 2):

> In the sixth consulship of Arcadius and Probus, Vandals and Alans came unto the Gauls, having crossed the Rhine, on the day before the kalends of January.

As far as late antique sources go, this is as specific as one can get, especially given Prosper lived through the event as a teenager. However, two other dates are suggested by other ancient authors, these Paulus Orosius and Zosimus, the latter using surviving fragments written by Olympiodorus of Thebes which cover the event. Orosius' *Seven Books of History Against the Pagans*, written in the second decade of the 5th century AD, mentions in passing that the crossing took place two years before the AD 410 Gothic sack of Rome, making the year of the Rhine crossing AD 408. Meanwhile in Zosimus' *New History*, likely written at the beginning of the 6th century AD, he details Gaul being ravaged in AD 406. Given this would be before any crossing of the Rhine on New Year's Eve of the same year, it has led to speculation the date of the event was actually the end of AD 405. In his recent analysis of the data, MacDowall says he is not particularly convinced by either alternative date, and I agree (2016, 35). Therefore I will continue to use New Year's Eve AD 406 as the date for the Vandal, Alan, and Suebi crossing of the Rhine.

In terms of how many Vandals, Alans, and Suebi crossed the frozen Rhine, here we again rely on our primary sources. Cross referencing Orosius (*Seven Books of History Against the Pagans*, 7.40.3), Zosimus (*New History*, 6.3.1), and Procopius (*The Vandalic War*, 1.3) we have a figure in the high tens of thousands. Pohl has this as just under 100,000 (2004, 36), while MacDowall says it is not unreasonable to suggest up to 60,000 Vandals and 30,000 Alans and Suebi (2016, 37). The Hasdingi Vandals were led by Gunderic, son of Godegisel who had earlier been killed by the Franks. It is unclear who led the Silingi Vandals at the time. Meanwhile, the Alans were still led by Respendial, and the Suebi by Hermeric.

It should be noted here that the mid-winter Rhine crossing was not a simple large-scale military incursion, but a mass migration of despairing Germans and Iranians hoping for a better life once they had forced their way onto imperial territory. In that context, the people's crossing featured all levels of their respective societies, including women and children, and also an extensive baggage train. No more than 40% at this stage were likely warriors.

The Destruction of Gaul

Most historians today locate the centre of axis for the mid-winter Rhine crossing at Mainz, based on Jerome's narrative which records the Roman city as the first to be destroyed. Here he provides graphic detail, saying that '...in its church many thousands have been massacred...' (*Lettres, Epistle to Ageruchia*, 123.20). However, given the scale of the crossing, it was most likely on a much wider front, especially with the river frozen over.

After this initial breach the Vandals, Alans, and Suebi quickly splintered into numerous smaller bands, no doubt desperate for provisions given the time of year.

Two broad fronts of ingress into Gaul are then evident, with untouched Trier to the west of Mainz the fulcrum. First, large numbers of barbarians headed south, following the Rhine upriver. They quickly reached Worms, and then Strasbourg. Both were brutally sacked. By this time most Roman cities in Gaul featured significant (though often small in diameter) defensive wall circuits built from stone. Many of these fortifications incorporated the latest in defensive military technology, for example projecting bastions able to enfilade an attacker as they approached. However, of the towns sacked now or later, only Worms is detailed by Jerome putting up significant resistance. Specifically, he says '...the people of Worms after a long siege have been wiped out...' (*Lettres, Epistle to Ageruchia*, 123.20). The ease with which the Vandals, Alans, and Suebi reduced the rest of the cities they attacked suggests only one thing: that the Roman system of defence in depth in Gaul really had failed completely, with those few *limitanei* Stilicho had left in place along the frontier overwhelmed, and the *comitatensis* (field armies) absent.

The Rhine crossing also represented a dramatic failure of Roman intelligence-gathering along the frontier. Clearly the imperial authorities were caught completely unawares, taking no extra precautions to ensure the cities across the region could better withstand a siege. By the early 5th century AD the built environment in Gaul had long been used to Germanic predation across the *limes*, with magistrates knowing if their city was besieged it would only be for a short time given the invader's lack of siege technology to breach a stone-built wall circuit. Further, they knew relief would soon be on the way. In those 'normal' circumstances, the Germans then quickly moved on to easier pickings in the countryside. Now, however, the cities had not been able to stock up on food and build additional shelter for rural refugees, both important given this was mid-winter, and a very cold one at that. Further, the town councils knew there was no prospect of swift relief. In such circumstances they were faced with a terrible dilemma, to resist and starve, or throw themselves on the mercy of the barbarians by opening the gates. In both cases the choice failed, and dramatically, with tens of thousands of Romano-Gallic citizens slaughtered.

The various disparate leadership groups among the Vandals, Alans, and Suebi were clearly astonished by the ease with which these first cities in Roman Gaul were overcome. Soon the thought of any accommodation with the empire disappeared. As winter turned to spring in AD 407, they surveyed the wider landscape before them, noting one thing in particular. There were no Roman military units to stop them. For now, they could do as they wished, provided their people were fed, watered, and sheltered.

By this point the eastern group of invaders had left Strasbourg in ruins and were continuing south along the Rhine, soon reaching the nearby river Doubs, this a left-bank tributary of the river Saône. Heading down the valley of the Doubs, some bands then branched out to target any easily accessible Roman settlements along the local road networks. Soon Langres (Roman Andematunum), Besançon (Roman Vesontio), Autun, and even Clermont-Farrand (Roman Augustonemetum) in the Massif Central were in ruins. Meanwhile, the main eastern group continued south on reaching the Saône and soon had Lyon in view. This was the principal city of Roman France, and a significant transport node where all the main regional trunk roads in Gaul met, many of these then passing through the Alps to Italy. Further, Lyon also featured the confluence of the Saône with the river Rhône, opening the way to the Mediterranean coast for the barbarians.

Sometime after the eastern group of barbarians headed down the Rhine to Worms and Strasbourg, a second disparate group headed west, targeting north-western Gaul. We are well served here by Jerome who carefully lists in chronological order the Romano-Gallic cities sacked. These were Reims (where the city's bishop, St Nicasius, and his sister, St Eutropia, were beheaded), Amiens (Roman Samarobriva), Arras (Roman Nemetacum), Tournai (Roman Turnacum) and finally Thérouanne (Roman Tarvenna). Of note, the latter was only 40km from Boulogne-sur-Mer (Roman Bononia) on the North Sea coast. Interestingly, the archaeological record shows that the key Roman fortresses on the lower Rhine, for example Cologne and Nijmegen, were untouched. This shows the western ingress focused purely on the rich hinterland, with the invaders following the principal trunk roads in a desperate search for sustenance as well as loot.

By the summer of AD 407 the eastern group of barbarians had almost reached the Mediterranean, while those in the west consolidated in place, no doubt pondering what to do next. By then Vandal, Alan, and Suebi numbers had been swelled by economic refugees from Gaul, these the victims of the economic dislocation caused by the invasion. With their livelihoods destroyed and homes burned, many chanced joining the barbarians. Others turned to brigandage, forming roving bands of *bagaudae*. These were a common feature in Roman Gaul, always emerging to predate state infrastructure in times of crisis.

To this point all had fallen before invaders, with Jerome painting a grim picture of events. He says (*Lettres, Epistle to Ageruchia*, 123.21):

> The savage tribes in countless numbers have overrun all parts of Gaul. The whole country between the Alps and the Pyrenees, between the Rhine and the Ocean, has been laid waste by hordes of them.

Other contemporary writers are equally apocalyptic, particularly the Christian Gallic poets for which Gaul was famous for at the time. For example, Orientus wrote that '…all Gaul was filled with the smoke of a single funeral pyre…' (*Orientii Commonitorium*, 2.184). Meanwhile, Prosper wondered if his generation was seeing the total collapse of their known world. He says (*Defence of St Augustine*, 17.25):

> He who once turned the soil with a hundred ploughs, now labours to have just a pair of oxen; the man who often rode through splendid cities in his carriages is now sick and travels to the deserted countryside wearily and on foot. The merchant who used to cleave the seas with ten lofty ships now embarks on a tiny skiff, and is his own helmsman. Neither country nor city is as it was; everything rushes headlong to its end.

Various contemporary saints' 'lives' now pick up the detail as the two axes of predation worked their way through Gaul over the next two years. These hagiographies, the written lives or biographies of various Romano-Gallic Saints, were designed to commemorate particular feast days. Here, they record either a city or town's destruction, a martyrdom, or the settlement's miraculous escape. In my narrative below, given I only aim to trace the two barbarian routes of ingress through Gaul to the Pyrenees, I don't distinguish between which unless it is specifically relevant.

The eastern axis soon hit the Mediterranean and, no doubt finding the Alpine passes to Italy heavily defended, turned west along the coast. Cities and towns targeted as they progressed included Arles (Roman Arrelate), Uzès (Roman Ucetia), and Béziers (Roman Baeterrae). Jerome also says that, in this later phase, Toulouse (Roman Tolosa) was besieged, and only saved from destruction by the intervention of its bishop Exuperius (*Lettres, Epistle to Ageruchia*, 123.25).

Meanwhile, in the west the group there first destroyed Laon (Roman Alaudanum) to the northwest of Reims, and Arcis-sur-Aube (Roman Artiaca) to its southeast. It then headed southwest towards Aquitaine. On the way it targeted Meung-sur-Loire (Roman Magdunum) and then, much further south, Bazas (Roman Civitas Vasatica) and Éauze (Roman Elusa).

It is astonishing to note here the initial inaction of the imperial centre when its two rich *dioceses* in Gaul were being systematically ransacked. Clearly the issues which had diverted Stilicho's attention away from the Rhine frontier in late AD 406 were still preoccupying him into AD 407 (Heather, 2005, 206). Perhaps the gravity of the situation only slowly dawned on the imperial leadership as, drip by drip, news of each city being sacked reached them in Milan and Rome. Indeed, the only success the Romans seemed to have had in Gaul prior to the intervention of the British usurper Constantine III (see below) was with a significant number of Alans under a leader called Goar. These found accommodation with the Roman authorities and agreed to settle around Orléans (Roman Aurelianum), a key regional town in central Gaul, as *foederate* mercenaries (MacDowall, 2016, 46).

The story of Constantine III is one of the more remarkable of those making a play for the imperial throne in late antiquity. By the first decade of the 5th century AD the *diocese* of Britanniae had long been in decline, even though still fully integrated within the empire. Then in AD 407 three leading figures in Britain usurped in succession. Zosimus directly links the event to the Rhine crossing by the Vandals, Alans, and Suebi, saying the military there '…were compelled through fear of their proceeding as far as their country…' (*New History*, 6.2.1). Given the proximity of the western group of barbarians to the North Sea coast, this is no surprise, with Britain effectively cut off from the nearest imperial territory on the continent. The seizure of Boulogne-sur-Mer, the key port in the region, would then have allowed raiding parties to cross to Britain. Also, fear of severe economic dislocation clearly played a role here, especially among the military in the *diocese*. As Lambshead points out in his recent survey of the fall of Roman Britain, at that point their pay was two years in arrears (2022, 137). Now cut off from the imperial mints in Gaul, they decided to act to ensure they were ultimately paid.

As detailed earlier, the usurpers in Britain were called Marcus (likely the *Comes Britanniarum* senior commander in the *diocese*), Gratianus (another military leader), and Constantine III. The first two never left the *diocese* and were assassinated by the disgruntled soldiery within months, but Constantine III did survive and then travelled to the continent in pursuit of the Western throne. At first he was highly successful, and for a time looked set to succeed. His original name is unknown, but on usurping he quickly adopted the regnal name Flavius Claudius Constantine III, renaming his sons Constans and Julian at the same time. He crossed to Gaul in early summer of AD 407 with the remaining *comitatensis* field army troops in Britain, and perhaps some *limitanei*, too. Once there, having surveyed the devastation in the northwest of the region after the initial barbarian onslaught, he gathered any remaining troops and set about restoring order to the Rhine frontier. On the way there he engaged a group of barbarians directly. These could have been *foederates* sent to challenge his usurpation by Stilicho and the emperor Honorius, though were most likely the Vandals, Alans, and Suebi still in the region. This battle took place in late AD 407, which Zosimus describes as follows (*New History*, 6.2.1):

> A furious battle ensued between them in which the Romans gained victory, and killed most of the barbarians. Yet by not pursuing those who fled, by which means they might have put to death every man, they gave them the opportunity to rally, and by collecting an additional number of barbarians, to assume once more a fighting posture.

Assuming these were indeed invaders from north of the Rhine, Zosimus' narrative indicates that despite this early victory over the barbarians, Constantine had too few troops to follow up his success and instead focused on rebuilding the *limes Germanicus* to prevent any further incursions across the Rhine. Further, it also explains why the Vandals, Alans, and Suebi he defeated then headed south into Aquitaine after sacking Laon and Arcis-sur-Aube.

Following their respective travels south, by early AD 409 both the eastern and western barbarian axes had re-joined again after reaching the Pyrenean frontier. By this point, as detailed later, order was being restored more broadly across Gaul by Constantine III. The Vandals, Alans, and Suebi now cast their eyes even further south to easier pickings in the rich Roman provinces of the Iberian Peninsula, where perhaps they might also find land to finally settle.

An Iberian Adventure

Having smashed their way through Gaul, the Vandals, Alans, and Suebi were now poised to continue their journey south, this time across the Pyrenees into modern Spain. To provide a full geographical understanding of their travels there, I first set out the political organization of the region in both Principate and Dominate.

I then narrate this next stage of their journey, beginning with the rise and fall of Constantine III on the continent, the usurper's story providing the backdrop for their crossing into Hispaniae. Finally, I then detail the differing experiences over 20 years of the Vandals, Alans, and Suebi in Spain, prior to Gaiseric's fateful crossing into North Africa in AD 429.

Roman Spain

In the Roman world the Iberian Peninsula was called Hispania. By the beginning of the 1st millennium BC the indigenous population there were largely Indo-European speakers, though the Basque language was still spoken in the far north, and was clearly a remnant dating to before the arrival of Indo-Europeans given it belongs to a totally different language group (see Chapter 3).

At the time of the First Punic War between Rome and Carthage, which began in 264 BC, the three broad population groups in the Iberian Peninsula were:

- The Celtibarians, four tribes who occupied central Spain. This was an amalgam culture that evolved after a large group of Meseta Celts migrating from Gaul merged with Iberian natives living there. They often served as mercenaries in other Spanish armies.
- The Iberians in the eastern and southern coastal region. Here, cultural exchange with their Carthaginian and Greek colonial neighbours is evident.
- The Lusitanians in the region of modern Portugal, this region also incorporating much of the Basque far north.

Roman victory in this conflict, in particular its seizure of Carthaginian territory on Sicily, led to the founding of major new Punic colonies on the eastern and southern coasts of Spain as Carthage sought to make good its territorial losses elsewhere. Carthage had long had a trading presence there, with the word Hispania a later Roman derivation of a Punic original. However, this was now greatly expanded, with their new colonies becoming key battlegrounds as Rome and Carthage fought their life and death struggle through the Second and Third Punic Wars for dominance of the western Mediterranean. By 146 BC Rome was totally victorious, with Carthage destroyed and Punic power never to return.

After this success the Romans began to settle in the peninsula, fighting a series of wars against the indigenous population. Ultimately, this led to the creation of their early provinces of Hispania Citerior on the east coast and Hispania Ulterior on the south coast, the latter where Gaius Julius Caesar was at one stage proconsul. Over the next century Rome then gradually expanded its control over the peninsula. The final conflicts there were the Cantabrian Wars fought by Augustus to conquer the far north between 27 BC and 14 BC, which though sanguineous in the extreme eventually led to total Roman control over the whole of Spain. Augustus then reorganised the peninsula as part of his wider imperial reformation, creating three new provinces to replace the original two. These were Hispania Tarraconensis in the northwest and east, Hispania Baetica in the south, and Hispania Lusitania in the southwest. All remained in existence throughout the Principate.

Hispania was well known in the Roman period as an exporter of fine wine, olive oil, *garum* (fish sauce), all made in industrial quantities, and precious metals and copper. The latter extractive industries featured some of the largest *metalla* operations in the entire empire, including the Rio Tinto mines in the region of modern Andalusia and the Vispaca mines in Portugal.

Hispania Tarraconensis was a province of contrasts. The urban and commercial environment along the eastern Mediterranean seaboard was largely Punic in origin, with key towns like Cartagena (Roman Carthago Nova) dating back to the time of Hannibal and the Second Punic War, though the provincial capital of Tarragona (Roman Tarraco) was an earlier native Spanish founding. Meanwhile the mountainous north retained much of its pre-Roman Basque character. Unusually for a province away from the frontiers of empire, Hispania Tarraconensis also featured a legion. In the late 2nd century AD this was *legio* VII *Gemina*, based at León (Roman Castra Legionis) to maintain order among the troublesome native northern Lusitanians.

Next, in the far south of the Iberian Peninsula, the Senatorial province of Hispania Baetica was one of the richest Roman provinces, featuring the key Atlantic port of Cádiz (Roman Gades, originally a Phoenician founding). With its provincial capital at Cordoba (Roman Corduba), Hispania Baetica was most notable in the Roman world for being the birthplace of the emperor Trajan.

Moving north, Hispania Lusitania sat on the Atlantic seaboard, encompassing much of the territory of modern Portugal. Its provincial capital was located at Mérida (Roman Emerita Augusta). The region had proved particularly difficult to conquer during the Republican wars, but by the late 2nd century AD it was a sleepy backwater, not requiring the close military attention needed in Tarraconensis.

As with Gaul, the administrative structure of Hispania was completely changed by the Diocletianic Reformation and the onset of the Dominate phase of empire. Gone were the three Augustan provinces, which were replaced with the single *diocese* of Hispaniae, within which six smaller provinces (all detailed in the table below) were created. It was this organisational landscape which the Vandals, Alans, and Suebi entered once they crossed the Pyrenees in AD 409. Note that the final province listed below, Mauretania Tingitana, is actually in North Africa. This was completely natural to the Romans, with their empire pan-Mediterranean in nature. It also shows the value they placed on maritime connectivity.

Diocese	Province
Hispaniae	Gallaecia
	Tarraconensis
	Carthaginiensis
	Lusitania
	Baetica
	Mauretania Tingitana (across the modern Straights of Gibraltar in North Africa)

Later, after Constantine I's creation of four even larger units of administration, Hispaniae sat within the *Praefectura praetorio Galliarum*. Given it was part of the Iberian *diocese*, this included Mauretania Tingitana, though the rest of North Africa was part of the *Praefectura praetorio Italiae*.

The Rise and Fall of Constantine III

The continental adventures Constantine III provide the backdrop for the passage of the Vandals, Alans, and Suebi through the Pyrenees into Spain in AD 409. By that time the British usurper had been resident in his new capital, Arles, for a year. His choice of the city was no surprise given it was the location of one of the few surviving imperial mints in Gaul, and so enabled him to at last pay his troops.

By that time, having seen off the Vandals in AD 407, his army had fought and won a second short campaign against another barbarian force. This time it had been a large band of *foederates* under Sarus, a Gothic chieftain and key subordinate of Stilicho (at that time still in post). Here, the imperial centre had moved far more quickly than earlier against the Vandals, Alans, and Suebi when they had crossed the Rhine in AD 406. This shows the emperor Honorius took a usurpation much more seriously than a barbarian incursion, providing fascinating contemporary, real-time insight into the mindset of the imperial court. Clearly, the emperor's advisors thought the onslaught of the Vandals and their allies just another large-scale predating raid that would dissipate over time. Events would prove them catastrophically wrong, but for now their focus was on Constantine.

At first Sarus had been highly successful, defeating in turn the two *legates* Constantine had sent against him, Iustinianus and the Frank Nebiogastes.

However, Constantine regathered his forces under two new leaders called Edobichus and Gerontius, recruiting large numbers of Frankish and Alamanni *foederates*. This new army then advanced on Sarus, winning a decisive engagement and forcing the Gothic leader and his troops back through south-eastern Gaul to the Alpine passes. There Sarus then had to bribe *bagaudae* to secure passage back to Italy. Hot on their heels, Constantine then secured the passes with his own troops, clearing them of *bagaudae* and installing garrisons to prevent Honorius sending another army to challenge him in Gaul. Finally, in May AD 408 Constantine reached Arles where he set up his own court, appointing Apollinaris, the grandfather of mid-5th century AD luminary Sidonius Apollinaris, his Praetorian prefect. Constantine's attention now turned to Spain, home of the Theodosian dynasty.

There, four cousins of Honorius still resided, these called Didymus, Theodosiolus, Lagodius, and Verianus. Mindful the emperor would encourage them to attack him through the Pyrenees while his own attention was focused on the Alpine border, Constantine quickly moved to secure his rear. First he removed his son, Constans, from the monastery where he had placed him for safe keeping. He then sent him to Spain as his newly appointed *caesar*, along with Gerontius (by now appointed *magister militum*) and a large force of *foederates*. On arrival they defeated the Theodosians, with Didymus and Theodosiolus captured and Lagodius and Verianus fleeing to Constantinople where they sought refuge with the newly installed Eastern emperor, Theodosius II.

The victorious Constans now set up his own court at Saragossa (Roman Caesaraugustus), capital of the province of Tarraconensis. It is noteworthy here he chose this north-eastern city, with its excellent transport links, rather than the *diocene* capital at Mérida (Roman Emerita Augusta) in the far south west. This shows the importance he placed on keeping open lines of communication with his father in Arles. Indeed, his first act was to place strong garrisons in the Pyrenean mountain passes. With matters secure in Spain, Constans then set off back to Gaul to report to Constantine, leaving his family in the care of Gerontius.

By this time events in Italy were moving swiftly, with Stilicho executed on 22 August after his swift fall from grace. Sarus, his loyal follower, then abandoned the Western army, taking his *foederates* with him. This left Honorius facing multiple threats across the west alone, including the Visigoths (now under the deceased Alaric's successor Ataulf) who by now had returned to Italy. In extremis, he was thus forced to seek accommodation with Constantine, recognising him as co-*augustus* and making him joint *consul* with himself for the following year.

However, this proved the high point for Constantine. Later in AD 409, as fully detailed below, the Vandals, Alans, and Suebi forced the Pyrenean passes into Spain. As Constantine prepared to send Constans back to Saragossa to deal with this crisis, word arrived that Gerontius had rebelled and set himself and a relative called Maximus up as co-emperors. Then, in early AD 410 Gerontius advanced into Gaul with the support of unknown barbarian allies, who may or may not have been Vandals, Alans, or Suebi given they were by then in Spain.

Now, with enemies to both his front and rear, Constantine realised his only chance to regain the initiative was to seize the Western throne from Honorius and become sole *augustus*. Encouraged by the emperor's *magister*, Allobich, a German who wanted to replace Honorius in revenge for the death of Stilicho, Constantine marched on Italy with most of his remaining troops. However, his invasion was a fiasco, and he was forced to retreat back to Gaul in late spring AD 410, with Allobich then beheaded.

Constantine's position now grew even more desperate. The *foederates* he had earlier sent under Constans to slow Gerontius' advance through Gaul were defeated at Vienne (Roman Vienna) in early AD 411. There his son was captured and killed. Then his new Praetorian prefect, Decimius Rusticus, a recent appointment to replace Apollinaris, abandoned Constantine for yet another usurper called Jovinus. With his forces depleted, Constantine was then besieged in Arles by Gerontius.

By this time Honorius had found a new general to lead his field armies in Italy and Gaul called Flavius Constantius, later briefly the emperor Constantius III. Arriving at Arles, he soon put Gerontius to flight and then took over his siege. However Constantine still held out, hoping Edobichus would return with newly recruited troops from northern Gaul. Sadly for Constantine, when this new force tried to reach Arles its was quickly defeated by Constantius. After this, Constantine's last loyal troops on the Rhine frontier deserted. With no other troops able to break the siege he was forced to surrender to Constantius, who first imprisoned him and then beheaded him in August or September AD 411.

Thus ended the final attempt to seize the imperial throne by a British usurper. However, the story of Constantine III actually forms the backdrop of two far more significant events. First, within a year of his arriving in Gaul the Romano-British aristocracy in the *diocese* threw out the Roman tax collectors, officially ending Britain's presence in the empire. Their rationale was that, given there were now no field army troops there, and with the *limitanei* on the frontiers also denuded, they were getting no return when paying their taxes. Sadly for them, mass predation by Germanic and Irish raiders quickly followed and they realised they had made a terrible mistake. Soon they were lobbying Honorius to be allowed back into the empire, interestingly bypassing Constantine III in Gaul, but he famously said no. As Zosimus puts it, 'the emperor sent letters to the cities of the Britons urging them to fend for themselves' (*New History*, 6.10). So ended the Roman occupation of Britain.

Meanwhile, the second significant event was the passage of the Vandals, Alans, and Suebi into Spain, which would ultimately have even more disastrous consequences for the empire. I will tell that story now.

Into Spain

For the next 20 years the story of the Hasdingi and Silingi Vandals, and their Alan and Suebi fellow travellers, is focused on Spain and the western Mediterranean. Our primary sources are numerous but patchy, though recent archaeological research has helped me piece together the chronology I set out here.

Their remarkable story starts off well with a strong contemporary reference, this from the Spanish writer Hydatius who says in his *Chronicle* that in AD 409 '…on a Tuesday, some say the 28th September, others 13th October…', the Vandals, Alans, and Suebi crossed the Pyrenean passes into Spain (49.1). Born around AD 400, Hydatius was the bishop of Chaves in Gallaecia (Roman Aquae Flaviae), this the north-western province in Hispaniae. His *Chronicle* was written in the AD 450s and is our best source for events in Spain in the first half of the 5th century AD, though his narrative is often apocalyptic, written to fit a world view set amid the decline of the Roman Empire in the west. Meanwhile, with regard to the disparity between his two dates, MacDowall suggest it may refer to the length of time it took for the tens of thousands of German and Iranian migrants to cross into Spain (2016, 55).

On arrival there, this at the height Constantine III's usurpation, they found northern Spain in chaos. Though by this time Constans had set up his court in Saragossa, his initial defeat of the Theodosians had failed to pacify the whole peninsula. Now with the Vandals, Alans, and Suebi also arriving, and in vast numbers, a 'bubbling human broth' had been created (Kean and Frey, 2005, 237).

The first priority for the barbarians was to gather supplies for the coming winter. By this point these were is short supply in Tarraconensis given the overwhelming demand. Soon the local road network was flooded with barbarians heading south and west, though interestingly they didn't overwhelm the Roman administration (by this time, most likely the usurpers Gerontius and Maximus), at least in Saragossa. There, the normal taxation regime remained in place, both through cash and in kind. Here Hydatius paints a grim picture, saying (*Chronicle*, 49.1):

> While the barbarians ran wild through Spain, and evil pestilence raged, the tyrannical tax collector plundered and the soldier used up the supplies stored in the cities. Terrible famine prowled, so that human beings were compelled to devour human flesh and mothers fed on the murdered and cooked bodies they had burned.

Strong words indeed, and even if a gross exaggeration, the situation was clearly unsustainable. On the one hand the Romans, divided and yet to see the endgame of Constantine III play out in Gaul, would never be strong enough to expel tens of thousands of Germanic and Iranian invaders, no doubt with their numbers bolstered by thousands of *bagaudae*. At this stage in the Dominate the *comes Hispanias*, in charge of the field armies on Spain, had eleven *Auxilia Palatina* and five *Legiones Comitatenses* units under his control, giving him a force of no more than 10,000 men. That was far too small to securitise the entire Iberian Peninsula. On the other hand, the barbarians needed food, shelter, and ultimately most of them wanted land to settle. An accommodation had to be reached, and that is exactly what I believe happened in AD 411.

Here, we must read between the lines written by our sources. First, Hydatius maintains his doom-laden narrative, saying that in that year (*Chronicle*, 49.1):

> ...they apportioned to themselves by lot the provinces [of the *diocese* of Hispaniae] for settlement: the Hasdingi Vandals Gallaecia, the Suebi that part of Gallaecia situated on the very western edge of the ocean. The Alans the provinces of Lusitania and Carthaginensis, and the Silingi Vandals Baetica. The Spaniards in the cities and forts who had survived the disasters surrendered themselves to servitude under the barbarians, who held sway throughout the provinces.

For context, Lusitania is in the southwest of modern Spain, Carthaginensis the centre and southeast, and Baetica the south. I have already detailed Gallaecia was in the northwest. Of note, Tarraconensis (where Gerontius had now left Maximus in charge in Saragossa) was not part of the division of territorial spoils. This indicates to me there is more to Hydatius' story here than meets the eye, with five factors needing consideration.

First, although Hydatius did live through these events, he wrote the chapter covering the Vandals, Alans, and Suebi in Spain 30 years afterwards in some of his earliest work, by which time the Romans had recovered direct control of 90% of the Iberian Peninsula (in some areas more than once). Further, the hysterical nature of his narrative reflects the fact he was writing from an extreme 'end-of-days' Christian perspective, reflecting his own bleak religious beliefs. While this actually proved well-founded given the collapse of renewed Roman authority in Spain in the years after the death of Majorian in AD 461, at the time he wrote this section things were still broadly stable.

Second, as had already been seen in Gaul, the Vandals, Alans, and Suebi had no homogenous command structure. Without this, the division of such a huge geographic area would have been impossible given the logistics required to move entire peoples around the peninsula, and then support them economically. Remember also that by AD 411 the barbarians were in poor shape given their hostile journey through Gaul, and then over the Pyrenees into Tarraconensis, where the local population had struggled to sustain them, hence the subsequent diaspora. Even in the best of circumstances, which these weren't, the arrival of tens of thousands of migrants was never welcome in the ancient world.

Third, even though AD 411 was the year Constantine III was executed and Honorius re-asserted control in the west, the usurpers Gerontius and Maximus were still able to effect rule over at least Tarraconensis in Spain given this wasn't part of the geographic spoils divided by the barbarians. There they clearly remained the representatives of the Roman state, even if unofficially. Also note that Mauretania Tingitana, across the Strait of Gibraltar in North Africa, also maintained full imperial control. Further, the Theodosian dynasty continued to rule the empire for decades, the last incumbent in the east being Marcian who died in AD 457 and in the west Valentinian III who died in AD 455. It is unlikely they would have given up their vast family estates lightly. Notably, these were in northern Carthaginensis, close to its provincial borders with Gallaecia, Lusitania, and Tarraconensis (Kean and Frey, 2005, 224).

Fourth, having acknowledged above the lack of any holistic barbarian command structure, one should also note the economic complexity of a Roman province, even in late antiquity. The Vandals, Alans, and Suebi who crossed the Rhine in AD 406 were not the more sophisticated German and Gothic peoples who crossed into the empire across the northern *limes* later in the century, with sophisticated elites able to take over the control of regional Roman administration as a going concern. That was definitely not the case here, where we are instead dealing with largely illiterate armed itinerants travelling in their tens of thousands in search of provisions, loot and, ultimately, land to settle. Even at the most senior level, the Germanic and Iranian leadership here was clearly not fit for the purpose of taking on the running of a sophisticated Dominate Roman province, with its complex post-Diocletianic Reformation administrative structure. The results would have been disastrous for all concerned, and the fact they ultimately returned to Roman control later in the century as going concerns indicates the barbarians didn't take sole control at this time.

Fifth, as Pohl points out, the land division was odd to say the least. He says (2004, 37):

> What is striking about this arrangement, besides the predominance of the Alans [certainly junior partners to the Vandals and possibly Suebi], is that the Vandals were settled apart from one another, and the Hasdingi royal lineage, from which Gaiseric and his successors descended, only received a very modest share of land. Their part was also more remote.

Again, note this is a vast geographic area we are considering, with a challenging climate of extremes including a mountainous centre and often arid south, neither ideal for northern Europeans and horse-riding Iranian steppe peoples.

To my mind another hypothesis is needed here to explain events, with Orosius (writing in Gallaecia within a decade of the land division) pointing the way when he says the barbarians 'took up the plough' in AD 411 (*Seven Books of History Against the Pagans*, 7.43.1). In late antique parlance, when Roman writers referenced those they considered barbarians in this context, it meant they were given farmland to settle on. Then, writing over 130 years later and with a degree of objectivity notably lacking in Hydatius, Procopius specifically says the land settlement was arranged by the Roman authorities (*The Vandalic Wars*, 3.3).

Reading between the lines here, which are confusing given the fast-moving nature of events, I go back to my original line on this subject. An accommodation was reached by all parties. The Roman state, either through Gerontius and Maximus (both to shortly fall from grace, the former dead by the end of AD 411) or whoever replaced them (Theodosian or otherwise), lacked the means to expel the invaders. By the same token, as Heather says, the Vandals, Alans, and Suebi '...needed to find, and settle, revenue-producing territories that would support them in the longer term...' (2005, 208).

The most likely explanation is that each of the various invading peoples were settled as *foederates* in the respective territories allocated to them, Gallaecia receiving both the Hasdingi Vandals and the Suebi, all with their own land to farm. There they provided muscle for the respective provincial governments.

Indeed, as noted earlier, they may have already served as *foederates* for Gerontius when he crossed into Gaul, setting a precedent. This was absolutely normal behaviour throughout the Roman world by this time, for example in Britain where the Romano-British elites (post separation from the imperial centre) were hiring Germanic *foederates* to replace the now departed Roman troops at the same time (Elliott, 2021b, 187). Whether the Vandal, Alan, and Suebi *foederates* had a seat at the administrative table in each province is a different question, and unknowable. But certainly, given the provinces continued to function economically, under this agreement I believe they were still run on a day-to-day basis by their Roman civil servants.

This seemingly elegant settlement endured nearly five years, but sadly for all was not to last, either because the Theodosians chose to reassert themselves, or the Vandals, Alans, and Suebi overstepped their licence and provoked the imperial centre. Most likely it was a combination of the two. By this time the Visigoths were resident in southern Gaul after their lengthy travels, under the rule of their new king, Wallia, after the assassination of Athaulf and his successor, Sigeric, in AD 415. Early in AD 416 Honorius encouraged Wallia to lead a force of Visigoths over the Pyrenees to target the Silingi Vandals in Baetica. For context, this was a long journey from Gaul to the southern coast of Spain and would certainly have needed the acquiescence of the Roman authorities in Tarraconensis to facilitate passage. Once in Baetica, the Visigoths forced a meeting engagement and captured a Silingi king called Fredibal who was sent back to Ravenna as a captive (MacDowall, 2016, 61). They then returned north of the Pyrenees for the winter.

However, again with the encouragement of Honorius, the Visigoths returned to Spain in each of the following two years, and this time in much greater force. First, in AD 417 they targeted the Silingi Vandals again, and a year later the Alans in Lusitania and Carthaginensis. Here Hydatius provides first-person insight, saying (*Chronicle*, 49.1):

> The Silingi Vandals in Baetica were wiped out by King Wallia. The Alans [then] suffered such heavy losses at the hands of the Goths that, after the death of their king Attaces [who had succeeded Respendial], the few survivors placed themselves under the protection of Gunderic, king of the Hasdingi Vandals who had settled in Gallaecia.

In fact, as is clear from other sources, some Silingi Vandals did survive, and it was they and the Alan remnants who fled to Gunderic in Gallaecia. There he then became king of all the Vandals, not just the Hasdingi, and also the remnant Alans. Indeed, later the Vandal kings of their North African kingdom were styled *Rex Wandalorum et Alanorum*, meaning king of the Vandals and Alans. As MacDowall says (2016, 61):

> From AD 418 there was only one group of Vandals [and Alans], and the term Hasdingi came to be used to describe the royal line rather than a single Vandal clan.

The real winners here though were the Visigoths. In later AD 418 they were recalled to southern Gaul by Constantius, still the leading *magister militum* in the west. There, with the blessing of Honorius, they were officially settled as *foederates* in the province of Aquitania Secunda. Wallia died soon after, with his replacement, Theoderic I, then ruling the Visigoths until AD 451 when he fell fighting with his army as an ally of the Romans against Attila the Hun at the battle of the Catalaunian Plains.

Back to Spain in AD 418, once Wallia had withdrawn his troops, Baetica, Lusitania, and Carthaginiensis fell back under Roman control given the power vacuum there. Gunderic now seemed bottled up in Gallaecia, which some modern commentators argue was a backwater compared to the rest of Spain (I address the Suebi presence there below). However, that was far from the case. In the first instance, the province had a long and well-established administrative structure. Despite Roman provinces in the Dominate being smaller than their Principate counterparts, and sitting within Diocletian's much larger *diocese* (in this case Hispaniae), they still maintained their pre-Dominate levels of organisation. These were based on a set of nested hierarchies, which Oosthuizen details in her analysis of the transition from Roman to post-Roman Europe (2019, 27):

> Broadly speaking these [hierarchies] ranged from *vicus*, a small local centre [as opposed to the *vici* civilian settlements associated with Roman forts], to *pagus*, the locality, to *civitates*, a region often reproducing a prehistoric territory.

Dominate Gallaecia featured three *civitates*, these being Conventus Bracarensis in the south west, Conventus Lucensis in the north west, and Conventus Asturicensis in the north east. Each had a well-developed *civitas* capital, these respectively Braga (Roman Bracara Augusta), Lugo (Roman Lucus Augusti) and Astorga (Roman Lucus Augusti). Braga served as the provincial capital for much of the Dominate, including at the time of the Hasdingi settlement there.

Gallaecia was also well connected with the rest of Hispaniae and Gaul by the excellent trunk road network in the region. The principal routeway travelled east through nearby León (Roman Legio), the main military base of the wider *diocese,* and then on to Saragossa before heading north over the Pyrenees.

However, even if these were blocked for a time after the Romans returned to Baetica, Lusitania, and Carthaginiensis (though there is no direct evidence such obstruction took place), Gallaecia still maintained excellent transport connections with the wider Roman world. This was because it was a maritime province. It featured numerous ports, with the principal ones at A Coruña (Roman Brigantium) and Oporto (Roman Portus Cale). From there, regional merchandise was transported along well-known sea routes dating back to the prehistoric period south to the Mediterranean, and north to Britain (even after is dislocation from the empire) and the continental empire.

Note should be taken at this point that in the post-Spanish migration settlement the Suebi contingent had also been settled in Gallaecia, '…on the very western edge of the ocean' (Hydatius, *Chronicle*, 49.1). I interpret this, based on later events and the fact the Suebi were the smallest of the three migrating contingents, as the far north-western tip of the province, perhaps including A Coruña (though I think this unlikely). Certainly, whatever the nature of the Suebi settlement in Gallaecia, it was soon a cause of friction with their larger Vandal neighbours. Three conflicts followed in short order, all indicating that by this time the *foederate* umbilical between the Vandals (and indeed Suebi) and the Gallaecian Roman administration had been severed.

First, in early AD 419 the Vandals defeated a Suebi army in battle somewhere on the northern Gallaecian coast, driving the survivors east into the Asturias Mountains, and perhaps even further to the border with Tarraconensis (MacDowall, 2016, 63). Here they encountered Flavius Castinus, the new *vicarius* of Hispaniae, now resident in Saragossa. Clearly a man of ambition, Castinus established an alliance with the Suebi, who together with their new Roman allies then mounted an invasion of Gallaecia late in AD 419. Here the Vandals were less successful, losing a battle near Hydatius' hometown, Chaves. Notably, this is in the far south west of Gallaecia and may indicate the invaders had arrived by sea, perhaps landing at Oporto. Some reports suggest Gunderic was then forced to retreat to Baetica, though given the distances involved and the fact this region was by now back under Roman control, I think it unlikely. However, Castinus refused to let up, and in AD 422 a full-scale war broke out between the Romans and Vandals. This time the former used Visigoth *foederates* as well as Roman regulars, and perhaps allied Suebi warriors again, too. Our main source is once more Hydatius, who says (*Chronicle*, 49.1):

> At this time an army was sent to Spain against the Vandals with Castinus as commander. By an unsuitable and unjust order he excluded Boniface, a man quite well known for military skill, from partnership in his expedition. As a result Boniface judged Castinus as dangerous to himself and unworthy to be followed since he [Boniface] found him [Castinus] quarrelsome and proud. So Boniface rushed quickly to Oporto and thence to Africa.

There is much to unpack in this short quote. First, we are introduced to the later *comes* Boniface for the first time, a central figure in the story of the Vandal invasion of North Africa. Second, he sailed there from Oporto, illustrating as mentioned earlier how well connected Gallaecia was with the wider Roman world. Finally, the war clearly didn't go well for the Romans and their allies.

Though Castinus had some early success on the borders of Gallaecia, Gunderic then seized the initiative with a full counteroffensive. Soon his army was deep within Tarraconensis, quickly reaching Tarragona (Roman Tarraco) on the Mediterranean coast, with the Vandals capturing the key port without a fight. However Castinus was hot on their heels and soon besieged them there. Sadly for the *vicarius*, he was then deserted by his Visigoths *foederates*. Unwisely, Castinus next decided to risk open battle with the Vandals, hoping his remaining troops would be sufficient. This proved a disastrous decision, with the Vandals totally victorious and Castinus fleeing to Saragossa with his few surviving troops.

Here Salvian of Marseille adds an interesting detail, saying the Vandals paraded a Bible as a standard before them in the battle (*De Gubernatione*, 7.7). This is an important reference given it is the first mention of the Vandals in a Christian context, though there is no mention of their denomination at the time, whether Catholic or Arian. Most commentators, then and now, argue the Vandals were still heathens when they crossed the Rhine in AD 406. If they did convert when they travelled through Gaul or in Spain, which seems likely given they are referenced as such on arrival in North Africa, then the most obvious vector would be through Catholicism. Indeed, Hydatius says that Gunderic's successor, Gaiseric, was originally a Catholic before converting to Arianism (*Chronicle*, 49.2).

Back to Spain, it was also likely in the aftermath of the Roman defeat at Tarragona that Boniface abandoned Castinus and made for North Africa, presumably with the acquiescence of the Vandals given he departed from Oporto in Gallaecia. This was likely the first time he was able to spend time with the Vandal leadership, with their permission certainly needed for him to travel through the territory they controlled. This meeting was an event that had major repercussions at the end of the AD 420s, as will be seen.

Finally, it was this engagement that dragged the Vandals away from Gallaeica to settle elsewhere in Spain. This is evident given the next actions of Gunderic, which took place against the backdrop of Honorius' death in August AD 423. For a time, chaos then ensued in Ravenna and Rome, with Spain again left to its own devices. There the Roman authorities, still nominally in charge in Tarraconensis, Baetica, Lusitania, and Carthaginiensis, now struggled to contain the Vandals. For a time we know they remained on the Mediterranean coast as they next mounted a predatory maritime campaign against the rich Balearic Islands in AD 425. This was a remarkable achievement, showing the Vandal propensity for osmosing bespoke skills from host populations, later a key feature of their time in North Africa. These new maritime skills were next in evidence when Gunderic sacked the key port of Cartagena (Roman Carthago Nova) in Carthaginiensis later the same year.

Then, in the late spring of AD 426, he crossed the Strait of Gibraltar to lead a mass raid on Mauretania Tingitana in North Africa, the first time the Vandals had visited the continent. There, Victor of Vita later wrote they found '…the whole land beautiful and flowering on all sides…' (*History of the Vandal Persecution*, 1.3). Gunderic then returned to Baetica, where the Vandals sacked Seville (Roman Hispalis). They then headed northeast into Carthaginiensis, raiding the key cities there, with the resident Alans only too happy to join in.

Gunderic then returned to Baetica in AD 428 where he again plundered Seville, which was only just recovering from his previous sanguineous visit. However, the king himself died while laying siege to the city's church, the last location there to hold out against the Vandals. He was succeeded by his half-brother, Gaiseric, one of Godegisel's younger sons whose mother was either a serf or slave, and may have been Roman originally. Given Gaiseric was unchallenged when appointed, he was clearly well placed in the Vandal court. Gunderic had two young sons who had their own champions among the Vandal elites, but Gaiseric's reputation as a fine warrior tipped things in his favour (MacDowall, 2016, 70). In the post-Roman world he was to prove one of the 5th century AD's greatest rulers, with Jordanes providing an enigmatic description of him (*Getica*, 33.168):

> He was of medium build and walked with a limp due to a fall from his horse; he was of spiritual profundity, taciturn, scorned luxury, was of violent temperament, extraordinarily resourceful and far sighted, and prepared to sow the seeds of discord and to spread hatred in order to stir the peoples up against one another.

In short, a fit ruler for his times. However, shortly after becoming Vandal king, Gaiseric's army was attacked from the northeast by the Suebi while still in Seville. Here, their former allies turned enemy had already occupied much of Gallaecia in the Vandals' absence. Under their new king, Heremigarius, ruler since AD 427, they had then travelled south and had recently captured the *diocene* capital Mérida on the provincial border with Baetica. Now Heremigarius targeted Seville, leading to direct conflict with Gaiseric. However again the Vandals were victorious, with the Suebi king fleeing, and later drowning in the Guadiana River.

Gaiseric had been victorious in his first war, this a pattern repeated time and again throughout his long life. By this point the Vandals and their Alan allies were the dominant power in Spain. However, at some stage all expected the imperial centre to re-assert itself once the succession in Ravenna stabilised. Gaiseric now turned his eyes back south again, to North Africa. This set the scene for the final, most fantastical stage of the Vandal migration which had begun 23 year earlier in the depths of a freezing winter on the Rhine. Because now, a new continent beckoned.

CHAPTER 5

Vandal Conquest

As AD 429 began, neither Gaiseric nor the Romans could have possibly imagined the epoch-changing events that were about to unfold in North Africa, the economic jewel of the Roman Empire. Here I tell the story of how the Vandals improbably conquered this extremely wealthy region, setting in train a series of events that see it very different to the rest of the territory of the Western Empire in today's world. I begin by detailing the history of classical North Africa to the point the Vandals invaded, and then narrate the incredible story of their conquest there in full.

North Africa in the Classical World

The North African territories conquered by Gaiseric had a rich history going back millennia. Here I briefly provide background detail regarding regional geography and the climate, before chronologically detailing the key phases of North African history through to AD 429, including a thorough description of the region in the imperial Roman period.

Geography and Climate

Today, the term North Africa describes a geographic area comprising (east to west) the Republic of the Sudan, the Arab Republic of Egypt, the State of Libya, the Republic of Tunisia, the People's Democratic Republic of Algeria, and the Kingdom of Morocco. In the context of this work we are only interested in the region as the Romans knew it, which to them were the territories of the latter four countries. Today, we call this the Maghreb.

As detailed in the Introduction, the physical geography of the Maghreb comprises two distinct regions, with Libya in the east and Tunisia, Algeria, and Morocco in the west. The latter region is a true north-south layer cake of different geological areas, these the coastal zone, the Atlas Mountains, the high plains, the Aures Mountains, and the Sahara. Meanwhile, Libya has a far more limited layer cake, composed of the coastal zone and the Sahara.

Also as detailed earlier, the climate in Roman North Africa was broadly similar to that today, though perhaps slightly wetter except in the Libyan desert. With the predominant easterly and north-easterly weather systems, winters were usually mild and wet, with rainfall continuing into the spring and then picking up again in the autumn. Summers were warm and dry, with the climate getting dryer as one headed further inland, especially approaching the Sahara.

These weather patterns, together with the regional geology, dictated agricultural land use. Thus, in the west, the coastal zone and Atlas range were fertile all year round, the high plains and the gorges of the Aures fertile seasonally (all year round if irrigated as by the Romans and Vandals), and the Saharan fringe fertile only for the hardiest crops. In the Libyan east the transition from the fertile coastal zone to the arid Sahara was far more marked, and it is only here we have evidence of classical world climate change in the Maghreb, with a centuries-long small but steady decline in rainfall leading to increased desertification.

The Berbers

North Africa has a rich history featuring a multitude of different peoples, some indigenous and some colonists, the latter including the Carthaginians, Romans, and Vandals. In that sense it features a chronological layer cake of a complexity to match that covering its geography.

In the historical record, the indigenous people of the region were the forebears of today's Berbers (also called the Imazighen). Then as now, the Berbers were a diverse collection of ethnic groups linked by their usage (for the most part) of Berber languages, which are part of the Afroasiatic language family. They are first referenced in dynastic Egyptian texts, with some believing their original homelands were in the eastern Libyan desert. By 2000 BC the archaeological record shows the spread of their distinct Berber material culture eastward towards the Nile Valley, and crucially for this book, westwards through the Maghreb, ultimately to the Atlantic coast of modern Morocco and beyond to the Canary Islands.

In our period of interest in the classical and late antique world, the primary sources reference three specific Berber peoples. These were the Garamantes who inhabited the Libyan Maghreb (broadly, a region today called the Fezzān), the Numidians who were resident in modern Tunisia and eastern Algeria, and the Mauri of Mauretania in western Algeria and Morocco. I detail each in turn here, using the term Berber when referencing more than one group.

The Garamantes were the dominant Berber culture in the Libyan interior from 1000 BC to the late 7th century AD. They are first mentioned by Herodotus when writing in the mid-5th century BC. He calls them '…an exceedingly great nation…' who farmed dates and herded cattle (*The Histories*, 4.183). Herodotus adds their main regional competitors were an unknown aboriginal population he calls Troglodytes (cave-dwellers in ancient Greek).

The Garamantes were a significant civilisation in their own right, with Darlington saying (2023, 42):

> They were a powerful and sophisticated autochthonous African kingdom, with a written script, stratified society, kings and luxury goods. Recent archaeological evidence has revealed forts, temples, pyramidal tombs, stone-built palaces and sophisticated towns.

At the height of Garamantian power their kingdom featured at least six known major settlements. The capital was located near modern Germa, 150km west of Sabha in south-western Libya. Archaeologists excavating the ancient site in the 1960s named it Garama, and that is the name by which it is still known today. At its largest extent the city had a population of 10,000, and from here the king of the Garamantes ruled an aristocratic elite famous in the classical world for riding into battle in four-horse chariots, long after they fell out of use in Egypt. Garamantian warriors were also renowned for wearing ritual tattoos and bearing facial and body scars. Meanwhile, reflecting the origins of the Berber-speaking peoples in the eastern Libyan desert, their religion was heavily influenced by that of dynastic Egypt. The 1st century AD Roman writer Silius Italicus says their main deity was called Ammon, clearly a derivative of Amun-Ra, the principal god of the Egyptian pantheon (*Punica*, 1.39). He adds that instead of using traditional temples they worshipped in 'prophetic groves'.

Unlike the Numidians to their west, the Garamantes remained a Saharan fringe culture, showing little interest in expanding their political reach north to the Libyan coast, even after the first Greek and Phoenician settlements were established there. In the case of the former, major Greek colonies began to appear in Cyrenaica to the northeast from the 7th century BC. By the Hellenistic period five major cities had been established there, these called Cyrene (later the Roman provincial capital), Ptolemais, Barca, Berenice, and Belagrae. Together they were known as the Pentapolis, with a separate major regional port also being established called Apollonia (Cornell and Matthews, 1982, 164).

Meanwhile, directly to the north of the Garamantes' core home territory, the three key cities of Tripolitania were established around the same time by

Phoenician settlers. These, which later flourished as part of the Carthaginian empire in the western Mediterranean, were called Leptis Magna, Oea (modern Tripoli) and Sabratha. Mattingly says that all became spectacularly wealthy (1995, 138), with Matyszak adding the Garamantes proved particularly adept at exploiting their relationship with these rich northern neighbours. He says (2022, 169):

> The Garamantes quickly established themselves as the middlemen in goods passing between the trans-Saharan region and the Mediterranean world, and traded with peoples to the south for gold, ivory and slaves.

The Garamantes also established a thriving trade supplying wild animals to the cities of Tripolitania. Early on these included the now extinct forest elephant for use in Hellenistic, Numidian, and Carthaginian armies. Later, these and other native species including the also extinct Barbary lion were supplied in industrial quantities for use in the Roman arena. The Garamantes also introduced the camel to the Sahara to assist their south-north trade from the Fezzān to the coast.

In extremis, the Garamantes also raided the coastal zone to their north, this reflected in the epithets used by the Romans to describe them which often focused on their martial nature. Examples of such epithets include savage, fierce, and indomitable. Intriguingly, recent paleo-osteological research on male and female Garamantian skeletons (these from a number of locations and a wide date range) have shown little sign of sexual dimorphism in the upper limbs of the individuals examined. Nikita says this best fits patterns of agricultural activity rather than warfare on the part of the male population (2011, 423). The inference here is that the Garamantes, in normal circumstances, were perfectly happy to maintain their thriving trading relationship with Tripolitania, only risking conflict with their northern neighbours when absolutely necessary. In particular, they knew that if they did, massive retribution would follow, for example the Roman expedition led by Lucius Cornelius Balbus in 20 BC. In Roman eyes this was a remarkable success given he not only defeated the Garamantes but also 'conquered the desert', leading to a triumph in Rome, the last by a person outside the imperial family (Mattingly, 190, 2006).

The most likely trigger of such high-risk raiding of the Mediterranean hinterland was climate change. Given the location of their kingdom on the Saharan fringe, the Garamantes were more susceptible to the vagaries of climate than the other Berber peoples of the Maghreb, who could always rely on precipitation caused by the Atlas and Aures ranges. In particular, the Garamantes faced the challenge of steadily declining rainfall, leading to the onset of desertification in the south of the kingdom. To counter this they became expert hydraulic engineers, eventually building a spectacular network of subterranean tunnels extending for thousands of kilometres to sustain their settlements from the natural aquifers deep within the bedrock. Nevertheless, the archaeological record shows that by the beginning of the 7th century AD population levels had started to diminish as some locals turned to transhumance as a coping mechanism. The Garamantian civilisation was finally extinguished in AD 669 when the Arab Conquest swept through the region.

Moving west, the Numidians inhabited the region of modern Tunisia and eastern Algeria. Here was a Berber ancient world civilisation fit to match any in the Hellenistic eastern Mediterranean or early Republican Roman world. Crucially, the Numidians were the first to make full use of the bountiful potential of the fertile western Maghreb, its rich agricultural return in stark contrast to the more arid landscape farmed by the Garamantes in the Fezzān.

The Numidians were originally a semi-nomadic people, arriving in the region as part of the second wave of Berber migrations after the first settled the Fezzān. They are first mentioned in contemporary literature by Polybius in the context of the First Punic War when he describes Numidian light cavalry in action (*The Rise of the Roman Empire*, 1.19). These became famous in the ancient world for their skill with the javelin, and also for the brutal hamstringing of foot opponents in the pursuit. This allowed them to continue the chase, and then later return to kill their immobilised prey. In his recent study of the Numidian military establishment Horsted calls them the most efficient light cavalry in the ancient Mediterranean (2021, 6). They are immortalised on Trajan's Column in Rome where Numidian horse auxiliaries are depicted chasing the emperor's Dacian opponents, resplendent with braided dreadlocks and clipped beards. Appian says the small horses they used were ideally suited for life on campaign given they were content to eat only grass, and rarely needed to drink (*Punic Wars*, 2.11). The Numidians also made use of war elephants, training for battle forest elephants that had been locally captured or reared in captivity.

The Numidians were early traders with the Phoenician settlers establishing colonies along the Mediterranean coastline to their north and east, particular around the Gulf of Gabes. These new cities were direct contemporaries of those being founded at the same time in Tripolitania. In particular, the founding of Carthage had a big impact on the Numidian tribes in the region. This city developed rapidly from one of the earliest Canaanite Phoenician colonies in North Africa to become the capital of a Carthaginian empire that came to completely dominate the western Mediterranean. Close proximity to this economic powerhouse soon saw the various Numidian peoples in the region coalesce into two distinct Numidian kingdoms by 250 BC. These were the Massylii in the east and the Masaesyli in the west. Matyszak is dismissive here of the newfound political structures of the Numidians, arguing that (2022, 171):

> Political 'unification' meant little more than the fact that disputes over grazing rights and the harvests at various oases were now resolved by a chieftain/king rather than through feuding as previously.

However, having travelled extensively through the region, I think this an oversimplification. There is abundant evidence there of significant Numidian settlement dating to this time, and also industrial-scale agricultural activity. The latter specifically catered for the Carthaginian cities on the coast and its hinterland.

Further, the finest tombs I have visited were Numidian and not Carthaginian, for example the colossal Mausoleum of Madghacen near Batna in modern Algeria in the high plains north of the Aures range. This immense rotunda is the oldest known funerary monument in the Maghreb. It has clear Hellenistic design features, including 60 Doric columns, and at 18.5m in height and 59m in diameter is a striking feature in the landscape visible for miles around. Indeed, watching the sun rise over its apex on a clear day, beneath copper-blue skies, it is a sight to behold. Further, the many fine museums in the region all feature large collections of distinctive Numidian tombstones, often featuring images of the light cavalry for which they were so famous.

As the Carthaginian Empire continued to grow, its relationship with the Numidians further blossomed, in effect becoming symbiotic. This can be seen in the later regional built environment, for example at Constantine (Roman Cirta) in modern Algeria, the city in the clouds. Founded by the Carthaginians on a plateau 640m high in the Atlas Mountains, it later became a regional capital for the Numidians.

Numidia continued to supply their famous light cavalry to fight in Carthaginian armies as the latter's conflicts with Rome progressed, particularly in the climactic Second Punic War which lasted from 218 BC to 201 BC. This no doubt seemed a shrewd move when Hannibal was victorious, winning his three famous Italian victories over the Romans at the Trebia, Lake Trasimene, and Cannae. However, when the tide turned in favour of the Romans, it soon became evident to many Numidians they were backing the wrong side. The first leader to begin negotiations with the Romans was Syphax, king of the Masaesyli, though the Carthaginians quickly ensured his loyalty by granting him extensive territory around Constantine. However, it was Massinissa, the young king of the Massylii, who finally made a break with Carthage and sided with Rome. This led to a spectacular rise in power as, after the end of the Second Punic War, the Romans also made him king of the Masaesyli, for the first time uniting Numidia. The unfortunate Syphax was taken back to Italy a prisoner and later died in Tivoli (Roman Tibur), though his reign was monumentalised with the immense Mausoleum of El Khroub near Constantine. From that point, Numidia flourished as a key trading partner with Rome, with grain, olive oil, and fruit its key exports to Italy, and the rest of the Roman world.

Things only soured for the Numidians after the ill-favoured Jugurtha, king from 118 BC, overreached his authority and fell out with Rome, the resulting Jugurthine War lasting until 105 BC. Despite initial Roman incompetence in the conflict they eventually won, with Jugurtha dying an ignominious death, executed by strangulation after the Roman victor Marius' triumph in 104 BC. The Romans then punished Numidia severely, ceding much of its territory to its western neighbour, the Roman client state of Mauretania. From that time the diminished kingdom of Numidia increasingly fell under Roman control, often finding itself engaged with one side or another in the civil wars of the late Republic (see below), and ultimately forming the core territory of the Roman province of Africa Nova.

Finally, Mauretania was the land of the Mauri whose territory stretched across a vast region from western Algeria to the Atlantic Moroccan coast. Although there are references to Carthaginian kings seeking alliances with those inhabiting the region, including Hanno I, who ruled from 340 BC to 337 BC, the name Mauri first appears in literature in Strabo's *Geography* at the end of the 1st century BC as a Latinised version of the Greek Μαῦροι (17.3.2). The first known historical king from the region, called Baga, ruled during the Second Punic War, supplying light cavalry to the Carthaginians, these fighting in exactly the same way as the Numidians.

Later, after the demise of Carthage with its destruction at the end of the Third Punic War in 146 BC, the Mauritanians initially forged close links with the Numidians. For example, King Bocchus made the mistake of supporting Jugurtha against Rome, though quickly changed sides and was handsomely rewarded with the Numidian territory previously detailed. From that point Mauretania then maintained a close relationship with Rome, though was perhaps too successful in its self-promotion given after the death of Bocchus II in 33 BC Rome began to establish administrative centres there. This soon led to indirect rule from Italy. Finally, Mauretania became a Roman client kingdom in 25 BC when Juba II of Numidia was installed as its king. His reign is monumentalised by the enormous rotundral Royal Mausoleum of Mauretania in Algeria, sitting high above the modern coastal route between Algiers (Roman Icosium) and Cherchell, the latter his capital. In this immense tomb he was buried with his wife and Queen Cleopatra Selene II, daughter of the late Republican warlord Mark Antony and Cleopatra VII Philopator, last ruler of Ptolemaic Egypt. On Juba's death in AD 23 his Roman-educated son, Ptolemy, succeeded him, though was later executed on the orders of Caligula in AD 40, having been invited to Rome as a friend of the emperor. Caligula's motives here are unclear, though Cassius Dio suggests he was jealous of the Mauritanian king's fabulous wealth (*Roman History*, 59.29.1). Mauretania was then directly annexed by Rome under Claudius in AD 44.

The Carthaginians

The next stage in North African history was a phase dominated by the Carthaginians, this already heavily referenced in the context of the Garamantes, Numidians, and Mauri. Originally Phoenician settlers from the eastern Mediterranean, the Carthaginians established key colonial cities along the southern Mediterranean coast of the Maghreb at key sites which provided safe shelter from the strong easterly and north-easterly winds there. This gave them access not only to the fertile interior of the region but also Spain, where their early colonies included the major Phoenician emporium at Cádiz (later, Roman Gadez) on the Atlantic coast. As time passed this maritime sphere of interest then greatly increased to cover the whole western Mediterranean, including Sicily, which brought them into conflict first with the Greek city states and then Rome.

This Carthaginian phase of regional ascendency is most visible today through the thousands of Punic tombstones to be found throughout the Maghreb, many featuring the distinctive symbol of Tanit, the chief Carthaginian deity. Another common symbol on Carthaginian tombstones is that most iconic manifestation of Punic military power, the war elephant. A fine example can be found reused in the later Roman theatre at Guelma (Roman Calama). Suffice to say the rise and fall of Carthaginian power established the western Maghreb as the economic powerhouse inherited by Rome, building on the earlier successes of the Garamantes, Numidians, and Mauri.

Roman North Africa

In terms of official Roman interest in North Africa, the experience was differential dependent on the region. In the eastern Maghreb Rome initially found it difficult to establish *Romanitas*. Birley says this was because, after the defeat of Carthage in the Second Punic War, Tripolitania was left largely to its own devices (1999, 29). Therefore, by the time of Carthage's final downfall at the end of Third Punic War, the region had enjoyed over 50 years of effective independence, with the three key cities there able to gather vast swathes of territory under their control, in the case of Leptis Magna over 5,000km². Thus, by the time Rome turned its full attention to prosperous Tripolitania, its principal city was already one of the richest in the Mediterranean. Nevertheless the Romans persevered, and by the beginning of the 1st century BC Tripolitania had become an official Roman province. However, even then its independent outlook long continued, with the first major manifestation of Roman power the classification of Leptis Magna by Augustus as a *civitas libera et immunis* (free community). This was a classic Roman conceit given it actually meant the regional governor had total control over the city. Even then the Punic origins of the region remained overtly visible, for example with the family names of the super-rich aristocracy there. Our best example is with the emperor Lucius Septimius Severus. In the late 1st century AD his great grandfather was the first generation of the family to change their Punic cognomen from Macer to Severus.

Further west, the Roman province of Africa grew out of the core Punic territories around Carthage after 146 BC, alongside the unified Numidian kingdom created at the end of the Second Punic War. It comprised much of the territory of modern Tunisia and north-eastern Algeria and was bordered to the west by Mauretania. Here the Romans, having obliterated Carthaginian culture (literally in the case of Carthage) at the end of the Third Punic War, installed a new administration under a proconsul (the governor of a province established by the Senate under the Republic) which rapidly set about re-ordering the local economy to ensure the vast wealth generated across the region quickly found its way to Rome. In particular, by the end of the 2nd century BC the supply of grain had been formalised under early iterations of the *cura annonae.*

Roman interest in North Africa then received a boost under Julius Caesar who championed full re-engagement in a region which many members of the Roman aristocracy still viewed with suspicion in the aftermath of the three Punic Wars. In 46 BC, after defeating his Pompeian and Numidian opponents at Thapsus, he established a third Roman province in the Maghreb after Africa and Tripolitania which he called Africa Nova, with the original African province now called Africa Vetus. However, after his assassination in 44 BC the Senate swiftly moved to unify the two with the single name Africa again, this finally taking place in 35 BC under the Second Triumvirate. The eastern province of Tripolitania was then added in 27 BC, around the time the Senate acknowledged Augustus as the first emperor. Shortly after, this new super-sized province was renamed Africa Proconsularis. By that time its economy was booming, with Scarre saying (1995, 104):

> Roman North Africa [at the end of the 1st century BC] was second only to Egypt as the supplier of grain for Rome, and such was the abundance of olive oil that only the poorest households were unable to afford oil lamps to light their homes.

In particular, the *cura annonae* from North Africa was a vital component of the regional economy. The Maghreb had long provided much of the grain dole for the population in Rome, surpassing Egypt as the main supplier by the mid 1st century AD. Given the imperial capital's population of one million, its none-arrival usually resulted in widespread rioting in the city, causing major problems for the sitting emperor. Even in the Dominate empire, when Rome had long been relegated to a spiritual rather than political role at the heart of the empire, the *cura annonae* was still vital in maintaining societal equilibrium there. Further, the vast surplus created by the export of agricultural produce from North Africa underpinned much of the Roman economy, particularly late on and in the west. As Heather says (2005, 281):

> The revenue surplus from North Africa was essential for balancing the imperial books. Without it, the west could never have afforded armed forces large enough to defend its other, more exposed territories.

To bring more land in the region under agricultural productivity, major construction and engineering projects were also carried out, largely by the Roman military. This included building dams, cisterns, aqueducts, and tunnels to further irrigate the Maghreb. A prime example is the enormous aqueduct and tunnel system constructed near the Algerian port city of Béjaïa (Roman Saldae) in the mid-2nd century AD. One of the tunnels here, built through the Atlas range, was over 500m long. Meanwhile, the various emporia of Roman North Africa were also major ports of transit for other goods too, for example gold, slaves, horses, and as detailed in the context of the Garamantes, wild animals for the arena.

The experience of those living in Roman North Africa was dependent on whether individuals were resident on the coast or interior. For example, Lavan has used archaeological data (including contemporary pottery assemblages) to show that access to the flourishing Mediterranean market economy was highly dependent on proximity to the thriving coastal settlements in the province, most of which were the original Phoenician foundings (2014, 1). As he explains, inland regions found it more difficult to take part in inter-regional trade because of the high transport costs when compared to goods moved by sea, though the extensive network of fine trunk roads throughout the region at least made this possible. Bonifay expands on this idea, using Africa Proconsularis as his specific example and basing his conclusions again on ceramic data (2014, 551). He argues that Mediterranean patterns of consumption are highly visible in the coastal zone, adding that in inland regions local production and markets substituted local goods for more recognisable Mediterranean products. The key here, he concludes, was again the differential cost of transport, a major element defining the provincial economy.

The Roman Maghreb in the Principate was not only very wealthy, but also one of the most articulate regions of the empire, renowned for its literature and as a source of leading lawyers throughout the Roman world. It was also home to some of the empire's wealthiest Senatorial and equestrian families who ran huge agricultural estates there.

By the late 2nd century AD, at the height of the Principate empire, the provincial capital of Africa Proconsularis had long been established at Carthage, which had been completely rebuilt after its total destruction at the end of the Third Punic War. By that time it had a population of 100,000, and was also home to the *Classis nova Libyca* regional fleet. Meanwhile, the Numidian west of the province was effectively a separate entity after being placed under the control of an imperial *legatus* in AD 40 by Caligula after he had annexed Mauretania. Septimius Severus then formalised this arrangement at the turn of the 3rd century AD, calling the newly detached province Numidia with its capital at the legionary fortress of Lambaesis near Batna in modern Algeria. Further west, Mauretania itself featured two distinct provinces from the time it became part of the Roman world under the Julio-Claudians, these Mauretania Caesariensis with its capital at Cherchell, and Mauretania Tingitana with its capital at Tangier (Roman Tingis).

Roman North Africa was protected in the south by the *limes Tripolitanus* (also called the *Fossatum Africae* in contemporary literature), this a series of fortifications built to defend the region from raiding by the Garamantes to the east, and a variety of Berber tribes living south of the Aures range along the Saharan fringe to the west. Whether the latter can be called Numidian as some modern authors do is problematic given Strabo calls them the Gaetuli (*Geography*, 17.3.2), so I will stick with Berber. In the far west, a number of Mauri tribes living south of the *limes* in the deep Saharan interior also caused occasional friction with the Roman authorities in Mauretania.

This fortified southern border had its origins under Augustus. For much of its length it was initially an east–west trunk road along the Saharan fringe, with fortifications built at key choke points where nomads from the far south could access the coast to mount raids. In the east in Tripolitania this was a simple matter for both parties, the Garamantes probing for weaknesses along the frontier which the Romans would then fortify, especially if they were oases. The fort at Bu Njem (Roman Gholaia) on the Libyan Saharan fringe provides a fine example. It is well detailed by Walas in her recent analysis of the extensive fieldwork undertaken there between 1967 and 1980. She explains that (2022, 48):

> The garrison at Bu Njem was founded in AD 201 and abandoned between AD 259 and AD 263. The site lies 192km east of a larger military base at Gheriat-el-Garbia [Roman name unknown]. Bu Njem's extraordinary preservation and its ostraca [inscribed sherds of pottery] have earned the site an important role in the archaeology of Roman frontiers. Epigraphic evidence shows the fort was built by a vexillation of legio III Augusta whose mother base was located over 1,000km away at Lambaesis, in modern day Algeria. In AD 238 legio III Augusta was dissolved as punishment for its participation in the revolt of Gordian I. Bu Njem was subsequently occupied by a detachment of auxiliaries with a decurion in charge. The legion is then attested epigraphically at Bu Njem again soon after its reconstitution in AD 253, and its detachment remained at Bu Njem until the site's abandonment.

Another key feature of the *limes Tripolitanus* in the Fezzān was the use of *centenaria* (fortified farmhouses) where veteran troops were settled after leaving the army. Some 2,000 of these are known in the southern peripheries of Leptis Magna and Sabratha alone, with examples including those at modern Gherait esh-Shergia and Gasr Banat (Roman names unknown). Here, the settled veterans were both *gendarmes* and farmers.

After its founding by Augustus, this section of the *limes Tripolitanus* was first expanded by Tiberius after Garamantes warriors fought with the rebel Numidian king, Tacfarinas, in the early AD 20s. It was then significantly expanded on three later occasions, first by Hadrian, then Trajan, and finally Septimius Severus. The latter carried out the last major Roman campaign against the Garamantes in AD 201 while returning to Leptis Magna, his hometown, as part of a triumphal progress through North Africa after defeating the Parthians in the east. Notably, all of the settlements he passed through in the region feature a significant Severan phase dating to this time, particularly Leptis Magna which he effectively rebuilt. At the time the Garamantes were causing trouble along the *limes Tripolitanus*, where vexillations of *legio* III *Augusta* under its *legate* Quintus Anicius Faustus had been fighting an intensive five-year campaign to stop endemic raiding into rich Tripolitania. Typically, on arrival Severus took matters in hand, personally leading a campaign far to the south of the *limes*, capturing several significant oasis settlements including Cydamus, Gholaia (the Roman fort there detailed above was founded at this time), Garbia, and the Garamantian capital, Garama. He incorporated much of this captured territory into Africa Proconsularis, and then further refortified the border which he extended south beyond the Saharan fringe.

However, in the western Maghred the Romans built a far more sophisticated system of defence in depth using the Aures Mountains as its anchor. Along the range's northern fringe sat the key military bases in the region, for example Lambaesis and its associated *colonia* Timgad where the retired veterans from *legio* III *Augusta* settled. From these sites the Romans built a road through each of the key north-south mountain gorges from the northern edge of the Aures to the Sahara. Two of the best known start at Lambaesis, literally from its south gate, before forking through two of the most important nearby gorges. Here, Blas de Roblès, Sintes, and Kenrick provide excellent detail on each route in their definitive narrative on Roman Algeria (2003, 226):

> The first, still today the main route of the N3 highway, followed the valley of the Oued el-Ksour past the ancient [Roman] settlement at Lambiridi to a point where the valley narrows and the stream cuts through the dramatic gorge of El-Kantara. The modern road and railway depart from the ancient route just at this point, and no longer pass over the stream where they did in Roman times. The Romans named this place Calceus Herculis (The Boot of Hercules) and constructed a road through the gorge. The abutments of the original Roman bridge are still in place [atop of which sits the French colonial bridge].

This was a crucial crossing of the Oued el-Ksour, a mountain stream dry in summer but a raging torrent after heavy rain in winter. Contemporary records from Lambaesis show it was guarded in the 2nd and 3rd centuries AD by vexillations of Syrian auxiliary archers from Emesa and Palmyra.

Meanwhile, of the second route they say (Blas de Roblès, Sintes and Kenrick, 2003, 226):

> Another route through the mountains, a little further to the east, passed by [Roman] Verecundo and then descended the valley of the Oued el-Abiod. Here again, the stream makes an abrupt change of course half-way along its length, carving a narrow defile through a mountain ridge at [modern] Tighanimine.

Here, just above the modern roadway, is a Latin inscription cut into the rock face by the vexillation of legionaries who actually built this section of road. I have seen this in person and it is truly astonishing, giving a direct link to the intensely hard labour of those Roman soldiers who carried out this incredible feat of engineering. Interestingly, the legionaries here are not from the regional *legio* III *Augusta*, but from *legio* VI *Ferrata*. From the inscription we know the work was carried out in the AD 140s, with some suggesting the legionaries who did the work were re-deployed to North Africa to spend time out of the frontline after the legion had taken part in the brutal putting down of the Bar Kokhba Jewish Revolt in the AD 130s. Also of interest, the modern road surface is not that built by the Romans, which in places may have been constructed with timber given Roman mortises have been cut into the rock face where sections today are missing.

Along the length of both routes, which converge to the south of the Aures at Biskra (Roman Vescera), another key feature of this system of defence in depth is also visible today, namely a string of stone built signal stations. While researching this book I had the pleasure of eating lunch in a Berber restaurant near modern Ghoufi, part way through the Oued el-Abiod. While there I noticed large amounts of Roman *spolia* reused in modern buildings. Asking the proprietor where this came from, he pointed across the gorge to a tumble of Roman building stone, describing it as a beacon. On investigating it transpired he was absolutely correct. It was indeed a Roman signal station. These allowed rapid communications from the frontier through the Aures range, alerting the regional headquarters in Lambaesis of any Berber raid massing on the Saharan fringe.

There, on the edge of the desert, could be found the final stage of this system of defence in depth, the physical *limes Tripolitanus* itself. In the western Maghreb this featured the same east-west roadway which marked the frontier south of Tripolitania to the east. However, some sections here also featured stone built wall sections in addition to the usual south-facing ditch and bank, and regularly spaced watchtowers. The main features, though, were the frontier forts along its length, for example those at Gemellae and modern Tehouda (Roman name unknown). The remains of both are still visible today, the latter particularly enigmatic given its later reuse as a defended settlement, with its fine Roman arches bricked up and plastered over, and only now revealed again by centuries of natural sand blasting. Here units of auxiliary cavalry patrolled the frontier, in the 2nd century AD this the *Ala* I *Pannoniorum* based on inscriptions in the local forts. This was notably a long way from their Danubian home.

As already detailed, for much of the Principate and Dominate phases of empire the *limes Tripolitanus* was manned by North Africa's only legion, *legio* III *Augusta*, and its supporting auxiliary units. The legion was originally based in the Numidian west at Haidra (Roman Ammaedara) but was later moved further south to nearby Tebessa (Roman Thevestis) where it remained until finally moving to its long-term home of Lambaesis. As already noted, this became the provincial capital of Severan Numidia. Meanwhile the key auxiliary bases, aside from those actually on the *limes*, were at Carthage and Utique (Roman Utica). The size of the various military installations in the Roman Maghreb indicates an overall military presence of around 20,000. D'Amato highlights the particularly regional nature of the equipment worn by the legionaries and auxilia here, including pseudo-Attic helmets of Hellenistic provenance, linen armour, and the use of round plank body shields (the latter, certainly in the case of legionaries, adopted earlier than elsewhere in the empire) (2019, 38).

As elsewhere across the empire, the organisational structure of Roman North Africa was consolidated as part of the Diocletianic Reformation when the new *diocene* administrative system was instituted, each with their own smaller, new provinces. This extensive and rich region featured three *dioceses*, these Oriens which comprised the eastern frontier, Egypt and Cyrenaica, Africa (which is our focus here), and Hispaniae, given this included (as detailed earlier) Mauretania Tingitana.

As already set out in the Introduction, the provinces in the new *diocese* of Africae were (east to west) Tripolitania, Byzacena, Africa Proconsularis, Numidia Cirtensis, Numidia Militiana, Mauretania Tabia, and Mauretania Caesariensis. Mauretania Tingitana then formed the western extremity of this late Roman provincial structure. Later, after the further administrative macro-restructuring of the empire by Constantine I, Roman North Africa became part of the Praefectura praetorio Italiae, excepting Mauretania Tingitana which maintained its Spanish connection as part of the Praefectura praetorio Galliarum. It is into this administrative landscape that Gaiseric and his Vandal and Alan warriors descended in AD 429.

Invasion

Having established the administrative structure of Roman North Africa, and the deep cultural history of the region, I now narrate the fantastical story of the Vandal conquest there. I begin by providing a short biography of one of the key protagonists whose actions played such a key role in this story, *comes* Boniface. I then cover the Vandal conquest itself in great detail, to the point when the entire region was finally under Gaiseric's rule.

Comes Boniface

I have already introduced *comes* Boniface in Chapter 4 in the context of his falling out with Castinus, the ill-fated *vicarius* of Hispaniae, when campaigning against the Vandals in AD 422. Also known as Bonifatius or Bonifacius, he was a leading Roman military and political leader in the Western Empire in the first three decades of the 5th century AD. Given the key role he played in the arrival of the Vandals and Alans in North Africa, I detail him here in full.

Boniface first appears in contemporary literature as a senior officer in the service of Constantius III in AD 413, campaigning against Athaulf. Here he gained early fame, successfully defending Marseille against the Visigoths and wounding their king in the process. Later in the decade he commanded an army of Gothic *foederates* fighting Mauri tribesmen in North Africa. While in the region he met and befriended St Augustine, by then bishop in Hippo Regius. Next, early in AD 422 he was recalled to Ravenna where he married Pelagia, daughter of the Gothic leader Beremudus. As part of the wedding dowry he inherited her father's *bucellarii*. This term, derived from the Greek for biscuit-eater, was used to describe mercenary heavy cavalry who served as bodyguards for late Roman military leaders. In the context of Boniface, they now gave him his own small private army, and were to serve him well for the rest of his career.

Boniface's stay in Ravenna was short, in fact only a matter of months given he is next referenced in Spain later that year abandoning Castinus after the Roman defeat to the Vandals at Tarragona. Departing Oporto in Gallaecia, he soon arrived back in North Africa. His decision proved sound as, far from being tainted by Castinus' disgrace after his disastrous campaign, he was promoted *comes Africae* in AD 423. This was a significant advancement, putting him in charge of all Roman *comitatensis* (field armies) and *limitanei* (border troops) in the *diocese* of Africae.

Here we can detect the support of a patron who was to play a key role in Boniface's later career, for good and bad. This was Gallia Placidia, youngest offspring of Theodosius I and paternal half-sister to Arcadius and Honorius. Placidia was one of the most powerful political figures in the late antique world, and when later regent for her son Valentinian III she ran the entire empire in the west for a time. Some argue her role in the promotion of Boniface's early career pre-dated his time in Spain with Castinus, whom she disliked intensely, which might provide background to the two men falling out. However, certainly now we can detect her involvement in Boniface's career progress at this time.

Honorius' death in August AD 423 then threw the Western succession into chaos. As referenced in Chapter 4, this formed the backdrop to the Vandals' later predatory campaigns in Spain. At the time, Placidia and Valentinian were resident in Constantinople after fleeing there in AD 421 when her husband,

Constantius III, died, he a late co-regent with Honorius. In her absence, the anti-Theodosian faction at court in Ravenna now took advantage. Led by Castinus, they placed the *primicerius notariorum* Joannes onto the Western throne early in AD 424. Kean and Frey call him an obscure clerk, but this is to misunderstand his actual role (2005, 214). In fact, as head of the *notarii* under Honorius, Joannes was one of the post powerful men in the Western Empire given he commanded the internal branch of the late Roman secret service (the external branch being called the *agentes in rebus*) (Elliott, 2023, 50). Unusually for a man in this post, he was also well liked at court, with Procopius calling him mild mannered and intelligent (*The Vandalic Wars*, 3.9).

Whatever his standing among the Roman elite, Joannes had clearly usurped against the long-in-power Theodosian imperial family, who acted with predictable aggression. In Constantinople, Theodosius II and Placidia made their opposition known immediately, encouraging the field armies in Gaul to rise against him. Here they were remarkably successful, with the new emperor's *praetorian prefect* in the region slain in Arles. More importantly, she also urged Boniface in Carthage to stop sending the *cura annonae* to Rome. Boniface complied immediately, showing their close links at the time. Heather says Boniface then refused to reply when entreated by Joannes to restart the grain supply (2005, 259). Interestingly, here Boniface was acting with the authority of a *diocene vicarius*. This indicates the original *vicarius* was a supporter of Joannes and had been forcibly removed by Boniface. Further of interest, Boniface showed no sign (either now or later) of wanting to take on this title in the civilian administration, preferring when in North Africa to use his military title.

In another setback for the new emperor, in early AD 425 Theodosius elevated Valentinian (still resident in Constantinople with Placidia) to become the new *caesar* in the west as Valentinian III. This was a direct challenge to Joannes who was now styling himself *augustus* and wanted to appoint his own junior emperor. In desperation, Joannes sent his most able *legate* to the Huns then camped north of the Danube to seek military help. This was the young Flavius Aetius, earlier a Hunnic hostage who knew them well and who was to later find fame defeating Attila the Hun at the battle of the Catalaunian Fields in AD 451. However, on this occasion, while he was away Theodosius launched a huge military assault against Joannes with an army under the command of his two leading generals, Ardabur and Flavius Ardabur Aspar. Placidia and the six-year-old Valentinian also travelled with them. Soon this was camped at Aquileia on the north-eastern coast of the Adriatic. Ravenna fell shortly afterwards without a fight when Aspar arrived with a flying cavalry column. This proved the end for Joannes, with Olympiodorus of Thebes saying (*Historikoi Logio*, 42.2):

> ...after a short struggle Joannes was captured through the treachery of his own officials and sent to Aquileia to Placidia and Valentinian. There his hand was first cut off as a punishment, and then he was decapitated [in the hippodrome, having been paraded around the city on a donkey], having usurped power for a year and a half.

The Eastern army then spent the next three days sacking Ravenna.

Shortly after, Valentinian III was elevated from Western *caesar* to *augustus* at the behest of Theodosius. Heather calls this '...a triumphant reaffirmation of the political unity of the two halves of the empire...' (2005, 260). However, to complicate matters, three days after the coronation Aetius returned with his newly hired Hunnic *foederates*. At first this led to a stand-off, with Aspar preparing his Eastern army for battle. An accommodation was soon reached though, with the Huns handsomely paid off with huge amounts of gold. Placidia, now regent and with the title *augusta*, then agreed to promote Aetius to her *comes per Italia* in charge of all Roman troops in Italy. This was a very senior post, only second to the *magister militum* who commanded the entire Western military establishment. At the time this was an aspiring Theodosian loyalist called Flavius Felix.

However, in the short term Boniface in North Africa was the key beneficiary, being promoted *comes Domesticorum* after resuming grain shipments to Rome following Joannes' downfall (Hornblower and Spawforth, 1996, 249). This was another very senior post in the imperial administration, though notably he chose to stay in North Africa where he had clearly established a significant power base.

Back in Ravenna, Placidia strove to balance the disparate ambitions of a court she thought she knew well through her time there with her father. However, by now a new generation of ambitious newcomers was moving to make their own mark, with Aetius the most overt. In the long run all underestimated her, and ultimately her period as regent was one of relative stability in Ravenna. However, initially trouble lay ahead, with Boniface the victim of the first round of political intrigue at court. Here, for reasons unclear, Felix accused Boniface of planning to usurp and form a break-away North African empire. Convincing Placidia the plot was real, she then ordered the *comes Domesticorum* to return to Ravenna. In a clear breach of imperial protocol Boniface refused point blank, clearly aware of the fate that awaited him if he complied (some argue here that Aetius had earlier sent him a warning telling him to ignore any summons by the regent).

Placidia then ordered Felix to send an army to North Africa to remove Boniface and ensure the grain supply continued to flow to Rome. The task was given to Felix's three leading generals, Mavortius, Gallio, and Sanoeces. The former two led field army troops from Italy, while the latter commanded Hunnic *foederates*, possibly those recently arrived with Aetius in Ravenna. Their army arrived safely, and promptly laid siege to Carthage, trapping Boniface inside. However, the three *legates* then turned on each other, with Sanoeces and his Huns killing Mavortius, Gallio, and their bodyguards, before he was slain himself. This promptly lifted the siege, with an astonished Boniface emerging victorious when all had looked doomed.

When news reached Ravenna of the disaster Felix doubled down, realising his own reputation was now at stake. He decided to risk another invasion. This time he appointed a German *comes* called Sigisvultus to lead the assault, with a large force of German and Gothic *foederates*. Again, at first the campaign went well, with Sigisvultus quickly capturing Annaba and Carthage. He was then declared the *comes Africae*, with Boniface fleeing into the Numidian interior. Clearly thinking his war won, Sigisvultus then appointed an Arian bishop in Carthage whom he sent to dispute theology with St Augustine in Annaba, a clear indicator of his own beliefs.

However, events soon turned against Sigisvultus. Boniface now led his *bucellari* on a two-year campaign against the Theodosian loyalists, avoiding direct engagement with Sigisvultus and his *foederates* every time they tried to engage him in battle. This may seem like classic guerrilla warfare, but the reader should note the battlespace in question was an enormous region running from the Mediterranean to the Sahara, in places heavily populated and with a multitude of cities and towns. Here, especially along the northern fringes of the Aures Mountains, it was easy for Boniface to establish a secure powerbase impossible to supress. At this time his daughter was also baptized by an Arian priest, which may reflect his origins if German, though these are obscure, or an attempt to placate his own *bucellari* and win over Salivates' Germans and Goths. This caused a falling out between Boniface and St Augustine.

Eventually the pragmatic Placidia realised the futility of Sigisvultus' ongoing campaign in North Africa, which again was threatening the grain supply to Rome. Therefore, in January AD 429 she sent an envoy to Boniface to open negotiations for his return to power there, a forged letter then being 'discovered' as the cause of their original falling out. This was very convenient, giving both an elegant way to back down without losing face. With the groundwork now set to allow Boniface to return to Carthage, in February a courtier named

Darius was sent from Ravenna to negotiate a lasting truce. As a result Boniface was restored to full authority in North Africa, with Sigisvultus returning to Italy. Darius remained with Boniface, no doubt acting as the eyes and ears of Placidia.

Later in AD 429 Boniface then faced a threat even more existential than Placidia's earlier attempt to remove him through Sigisvultus, and one he has been associated with ever since in a very negative way. This was the invasion of North Africa by Gaiseric's Vandals and Alans from Spain. I fully detail this later in the chapter, though suffice to say things did not go well for the Romans.

Two years later it was evident Boniface was losing his war in North Africa against a relentless Vandal advance. In normal circumstances he would have been recalled and replaced in disgrace. However, these weren't normal times. In May that year Felix suffered a dramatic fall from grace when he, his wife, Padusia, and a church deacon associated with the family were accused by Aetius of treason, and then quickly arrested and hanged in Ravenna. Placidia cast around for a loyalist replacement as *magister militum* but, with none to hand in Ravenna, alighted on Boniface in North Africa. In early AD 432 he was appointed and recalled to Italy, despite his unsuccessful record against Gaiseric, indeed losing another battle against the Vandal king before heading back to Ravenna (see below). Ammianus Marcellinus says that on arrival in AD 432 he was also promoted to the post of *patricius*, this the regent's most senior political advisor (*The Later Roman Empire*, 43.2). If true, then given he now held the key military and civilian leadership posts in the west, he was the senior figure at court (excepting Placidia). He then faced a predictable and immediate challenge by Aetius, who at the time was in Gaul where Hughes suggests he was planning to cross the Pyrenees to challenge the Suebi, who were now the dominant power in Spain after the departure for North Africa of the Vandals and Alans (2012, 85).

Soon civil war broke out, with Aetius leading his Gallic field army south through the Alps into north-eastern Italy. Battle was joined in late AD 432 at Rimini, where Boniface, alongside his son-in-law, Sebastianus, led the Italian field armies to a famous victory. However it was at a terrible personal cost to the new *magister militum* who, fighting in the thick of the action, was fatally wounded by a lance. Depending on the source, it took him between a few days and three months to die.

In the aftermath of this key battle Aetius was allowed to quietly retire to his own personal estates, with Sebastianus becoming Placidia's new *magister militum*. However, Sebastianus then overplayed his hand at court and tried to have Aetius assassinated in AD 433, the latter surviving and fleeing to the Huns to seek their support again. Sebastianus then prepared to emulate his father-in-law and engage Aetius in battle, leading an army of Visigoth *foederates*. However, at a crucial moment he lost the support of the military in Italy, with whom he was unpopular, and was exiled by Placidia who realised she needed to find a lasting accommodation with Aetius to protect Valentinian III. Sebastianus was then exiled to Constantinople where he remained for over a decade, with Aetius becoming the new *magister militum*. He was then further promoted to become *patrician* in AD 435, and was ultimately the dominant political and military figure in the Roman west for the next two decades until his own assassination in AD 454 (Heather, 2005, 262).

Into Africa

I now return to AD 429 and a momentous event in the history of the Western Empire, and late antiquity more broadly. This was the crossing from Spain to Africa of Gaiseric and his Vandals and Alans. First, three questions need to be answered: What was the actual date he crossed? Why did he and his followers cross? And, how many crossed with him?

In terms of the date, some have argued it was earlier than AD 429, and some later. However we have one piece of hard data, this from Hydatius, who specifically says the event occurred in May AD 429 (*Chronicle*, 42.8). That makes absolute sense to me. The year fits the chronology of how the Vandals under Gunderic and later Gaiseric predated their way through Spain in the AD 420s, including the former's initial raid to North Africa in AD 426. Further, in terms of the month, it was the right time of year to carry out such an ambitious maritime expedition. In the pre-modern world, except in extremis, sailors would rarely choose to sail out of the sailing season, in the Mediterranean this between late spring (as with Gunderic's earlier raid across the Strait of Gibraltar) and late autumn. Further, crossing in May would have allowed Gaiseric the time needed over the preceding winter and early spring to gather his force, obtain the provisions he would need to maintain them after their initial landing, and crucially to muster the necessary maritime assets to carry his migrants over. Logistics are the key to success with any military operation on this scale, particularly one as risky as a huge maritime crossing over open water, whether opposed or not. Time and again in the ancient world such endeavours came to grief, and on a quite spectacular scale. In that regard, and to put Gaiseric's crossing into perspective in terms of sheer ambition, the Visigoths had earlier planned two invasions of North Africa of their own, one from Italy and one from Spain. Both came to nought given the scale of the task (Pohl, 2004, 38). For the Vandals to be successful, meticulous planning was required, which to his credit Gaiseric carried out exceptionally well. Thus all of the anecdotal data points to Hydatius being correct. The Vandals crossed to North Africa in May AD 429.

Next a far more significant question: Why did they cross? First, Gaiseric's timing was perfect. As detailed, the Vandals and their Alan allies knew that at some stage the imperial administration in Ravenna would get its act together, which to a large extent it did in the aftermath of Boniface's death at Rimini in AD 432, and Sebastianus' exile to Constantinople a year later. That meant renewed Roman interest in Spain, especially given the Theodosian family estates there. Additionally the Suebi, recently in conflict with the Vandals, had taken advantage of the latter's adventures in eastern and southern Spain to secure their powerbase in Gallaecia. Initially, this was a land grab in a province previously under Vandal rule. However, soon they began an eastward and southerly expansion, filling the power vacuum left while Vandal attention was elsewhere, and with no imperial resistance given the succession crisis in Ravenna. Even after the Romans did return, the kingdom the Suebi carved for themselves proved very resilient, with their Gallaecian territories surviving intact until late in the 6th century AD (Pohl, 2004, 38). Finally, Gaiseric was also keenly aware of the recent turmoil in North Africa after Placidia's botched attempts to remove Boniface from power there, first with Mavortius, Gallio, and Sanoeces, and later Sigisvultus.

I next ponder the role of another protagonist when considering why the Vandals crossed to North Africa. This is Boniface, who is often thought the villain of the story given many historians argue it was he who invited Gaiseric across. This belief is based on two specific passages written by historians over a century later, and one less clear but near contemporary. The first is by Procopius, writing in the mid AD 540s, who says (*The Vandalic Wars*, 3.3):

> Boniface accordingly sent to Spain those who were his most intimate friends and gained the adherence of the sons of Godegisel [Gaiseric, as king, clearly the most prominent] on terms of complete equality. It being agreed that each one of three, holding a third part of Libya [here used as a generic term for North Africa by Procopius] should come to rule his own subjects but if a foe should come against any one of them to make war that they should in common ward off any aggressors. On the basis of this agreement the Vandals crossed the Strait of Gibraltar and came into Libya.

So far so clear, noting Boniface already had strong connections with the Vandals after bolting through their territory when fleeing Castinus after the Roman defeat at Tarragona. Next we have Jordanes, writing in the early AD 550s, who says (*Getica*, 33.168):

> Gaiseric, king of the Vandals, had already been invited to Africa by Boniface, who had fallen into a dispute with the emperor Valentinian and was able to obtain revenge only by injuring the empire. So he invited them urgently and brought them across the narrow strait known as the Strait of Gades, scarcely seven miles wide, which divides Africa from Spain and unites the mouth of the Tyrrhenian Sea [actually the Mediterranean] with the waters of Ocean.

Again, this is very clear. Finally, and earlier, we have an ambiguous reference by Prosper of Aquitaine. When speaking in the context of Boniface's conflict with Placidia and Felix, two sequential entries say (*Defence of St Augustine*, 17.26):

> After [Boniface's defeat of Mavortius, Gallio, and Sanoeces,] access to the sea was gained by peoples who were unaccustomed with the use of ships, who were then called on to help the rivals. The conduct of the war against Boniface was transferred to comes Sigisvultus.

This seems a clear reference to the Vandals in Spain given the maritime reference, especially as the next entry simply reads (*Defence of St Augustine*, 17.26):

> The Vandal people crossed from Spain to Africa.

Some argue that, when taken together, Prosper's two comments indicate it was Boniface who called on the Vandals for help. We therefore have two strong sources in favour of Boniface inviting the Vandals to North Africa, and one more equivocal.

However, in recent years some historians have begun to question this version of events. For example, Hughes, in his balanced biography of Boniface's arch rival, Aetius, says (2012, 72):

> The claim that Boniface was responsible for inviting the Vandals into Africa is also extremely unlikely. Although in revolt against the government in Ravenna, he will have suspected that it was not Placidia herself that was responsible but Felix: Boniface's loyalty had been rewarded in the past and his faithful service would expect continued loyalty from Placidia. Such an invitation would have been seen as the ultimate treachery in Ravenna. However, the strongest argument against Boniface inviting the Vandals into Africa is the complete silence of contemporaries, who in reality would have made the most violent complaints had this been true.

Indeed, the first time contemporary writers reference Boniface and Gaiseric in the same passage it is not in the context of the former inviting the latter over, but of Roman resistance to the Vandal invasion.

Further, one should note that Boniface was one of the empire's most senior military leaders. He had decades of experience fighting the enemies of Rome across the empire. As detailed above, to this point he had been highly successful as a field commander, and would only later suffer serious defeat when facing Gaiseric. Indeed, even his accuser, Procopius, was a fan of his martial track record, saying of he and Aetius (*The Vandalic Wars*, 3.3):

> There were two Roman generals, Boniface and Aetius, especially valiant men and in experience of many wars inferior to none of that time at least.

Boniface well knew the risks of inviting a barbarian leader with armed troops into his super rich *diocese*. As indeed happened, he knew that once any Vandals travelled across the Strait of Gibraltar with a view to a lengthy stay, the chances of them leaving North Africa were nil.

A final reason also mitigates against Boniface inviting Gaiseric to North Africa. This is the fact that at the point the Vandals crossed, Boniface's many allies in the imperial court were already working to rebuild his relationship with Placidia after the failure of Felix's various attempts to remove him. Boniface was keenly aware of this and would never risk anything that might impact his return to imperial favour.

Based on this historical data, limited to be sure, and on the anecdotal factors I have set out, we are then left to make a judgment on whether Boniface is a guilty man or not. Certainly MacDowall thinks he is, saying (2016, 69):

> Despite the tendency of many modern historians to try to rehabilitate Boniface's reputation, for me the stories ring true.

However, I think things are more nuanced, with the key factor the speed of events at the beginning of AD 429. As the year began, Boniface was still leading his insurgency deep within the Numidian interior against Sigisvultus. Then in January Placidia sent her first peace envoy, with the key emissary, Darius, following in February. Boniface was then restored to full authority in the *diocese*, immediately before Gaiseric crossed to Mauretania Tingitana in May. Clearly, after being restored to power by Placidia, Boniface had no need to recruit Vandal *foederates* given he now had access to the full military establishment in Roman North Africa, whose earlier loyalty to Sigisvultus is debatable given the latter's reliance on his Goths. Thus, if Boniface did invite Gaiseric to join him, it must have been earlier, while he still felt under threat from Ravenna.

Here we should next consider two important statistics relating to time and distance. First, how long would it take for a messenger to travel from Ravenna to the Numidian interior in the late Roman world, and second, how long would it take for a messenger to travel from the Numidian interior to southern Spain? In the first case, using horse relays along major imperial trunk roads and fast maritime transport, seven days. In the second case, eight days. Thus it is entirely feasible that as AD 428 came to an end Boniface, not realising his rehabilitation was imminent, sent word to his Vandal friends that he needed military aid, and quickly. If that was the case, this message to the Vandals may have already been in play at the point Placidia's first envoy set off to North Africa. That would then explain why there is no mention of any invite to Gaiseric in the contemporary sources. Under this hypothesis, and from a Roman perspective (for, as usual, that is all we have), the whole episode would have been a huge embarrassment, to be brushed under the carpet. On balance, I therefore believe this scenario is the most likely, based on the data we have and some common sense. Boniface did invite Gaiseric, but then promptly disowned the Vandals once back in Placidia's favour. Importantly, however, it was too late to stop the crossing. Gaiseric was on his way.

Finally, when considering why the Vandals made the crossing, some have also suggested there was a theological motive. The key here is Victor of Vita, writing a few years after AD 485 in the context of his damning account of Vandal North Africa, and particularly their subjugation of the region. Noting his hard-line Nicene perspective, where he viewed Arianism (along with Donatism) as a heretical form of Christian worship, Victor dwelt at length on the brutality of the Vandal conquest (*History of the Vandal Persecution*, 1.3). In particular, he noted their singling out of bishops, priests, and members of the Catholic Church. In many cases he says they were tortured by the Vandals to reveal the location of their places of worship. Written depictions such as this gave rise to a traditional understanding of the Vandal conquest as a form of persecution, with their Arian beliefs a motivating factor. However, as part of the broader pushback against negative views of Vandal North Africa in recent years, this has now been challenged. Those countering it reflect on the key role of St Augustine in his highly negative depiction of the invaders as persecutors, highly understandable in the circumstances he found himself in. This created a theological framework of interpretation in which Nicene clerics like Victor of Vita were later able to cast the Vandals as the enemies of God. In his expert analysis of the subject, Fournier counters this, saying (2017, 701):

> Sources writing independently of the Augustinian tradition do not present the Vandals as cruel persecutors. Of course, this does not imply that the Vandal period in Spain and the conquest of Africa were peaceful times, in fact it was quite the opposite. But in contrast with later sources like Victor of Vita, which depict the Vandals as targeting and abusing Nicene clerics specifically because of their religious beliefs, earlier sources attest mainly to the pillaging and general violence associated with a war of conquest.

This then begs the question, when did the Vandal elites convert to Arianism? They had certainly done so by the time they arrived in North Africa in AD 429 if one takes the primary sources at face value. Earlier, most modern commentators also believe they were still heathens when they crossed the Rhine with the Alans and Suebi in mid-winter AD 406. Therefore the initial conversion event to Christianity must have taken place as they traversed either Gaul or Spain. There, the predominant Christian denomination in both territories was the Catholic Church, and as I have earlier argued, it was most likely to this creed they were first baptised. Hydatius is very clear here, saying Gaiseric was originally a Catholic and then converted to Arianism (*Chronicle*, 80.1). We then have two other references to the Vandals in a Christian context before they arrived in North Africa. First, Salvian of Marseille saying the Vandals paraded a Bible as their standard at Tarragona against Castinus (*De Gubernatione*, 7.7). Given Salvian was a Catholic, it seems unlikely he would mention this if the Vandals were Arian at the time. Second, another very interesting comment by Hydatius in which he depicts Gaiseric as the divine instrument of God when later fighting the Suebi, just before the Vandal crossing to North Africa. Noting Hydatius was also a Catholic, again it would be odd for him to describe the Vandal king as such if the king were an Arian, especially given his broader negative view of the Vandals (*Chronicle*, 80.2). Taken together, these comments suggest the Vandal elites were Catholic almost to the point they travelled to North Africa. Therefore, once more, common sense is required. The Vandal elites were certainly still heathen when they crossed the Rhine. They then converted to Catholicism as they travelled through Gaul and Spain, most likely the latter. Finally, in an undetailed event, they converted once more, this time to Arianism just before travelling to North Africa.

One could then make the argument that converting to Arianism so close to the Vandal conquest of North Africa may have lent an evangelical bent to the campaign. However, as detailed, the specific primary source narratives suggesting this were added much later by Victor of Vita and others. Indeed, there is no contemporary direct reference to it at all, even by St Augustine. Also of note, to this point the Vandals had been highly practical on their travels through much of the Western Empire. Therefore, I think religion had little to do with their North African adventure, and that it was for much more pragmatic reasons.

So to recap on why the Vandals crossed to North Africa in AD 429, I make three broad points. First, it was a good time for them to leave Spain. Second, Gaiseric had most likely been invited to travel across the Strait of Gibraltar by

Boniface, who then quickly changed his mind after Placidia's rapprochement at the beginning of the year. Finally, theology had little to do with it.

Lastly, how many Vandals and Alans crossed with Gaiseric? Here we have three primary source references. First, Victor of Vita says that before he set out, the Vandal king gathered an entire assembly of young and old men, women, children, and slaves (*History of the Vandal Persecution*, 1.2). In total they numbered 80,000. He specifically emphasises these represented the entire population, not just warriors, as other contemporaries had reported. This last is a reference to now-lost primary sources.

Next, Procopius addresses Victor of Vita's lost sources directly by saying they report Gaiseric divided the Vandals and Alans into 80 *chiliarchies*, each commanded by a *chiliarch* (*The Vandalic Wars*, 3.5.18). A *chiliarchy* is a classical and late antique reference to a military unit of 1,000 men. It is Hellenistic in origin, hence Procopius using it given he was writing in Greek. However, he then seems to doubt this figure, saying the Vandals and Alans may actually have numbered only 50,000, making no distinction regarding the composition of those travelling.

Meanwhile Hydatius is a final primary source, and much closer to the events being described (*Chronicle*, 80.2). Though he doesn't give a number, he says the Vandals and Alans went to North Africa with their families and followers.

Based on the above historical data, and subsequent events, it seems reasonable to accept the Vandals and Alans travelling to Mauretania Tingitana numbered 80,000, this their entire population, of which no more than 25,000 were warriors. That being the case, if Boniface did indeed initially invite Gaiseric to travel to North Africa, the Vandal king took this at complete face value, taking his entire population with him rather than an initial cadre of *foederates* as some suggest. Such a conclusion also fits with my earlier hypothesis regarding timing. A message from Boniface to Gaiseric in Baetica in late AD 428 would have given the Vandal king plenty of time to set in train the huge logistics operation needed to transport his people to North Africa. Thus, when the time came to cross, it was with his entire nation.

In terms of the warrior component among the migrants, by this time most Vandal fighting men were heavy shock cavalry. This transition occurred during their travels through Gaul and Spain, reflecting their exposure to the fighting techniques of the Alans and other mounted warriors, for example Radagaisus' remnant Ostrogoths if they had joined the Vandals after defeat by Stilicho. For organisation, the Vandals remained a feudal society, with a warrior class who fought alongside nobles with whom they had a societal obligation. They were certainly not organised into formal *chiliarchies*, as suggested by Procopius.

The principal weapon of the Vandal heavy cavalryman was a long spear which could be used as a lance or thrown. Additionally, many also carried the *spatha* (long sword). Armour was variable, depending on status, though most warriors carried a large, round shield of plank construction. Many also wore helmets, mostly *spangenhelms* and ridge helmets captured from the Romans. Armour, when worn, was either *lorica hamata* (chain mail) or *lorica squamata* (scale mail), again mostly captured from the Romans. The principal Vandal battle tactic by this time was a surging cavalry charge to contact, sometimes preceded by a shower of spears. This seems an inflexible approach, and indeed Procopius does detail a later occasion when Vandal cavalry struggled against a dense formation of Berber foot (*The Vandalic Wars*, 3.8.27). However in North Africa, with its rolling green hills, for the most part it proved ideal, as the Romans were about to find out.

We can now move on to the invasion itself. In truth, we have no idea of the route taken by the Vandals. Most historians argue the port of departure was modern Tarifa (Roman name unknown) on the southern tip of Baetica, to the west of Algeciras (Roman Portus Albus). However, given the vast number of people travelling, I believe all the regional ports would have been used, not just one. This would have included Cádiz, Algeciras, Gibraltar (Roman Calpe), and Malaga (Roman Malaca). Further, as Heather points out, such an immense undertaking would not be possible in one crossing given the number of ships available to the Vandals. In his detailed analysis, he says (2005, 268):

> On simple logistics grounds, it is nigh on inconceivable that Gaiseric could have got together enough shipping to move his followers en masse across the sea. Roman ships were not that large. For example, in a later invasion of North Africa an east Roman expeditionary force averaged about 70 men (plus horses and supplies) per ship [this covered in Chapter 6]. If Gaiseric's total strength was anywhere near 80,000, he would have needed over 1,000 ships. But in the 460s the whole eastern empire could raise no more than 300, and it took the combined resources of both empires to assemble 1,000. In AD 429 Gaiseric had nothing like this catchment area at his disposal. It is overwhelmingly likely, therefore, that he would not have had enough ships to move all his followers in one go.

Having established a departure from multiple ports and over a lengthy period of time, perhaps the entire month of May AD 429, we can then look to Gaiseric's destination in North Africa. Some have argued his invasion fleet, or fleets in the above scenario given the time needed, headed directly to the North African coast and then sailed east to western Numidia. That would certainly have taken them straight to the heartlands of Roman North Africa. However, a cursory glance at today's map shows how unrealistic this would have been. If the target was Cherchell in modern Algeria, that would be a distance of 700km as the crow flies, and substantially more hugging the coast as pre-modern vessels would have done. MacDowall calls this an impossible task, (2016, 73), and having travelled along the coast there I agree given the sparsity of safe harbours to accommodate large ships, even today. Further, as Heather points out, a maritime journey to the heart of the *diocese* of Africae would have been suicidal, '…offering the Romans the first contingent on a plate, while the ships went back for the second' (2005, 269). Therefore, and again using common sense, it seems far more likely Gaiseric ferried his Vandals and Alans using the most direct route possible. That would be to Tangiers (Roman Tingi), provincial capital of Mauretania Tingitana, and any other nearby ports, including Ceuta (Roman Septum).

Next, what Roman forces were waiting for the Vandals when they arrived? On paper, in this case literally given we have the *Notitia Dignitatum* as our source, the Roman military establishment in Africae numbered around 15,000 *comitatensis* (field army troops) organised into 31 regiments of various sizes, and 10,000 *limitanei* (border troops) organised in 22 regiments, again of various sizes. To this we can add the small number of troops in Mauretania Tingitana, mostly the *limitanei* garrison in Tangiers, given the province was still administratively part of Spain.

On paper this was a military force equivalent in size to that of Gaiseric. However, one should note it was spread across a vast region, with the *limitanei* mostly deployed along the Saharan *limes*. Further, as AD 428 came to a close, the regional military would have been closely watching Sigisvultus' campaign against Boniface in the Numidian interior. In fact, many regular troops may have been confined to barracks, with the court in Ravenna unsure of their loyalty. Finally here, if Boniface had indeed invited Gaiseric at the end of AD 428, and then belatedly changed his mind, word of his change of heart may not have reached Mauretania Tingitana in time. Therefore, most likely, when Gaiseric landed he was not only unopposed, but perhaps even welcomed by the local Romans with whom Boniface was popular.

If initially invited by Boniface, Gaiseric was no doubt bemused when word reached him (before or after travelling) that the *comes Africae* had changed his mind. However it was too late for the Romans. The last thing Gaiseric could afford with his nobles and warriors was to lose face. He therefore determined to take any land the Romans had agreed to hand over anyway, and more besides. Soon he was leading a huge force of cavalry east along the coastal trunk road, targeting each major population centre in turn. First Mellila (Roman Rusadir) in Mauretania Tingitana fell, then Portus Magnus, Ténès (Roman Cartenna), and Cherchell in Mauretania Caesariensis, next Algiers in

Mauretania Tabia, before finally he arrived on the border of Numidia Cirtensis in early AD 430. There Gaiseric was met by Darius, Placidia's envoy sent to Boniface at the beginning of the previous year. Platitudes were no doubt exchanged, and misunderstandings acknowledged. Maybe a ceasefire was also agreed. However, this was only an attempt by Boniface to buy time so he could ready his defence of the key heartlands of Africae. Soon he arrived in person to confront the Vandals with an army of field army troops and Gothic foederates. Any ceasefire agreed with Darius then broke down and battle was joined near modern Guelma in Algeria (Heather, 2005, 271). The result was total victory for Gaiseric, with Boniface fleeing with his surviving troops to nearby Annaba (Roman Hippo Regius).

Gaiserics' lightning conquest campaign is often described as a journey through the desert, but it was far from that. The lush coastal zone the Vandals sped through comprised rolling green hills and fields growing arable and fruit as far as the eye could see. Further, Gaiseric had used his time in Spain well and learned from the Romans how to use maritime transport to help speed travel along the coast when on campaign. This was the real secret behind his speedy advance, the use of combined arms in a way which surely shocked the local Romans. As he flew along the coast he also sent cavalry squadrons inland to secure the key cities in the Atlas range which controlled the routes to the North African interior, for example Setif in Mauretania Tabia and Constantine in Numidia Cirtensis. Intriguingly, we have a funerary inscription dating to this lightning campaign from the town of Ouloud Mimoun (Roman Altava) in western Algeria. This references an official there who died '...by the barbarian sword...' in late summer AD 429.

Meanwhile, we have no idea why the key cities on Gaiseric's route fell so easily, with most well-fortified by this time. One theory is his speed of advance caught them all by surprise, especially if squadrons of ships jumped ahead of the cavalry columns to seize key harbours in advance. Also, perhaps disfunction in the regional military in the wake of the recent civil war also played a role. What is clear is the trail of destruction the Vandals left in their wake, especially if we take Victor of Vita's vituperative narrative at face value. He says that on finding a peaceful province (*History of the Vandal Persecution*, 1.3):

> ... they set to work with their wicked forces, laying it waste by devastation and bringing everything to ruin with fire and murders. They did not even spare the fruit-bearing orchards, in case people who had hidden in the caves and the mountains would be able to eat the foods produced by them after they had passed. So it was that no place remained safe from being contaminated by them, as they raged with great cruelty, unchanging and relentless.

For once it is likely here he is telling something close to the truth. Indeed he goes further, later in the same passage naming Pampinianus of Vita and Mansuetus of Urusi as two of the key regional bishops tortured by the Vandals.

Meanwhile, Gaiseric was keen to bring his campaign in North Africa to an end as soon as possible and pursued Boniface immediately. On arrival at Annaba sometime in May or June AD 430 the Vandals finally found a key settlement ready for a fight, though one full of refugees, including Boniface. The Roman city there is highly defendable, sitting beneath an acropolis atop which today sits the beautiful St Augustine Basilica. Gaiseric was therefore forced to take the city under siege. Inside, its bishop St Augustine and his priests prayed for relief from the Arian invaders, believing the city's fall would likely mean forced conversion or death for the Nicene Christians there. These are the fears which haunt his final letters to fellow North African bishops (Pohl, 2004, 39). Sadly he died while still under siege on 28 August, and his last thoughts bemoan the once verdant and abandoned wheat fields outside the city. The siege continued, given the Vandals lacked the technology or experience to force the walls. Soon hunger and disease were ravaging those inside, and also the Vandals outside. Finally, in July or August AD 431, the city capitulated, with Boniface again fleeing, this time for Carthage. There he joined the recently arrived Aspar who we last met fighting Joannes, now sent to North Africa by Theodosius II with reinforcements from both the Eastern and Western Empires. Belatedly, it seems Ravenna and Constantinople were waking to the fact that Gaiseric was a serious threat. This fear was reinforced when, shortly after, Gaiseric made Annaba the first Vandal capital in North Africa.

By early AD 432 the Romans, now under the dual leadership of Boniface and Aspar, were ready to engage Gaiseric in battle again. Procopius narrates this second engagement in detail, saying (*The Vandalic Wars*, 3.5.20):

> Since a numerous army had come from both Rome and Constantinople and Aspar with them as general, Boniface decided to renew the struggle. And a fierce battle was fought in which the Romans were badly beaten by the enemy and they made haste to flee as each one could.

Here Procopius is describing the Romans in full flight from the battlefield, indicating the severity of the loss. MacDowall makes an interesting point that the Roman army in this engagement featured elite units from both the Eastern and Western field armies, and further that Boniface and Aspar were experienced field commanders fighting on territory the former knew intimately. He concludes the Vandal victory was therefore down to Gaiseric's leadership and the high quality of his shock cavalry (2016, 85). They certainly made a big impression on the Romans, with Vegetius writing shortly after that the mounted prowess of the Vandals began to influence Roman heavy cavalry practice (*De Re Militari*, 1.20). This is intriguing given the Romans had been fighting high-quality shock cavalry for centuries. However, in the previous 50 years their principal threat had been the bow-armed Huns. This has led to speculation that perhaps, having changed tactics to deal with that threat, they were now caught out again by hard-charging lancers.

After this battle the Vandals then began a rapid advance through Africa Proconsularis and Byzacena, cutting through the heart of Roman North Africa.

Here they were aided by more tribulations in Ravenna, where Felix had fallen from power the previous year. As detailed earlier, at the beginning of AD 432 Placidia decided to make Boniface her new *magister militum* to counterbalance the growing power of Aetius. He was appointed shortly after and ordered to return to Italy. It is not clear if this was before or after his defeat by the Vandals alongside Aspar, but in the aftermath he quickly beat a hasty retreat to Italy, where on arrival he was also made *patricius*. By the end of the year he was dead, killed while defeating Aetius at Rimini.

Aspar remained in Carthage and was soon promoted *consul Africae*, a new Western post created specifically for him given he was an Eastern general. However, after his defeat alongside Boniface he no longer had the manpower to tackle the Vandals on the battlefield. Meanwhile Gaiseric, soon outside the walls of Carthage, was also unable to bring matters to a conclusion. Carthage was a far different proposition to Annaba. Still the fourth-largest city in the Roman world after Rome itself, Alexandria, and Antioch-on-the-Orontes, the Vandal king knew he didn't have the manpower to besiege the enormous city with its sophisticated defensive fortifications, let alone storm it. He therefore returned to Annaba. An uneasy stand-off followed, with occasional skirmishes between the two sides on the borders of Numidia Cirtensis and Africa Proconsularis, but no set-piece engagement.

By AD 435 both sides needed a break from the ongoing friction. Gaiseric, having conquered an enormous swathe of the western Maghreb, needed time to give his people what they had been promised for years, peace and stability in their own land. Meanwhile, Constantinople and Ravenna needed time to develop a coherent strategy for dealing with the 'new normal' in Roman North Africa. Though in the long term the Roman leadership in both Eastern and Western Empires was committed to reclaiming their lost lands there, they knew in the short term this was not possible. In particular, the Western Empire was beset with an ongoing series of foreign policy crises, not least the Huns on the upper Danube and Burgundians and Visigoths in Gaul.

This meant all available field army troops were now committed on those two fronts, with none available to reinforce Aspar. Further, the Romans were keen to ensure the Vandals continued to export vital agricultural produce to the rest of the empire.

The result was a peace treaty between Gaiseric and the Romans, signed in AD 435, with the Vandal king the real winner given it formally ceded Mauretania Tingitana, Mauretania Caesariensis, Mauretania Tabia, and parts of Numidia Cirtensis and Numidia Militiana to the Vandals. Here Procopius is full of praise for Gaiseric, saying (*The Vandalic Wars*, 3.5.20):

> After defeating Boniface and Aspar in battle, Gaiseric displayed a foresight worth recounting, whereby he made his good fortune thoroughly secure. For fearing lest, if once again an army should come against him from both Constantinople and Rome, the Vandals might not be able to use the same strength and enjoy the same fortune. He was not lifted up by the good fortune he had enjoyed, but rather became a moderate because of what he feared and so he made a treaty with the emperor Valentinian [III] providing each year he should pay the emperor tribute from Libya [this referencing the *cura annonae* from the western Maghreb].

This displays a serious understanding of the realities of his situation, especially given he agreed for the Romans to style his Vandal warriors *foederates* to allow Constantinople and Ravenna to save face. However, nothing could be further from the truth. Gaiseric was a conqueror, with both sides knowing it, and their new lands were far from the Vandal reservation Heather suggests (2005, 288).

One issue Gaiseric faced here was the land settlement for his nobles. As I detail in the next chapter, this was often a simple matter of his societal elites replacing those of the Romans, many of whom were absent living elsewhere in the empire. However, though many were happy with the land gifted them, others were not. The latter then quickly began eyeing any chance to accrue more Roman property. This proved a difficult situation for Gaiseric in his new court at Annaba. Soon he was casting around for opportunities to distract the most disgruntled of his followers. The answer was more plunder, and so he planned his first maritime raid using the naval power he had been building since the mid-AD 420s in Spain. Gaiseric's first target was Sicily in AD 438. The raid proved a great success and was the first of many piratical Vandal maritime adventures across the western Mediterranean. However, it wasn't long before the promise of Roman booty began to wear thin with those still looking for better land.

In the Vandal court things came to a head a year later when the king accepted the inevitable and decided to break his treaty of Rome. He then launched a lightning heavy cavalry strike into Africa Proconsularis, and by

19 October AD 439 had captured Carthage. This was an incredible feat, as MacDowall details (2016, 89):

> The ease with which he did this is astonishing. Hippo Regis had held out for fourteen months in AD 430/ 31, and after defeating Boniface and Aspar the Vandals were never able to breach Carthage's walls. In both cases, however, the Romans had good troops within the walls and were fully expecting an attack. Perhaps they had been lulled into complacency after the treaty, but even if the bulk of Boniface and Aspar's troops had been withdrawn... it is inconceivable that the Romans would have left Carthage without an adequate garrison.

Notably, the city was captured without a fight in what seems to have been a brilliantly planned surprise attack. Indeed, many inhabitants were attending the races in the hippodrome at the time. They had no idea they were under attack until the Vandals were within the city walls. Soon the Catholic clergy were fleeing Africa Proconsularis for Italy, together with any others who could afford the passage, especially the regional nobility. This left Gaiseric the unlikely master of the entirety of Roman North Africa, with Byzacena and Tripolitania soon joining Africa Proconsularis as Vandal acquisitions. His next move was the true statement of a conqueror: he moved his court to Carthage. There he now styled himself *Rex Wandalorum et Alanorum* (King of the Vandals and Alans). This sent shock waves through the Roman world, with some writers comparing events to Brennus' sack of Rome in 387 BC. For a time, many leading Romans refused to believe the news. Indeed, Gaiseric's kingdom was not officially recognized in the west until AD 442, and the east until AD 472 (Hornblower and Spawforth, 1996, 1581). I leave the story of the acquisitive Vandals there for now, picking up the next wave of their foreign adventures in the next and final chapter.

CHAPTER 6

Vandal Apocalypse

The North African *Regnum Vandalorum et Alanorum* (Kingdom of the Vandals and Alans) lasted 99 years, from AD 435 when Gaiseric captured Carthage to AD 534 when Gelimer surrendered to Belisarius. Until the Byzantine reconquest, it proved one of the more successful post-Roman Germanic kingdoms in the west. Here, I first set out key aspects of Gaiseric's great achievement, detailing his new kingdom's economy, cultural life, and religion. In the case of the former two, I show how, for much of the time, post-Roman North Africa thrived under the Vandals. In the case of the latter, I then detail the clash between Arianism and Catholicism, a key differentiator with the post-Roman experience in Gaul, Spain, and Italy, before outlining how an accommodation was finally reached as the kingdom neared its end. I then provide a chronological narrative outlining key events in the fractious relationship between Vandal North Africa and the Eastern and Western Roman Empires. On the one hand, this featured a series of increasingly ambitious Vandal raids across the Mediterranean, not least the infamous sack of Rome in AD 455. On the other, I cover the various botched Roman attempts to reconquer its richest former territory. I conclude with the campaign of Belisarius which finally succeeded, bringing an end to Vandal North Africa and the Hasdingi dynasty. As a final note, when reading this chapter the reader is encouraged to remember that all of our key primary sources are pro-Roman, with no Vandal voice to be heard at all. Therefore archaeology has a particularly important role to play here.

Vandal Heaven

The political history of the Kingdom of the Vandals and Alans is well known, forming a central part when narrating Justinian I's reconquest campaigns in the former Western Roman Empire. Here, through the narrative of Procopius and others, the lightning offensive of Belisarius in AD 533 is portrayed as a liberating campaign in a region in decline. However nothing could be further from the truth, as I now detail.

Economy

All key primary sources covering the Vandal conquest of North Africa, for example Victor of Vita, Possidius of Calama, and Fulgentius of Ruspe, present the event as an economic catastrophe, leading to an age of destitution and poverty. This view is not surprising, given all are pro-Roman and reflect the inherent Nicene antipathy to Arianism. Raven called their narratives '…atrocity stories spread by alarmed ecclesiasticals…' (1969, 196).

However, in terms of the regional economy, the reality was the opposite of what the primary source narrative suggests. Vandal North Africa has been the subject of much scholarly attention in recent decades, leading to a thorough reappraisal of traditional interpretations of the region in the period. In particular, Christian Courtois' 1964 *Les Vandales et L'Afrique* proved a key text which systematically countered much of the vituperative Nicene narrative. From that point onwards more open-minded historical research has become the norm, for example Averil Cameron's *The Mediterranean World in Late Antiquity* where she says (1993, 37):

> …it now seems that Vandal Africa was less isolated economically from the rest of the empire than has been traditionally supposed.

More recently, well-published archaeological research has shown that to be an understatement, providing a degree of analytical granularity previously lacking. It is now clear the Maghreb, particularly in the west, was not only extremely wealthy under the Romans, but remained so under the Vandals. In short, Gaiseric took over the entire region as a going concern, believing it easier to gather its vast wealth through taxation rather than predation. Here, I will first look at the nature of the regional economy in the 5th century AD, then the process by which the Vandals took this over, before presenting specific examples to show economic continuance both during the transition, and afterwards.

The *dioceses* of the later Roman Empire, and their constituent provinces, were finely tuned fiscal units designed to wring maximum revenue from each region. By the time the Vandals conquered North Africa that was even more the case, given the cost of fighting conflicts on multiple fronts throughout the empire.

The Diocletianic Reformation detailed in Chapter 4 provided the imperial centre with numerous means of extracting surplus wealth from a *diocese*. Given the Vandals inherited this system, I detail them in full here. They included:

- Targeting the property of the landed classes. This was always at risk of state exploitation through gains from legacies, disposals, land rentals, and sales, all of which gave the state an opportunity for additional taxation, or in extreme circumstances physical seizure.
- Gathering revenue direct from land controlled by the state itself. At its most extreme this was in the form of imperial estates owned by the emperor, which could either be industrial or agricultural in nature. The former included most of the larger *metalla* extractive industries, for example quarrying and mining. Meanwhile, the latter were a particular feature of Roman North Africa which featured more agricultural land under imperial control than any other region of the empire (see below).
- Exploiting the wider population through regular taxation, tribute demands, liturgies, labour requirements, military recruitment, and slavery.
- With regard to rural populations, the use of exploitative tools such as rents, dues, price fixing, requisitioning, and once again tax.
- Profit derived from the existence of harbours, markets, and trade, again through taxation and also surcharges. Also included here are customs charges at the borders of the empire, either from within-to-without, or between *diocese* and provinces.
- The system of military supply through *fabricae* (state-run manufactories).

A key theme running through all of the above was taxation. In particular, two direct taxes were levied. These were the *tributum soli* (based on land) and the *tributum capitis* (based on capitation). Such *tributa* (direct taxes) were ultimately paid to the *vicarius* of the *diocese*, with Mattingly saying tax-farmers (working under state-contracts), imperial fiscal officials, and local authorities often acted as middlemen to ensure the smooth running of the system, even in the later empire (2006, 496). Meanwhile, *vectigalia* (indirect taxes) (for example harbour dues) were collected by contractors called *publicani*. While such methods of taxation were the rule, there was also regional and inter-*diocene* variation across the geography of the empire, with individuals and communities often seeking exceptions in some shape or form.

However, the most ergonomic way revenue could flow from a *diocese* into the emperor's *fiscus* (treasury) was through his imperial estates. These were the personally owned landed property of the emperor. They came into imperial possession in a variety of ways. Mattingly (2006, 455) says that imperially owned land was often the result of confiscation at the point of conquest from regional elites, or land formerly owned by Roman nobles confiscated after failed usurpation attempts. Others could be the result of an inheritance, with the deceased seeking to gain imperial favour in some way. In her excellent study of agricultural imperial estates in Roman North Africa, Crawford gives a good example based on contemporary written records (1976, 36). This is Hadrian's sister-in-law, Matilda, bequeathing extensive agricultural estates around Setif to the imperial household.

Having established how the Roman state extracted wealth from a *diocese*, I now look at how the Vandals turned this system to their own benefit in North Africa. There is no doubt the initial phases of Vandal conquest led to enormous economic dislocation, especially in the coastal region of the western Maghreb. However, this was no different to any conquest campaign in the classical and late antique world, including those of the Romans. Gaiseric's masterstroke was managing the ambitions of his avaricious followers while transitioning to a civil regime where he took over the running of the region. Crucially I believe he planned for this given, no matter why he travelled to North Africa, he predetermined he would stay there with his people. To reiterate, he was offering them peace and stability in land they owned. As Raven said, 'The Vandals did not come to North Africa to destroy, but to settle' (1969, 196).

As we have seen, there were two key phases of Vandal conquest in North Africa. First, the initial dash along the Mediterranean coast and capture of Annaba, with the later peace of AD 435 securing significant land which Gaiseric could redistribute to his elites. Second, the rapid fall of Carthage in AD 439 after which he seized the entire *diocese*. The initial transition from Roman to Vandal control began as the first phase came to a close, and was completed after the second.

For context, in his analysis of the wider post-Roman transition of power to Germanic successor kingdoms, Wickham shows how closely the Vandal experience in North Africa paralleled that of the Franks in Gaul, Visigoths in Spain, and Ostrogoths in Italy (2010, 48). He shows how, rather than unpicking the finely tuned Roman administrative system, the Vandals simply adopted it once their elites had replaced those of the Romans. In many places this was an easy process given the number of huge imperial estates in the region, and the fact that much of the remaining land was owned by absentee landlords. Legal documents of the time show how local North Africans continued to manage the local currency and taxation system after the change of leadership, though with the surplus wealth now flowing into Gaiseric's coffers, rather than the emperor's. In his analysis of religious friction in the region post the Vandal conquest (which I consider later) Brown asserts there was a harder edge to the transfer of power in North Africa then elsewhere in post-Roman Europe (2012, 400). I have found no evidence of this in my research. However, he has rightly identified that after his victory in AD 439 Gaiseric settled many of his leading followers around Carthage, with Brown calling it a militarised glacis. This is not surprising given the martial nature of Vandal society, with MacDowall saying it made sense for Gaiseric to settle his better warriors around Carthage, the '…jewel in his crown…' (2016, 97).

Mattingly highlights here that the transfer of power worked on two levels, with some direct and some indirect. He says (1995, 215):

> For much of Roman Africa the Vandal conquest did not result in cataclysmic change. The conquerors seized some of the best land for themselves without displacing the dependent peasantry. Elsewhere, the Romano-Africans continued to farm the land as before, as is clear from the Albertini Tablets, a cache of late 5th century AD documents from a pre-desert estate on the Algerian/Tunisian border. The cultivation of this estate was carried out by many tenant farmers working small plots of land in the wadi beds.

What happened to the Roman elites in North Africa once the Vandals took over? First, as noted, Roman North Africa featured a large number of imperial estates, and also absentee landlords. The transfer of ownership here was relatively easy, with no elites in situ to replace. Second, many at the top end of Roman society fled either after the peace settlement in AD 435, or later after Gaiseric's capture of Carthage in AD 439. Indeed, contemporary writers detail that Rome was flooded with wealthy refugees from North Africa. Most expected to be away from their North African property for only a short time, but soon it became clear there would be no easy Roman reconquest. They were then forced to make longer-term arrangements in Italy and elsewhere, hoping one day to return home. Thus the transfer of their land to its new Vandals owners was also relatively straightforward.

For those Romans who remained in North Africa, the experience was similar to those living through the same transition of power in post-Roman Gaul, Spain, or Italy. Most survived the process well, striving for new ways to preserve their political, economic, and social status in the newly emerging post-Roman world. In many cases this meant working alongside their new masters, with many going 'native' within the new Vandal regime to maintain their societal standing. In fact everywhere in the post-Roman West, where the incoming elites kept the old Roman system of taxation and provincial governance in place, opportunity remained for the natives to continue as before. As Dodds details (2016, 3):

> An educated Roman might have found employment in barbarian service carrying out tasks which were indistinguishable from those he would have performed for a Roman emperor.

In a Vandal context, here one can see Gaiseric's true genius, as he realised it would be impossible to rule his new kingdom at the point of a sword only. MacDowall uses an excellent modern analogy to contextualise the Vandal king's strategy, saying (2016, 95):

> Unlike the American-led coalition in Iraq in 2003, Gaiseric did not dismantle the Roman apparatus of government. Roman officials continued to administer the bureaucracy and without their help he could not possibly have managed his far-flung domains, gather taxes and keep things running in a profitable manner. Many Romans held key positions in his government, the main requirement being loyalty to their new masters.

Thus Latin remained the official language of Vandal North Africa, while post-Roman officials retained Roman titles, for example *proconsul* for key positions in Gaiseric's court. However, in his analysis of North African literature under the Vandals, George argues it is important to consider one key fact in particular (2016, 95). This is the ratio of North Africans to Vandals in Gaiseric's new kingdom, which he estimates at 40:1. This explains why, at least at first, the Vandals kept their own legal system separate. Further, local North Africans were not allowed to serve in Vandal field armies. Both moves show Gaiseric realised the need to remind locals on a regular basis that he was their new master, not Ravenna or Constantinople.

Gaiseric also went to great lengths to develop strong links with the native Berber population of the Maghreb, concluding his own treaties of mutual support with many of the Berber kingdoms south of the southern *limes* he inherited, particularly in Mauretania (Mattingly, 1995, 215). Interestingly, along the Saharan frontier it seems he also kept in place many of the units of native *limitanei* the Romans had based there to help maintain the integrity of his kingdom. This is not surprising given most were Berbers, serving in areas where they either originated or had made their home. This process is visible in the ongoing use of frontier fortifications well after the Vandal conquest, although there is no evidence such *limitanei* served in Vandal field armies.

Specific examples show us how normal daily life continued unabated for most in Roman North Africa after the Vandal conquest. The built environment is a case in point. For example, in Carthage von Rummel highlights that although there is destruction evident from the time of the Vandal capture of the city (and also earlier, dating to Boniface's conflict with Sigisvultus), it was quickly repaired, excepting perhaps some of the outer suburbs (2016, 114). There could be found many of the Nicene ecumenical estates now deemed surplus to requirements given the Vandal adherence to Arianism, and the fact many Catholic clergy had already fled (MacDowall, 2016, 96). Von Rummel also highlights the fact that many of the properties in the wealthiest quarter of Carthage went undamaged by Gaiseric's rapid capture of the city, perhaps reflecting their early identification as prized possessions for the Vandal elites taking over. Many of these structures then underwent '…sumptuous reconstructions…' in the later 5th century AD, showing the new Vandal ruling class utilising their new-found affluence with overt displays of wealth (von Rummel, 2016, 114). This included grand domestic mosaics built in the same style as those of the previous Roman owners. In these fine town houses the newly ruling Vandal aristocracy entertained in *triclinia* just as their Roman predecessors had, resplendent in the latest Roman fashions. Indeed, Victor of Vita says the only aspect of their appearance which remained Germanic was how they wore their hair, long rather than short like the Romans (*History of the Vandal Persecution*, 1.3). Even Procopius, always keen to denigrate the Vandals, reports they enthusiastically took to traditional Roman ways of life, particularly games in the arena and hunting (*The Vandalic Wars*, 6.6).

Elsewhere in Carthage much also remained the same, the only grand public building notably destroyed being the Odeon, though others were clearly damaged by Gaiseric's lightning strike in AD 439. However, most were soon repaired, with poets in Vandal North Africa referencing amphitheatres, theatres, and public libraries in normal, regular use (George, 2004, 134). Recent archaeological investigation has also shown the Roman pre-planned street grid remained the same throughout the Vandal period. Interestingly, Procopius also says Gaiseric kept the late Roman walls of Carthage intact, though elsewhere in his new kingdom he says the king dismantled them (*The Vandalic Wars*, 3.5.21). This seems an odd thing to do given the certainty that the Romans would attempt to reconquer their lost lands in the Maghreb, with archaeological evidence showing that in many places Procopius' assertion simply wasn't true.

Evidence for continuity in the use of the built environment can also be found in many other places in Vandal North Africa. For example in Annaba in Numidia Cirtensis tombs within the largest basilica in the Christian quarter include those specifically Vandal. A fine example is that of Ermengon, Suebian wife of the Vandal Ingomar. Meanwhile, at Cherchell in Mauretania

Caesariensis excavations in the 1970s and 1980s identified new grand public structures being erected under Vandal rule, and also the continuance of the normal Mediterranean economy there given the huge numbers of eastern Mediterranean *amphorae* found in excavations in the *forum*. Similarly large amounts of African Red Slip ware, exported west along the coast from Africa Proconsularis, were also found. Recording the excavations, Benseddik and Potter say (1993, 379):

> ...it would be fair to say Caesaria continued to play a considerable role in overseas trade, demonstrating that life in the territorium was maintained with some vigour into late antiquity.

Meanwhile Merrills has challenged those arguing the Maghreb suffered economic instability in the wake of Gaiseric's conquest, using the African Red Slip ware industry as his key evidence (2004, 11). Brown goes further, suggesting the export of goods from Vandal North Africa thrived given the removal of the export levies earlier imposed by the Romans (2012, 401). He says African ceramics and wines flooded into markets throughout the Mediterranean.

In terms of agriculture, this also clearly thrived. Merrills cites examples of olive farming in the Kasserine Valley in Byzacena in modern Tunisia to show intensive agricultural activity there continued throughout the Vandal period (2004, 13). Raven also highlighted the continuance of unabated intensive agriculture in North Africa under the Vandals, saying (1969, 196):

> In fact, vineyards and olive groves survived to amaze the army of Belisarius a hundred years later just as, a millennium before, other crops and orchards had amazed the army of Agathocles of Syracuse.

Literature

North Africa was renowned as a powerhouse of literature throughout the Roman world. The traditional view is that, although this did continue under the Vandals, it was as a cultural refuge for literate Romans keen to maintain any links possible to a lost past. Under this school of thought, even the most positive commentary on literature in the Kingdom of the Vandals and Alans is begrudging. For example, when writing about the Carthaginian Latin poet Luxorius (who wrote in the AD 520s), Rosenblum said (1961, 25):

> Even under the Vandals, whom they looked down upon as barbarians, a group of poets wrote for readers and listeners who loved poetry, whether or not their ears were attuned to the nuances of Latin pronunciation. These poets looked to the past for their models and wrote in the tradition of their predecessors; perhaps this was their fixed point in a changing world, as all was tottering and crumbling about them.

However this is misdirection. In fact literature flourished under the Vandals in North Africa, supported by political and cultural patronage. A detailed study of poetry there in the Vandal period reveals a cultured and literary world which celebrated art and society in ways both recognisably classical but also markedly different in tone, fusing literary *Romanitas* with the new reality of Vandal rule. Thus, just as with the built environment and fashion, here the Vandals were keen to promote themselves as the cultural equals of their new subjects, and to overtly show it. Again, this is a pattern seen across the Germanic kingdoms of the post-Roman world. For example, as George says (2006, 133):

> These North African poems are representative of the same evolutionary phase as Latin poetry in other parts of the [post-] Roman world, as Germanic and Romano-African cultures intermingled and the Latin literary tradition found new life and changed modes of expression.

Of note, while the literature of Vandal North Africa naturally reflected the rebalancing of power there, it was still recognisably Roman. Specifically, it reimagined the North African experience of the individual and state relative to the new centres of power.

Most key poets writing in Vandal North Africa are usefully detailed in a 19th-century anthology called the *Anthologica Latina* which has been much revised since. Though its provenance is much debated, I list them here for completeness. These are Avitus, Bonosus, Calbulus, Cato, Coronatus, Felix, Florentinus, Lindinus, Luxorius, Modestinus, Octavianus, Ponnanus, Regianus, Tuccianus, and Vincentinus. Of these, Luxorius is the only one for whom we have much detail. Of the rest, we are lacking even the dates they were writing.

To these we can add one other poet who for some reason was not included in the anthology, namely Blossius Aemilius Dracontius who wrote in the AD 480s. This is unusual given more of his work has survived through to our day than any of the others, perhaps reflecting provenance issues at the time the 19th-century list was compiled. Interestingly, Dracontius spent much of his life under Vandal rule in prison for writing a poem praising a Roman emperor (Raven, 1969, 197).

Two key themes are evident in surviving literature from Vandal North Africa. First, celebrating key aspects of *Romanitas* under Vandal rule, for example hunting. Second, *epithalamia* (poems written to celebrate a marriage) which have been written for Vandal patrons. Here we have surviving works from Luxorius and Darcontius. The former wrote one for a leading Vandal noble called Fridus, who he styles a *vir clarissumus et spectabilis* (literally, a very famous man). Meanwhile, the latter wrote two which survive, one for the double wedding of two unnamed Vandal brothers and their wives, and the second for a Vandal noble called Johannes and his unnamed bride.

What is evident through the whole body of literature dating to the period of Vandal control in North Africa is the continuance of a cultural way of life similar, for the most part, to that under the Romans. Therefore, far from being a barren literary wasteland as contemporary ecclesiastical historians would have us believe, North Africa under the Vandals provided a rich cultural setting for poets and their poetry.

Religion

As earlier detailed, the Arian Gaiseric targeted the Nicene Church in North Africa from the moment he arrived. Here I set out a brief narrative of this well-known persecution, before providing context to show a broader picture.

Vandal harrying of the Catholic Church was violent from the very beginning. Victor of Vita details their '...wicked ferocity...' (History of the Vandal Persecution, 1.3), while Honoratus Antoninus, Bishop of Constantine, says that '...before our eyes men are murdered, women raped and we ourselves collapse under torture' (Merrills and Miles, 2010, 181). St Augustine wrote similarly, his distressed anxiety detailed in Chapter 5. Things got worse once Gaiseric secured his first peace deal with the Romans in AD 435, as Merrills and Miles detail (2010, 180):

> He worked to destroy the power of the Nicene Church in his new territories by seizing the basilicas of three of the most intransigent bishops and expelling them from their cities.

Gaiseric continued this policy after the capture of Carthage in AD 439, where as earlier detailed ecumenical properties in the suburbs had been abandoned. He now closed all Nicene places of worship in the city centre, including the cathedral (notably not installing his own Arian bishop) and three largest churches. The king then banned all forms of Nicene worship and exiled all Catholic bishops as heretics using anti-Donatist legislation dating to the AD 410s (Brown, 2012, 400). Further, unlike secular officials across North Africa who were encouraged to continue their service with the state, Catholic laymen were first excluded from church office, and later state office. Many also suffered confiscation of their property.

However, matters soon improved for the Catholic Church in North Africa when diplomatic considerations took precedence. In AD 454 Valentinian III requested Gaiseric install Deogratias as the new Catholic bishop of Carthage, the first there for 14 years. Deogratias proved particularly pious, selling off any gold, silver, and works of art still owned by the church to buy back locals enslaved by the Vandals. He then opened the Basilica Fausti and the Basilica Novarum, two of the city's churches, and filled them with bedding to provide accommodation for the homeless, opening a canteen to provide daily food. Heather says his appointment was a deliberate move by Gaiseric to help improve Vandal relations with the Romans while the king negotiated the marriage of his son, Huneric, to Eudocia, daughter of Valentinian III (2010, 141). It is also clear that, by this time, Gaiseric had changed course somewhat and was allowing other Catholic bishops to lead worship in North Africa. However, after Valentinian was assassinated in March AD 455 relations between the Vandals and Romans deteriorated again, with Gaiseric once more renewing his repression of Catholicism. He then left the bishopric in Carthage empty again when Deogratius died in AD 457.

When Huneric succeeded his father in AD 477 he intensified repression of the Nicene Church, with much of Victor of Vita's scathing narrative directed at this period of Vandal rule. Here the new king focused his attention on the lower levels of Nicene worship, banning priests from practicing the liturgy, destroying Catholic texts, and banishing 5,000 clergy to the desert interior of Tripolitania. Then in AD 483 Huneric issued a royal edict ordering all the Nicene bishops in North Africa to attend a debate with their Arian counterparts. After the one-sided event he forbade Nicene clergy from carrying out baptisms and ordinations, and ordered all remaining Nicene churches to close, with their property confiscated.

Huneric's successor, Gunthamund, was far more tolerant of Nicene worship than his uncle. By way of example, he ended the desert exile of Eugenius who had been elected in AD 480 to become the first bishop of Carthage after the death of Deogratius. Gunthamund also restored the shrine of Saint Agileus in Carthage, famously championed by St Augustine before his death. Things again took a turn for the worse under his successor, Thrasamund, who became king in AD 496, though here he specifically targeted the Nicene clergy, not the regional lay elite.

Then, when Hilderic became king in AD 523, relations between the Vandals and Catholic Church improved dramatically, this in the context of greatly improved relations with the Byzantine Empire under Justin I and Justinian I. Hilderic allowed a new Catholic bishop to take office again in Carthage, and notably some Vandals converted to Catholicism. This proved the highpoint of the relations between the Vandals and Nicene Church in North Africa, though it alarmed many Vandal nobles, providing the backdrop to the revolt against Hilderic by his cousin, Gelimer.

The narrative set out above is clear at first glance. The Vandals brutally targeted the Nicene Church as soon as they arrived in North Africa. They then continued to do so (to a greater or lesser extent) until the accession of Hilderic, an earlier high point in relations being the reign of Gunthamund. However, I believe there is more to this than meets the eye. I now consider three contextual themes.

First, was political coercion the real objective, certainly for Gaiseric, who was the longest serving king in Vandal North Africa? This would have worked for him in two ways. In the first instance, the Nicene Church was deeply embedded in all levels of Romano-African society. Targeting it directly, and then keeping the church under pressure over decades, was the easiest way to manipulate the social order there, especially at the top. This clearly worked, given Brown's observation that the failure of non-ecclesiastical elites there to stand up for the Catholic Church is noteworthy (2012, 401). As he says, those at the top of Roman society in North Africa '...settled down to thrive [under the Vandals] with indecent vigour...' Additionally, Heather suggests Gaiseric's promotion of Arianism was specifically aimed at his own Vandal followers as a means of internal coercion (2007, 139). He highlights key differentiators when comparing Gaiseric's extreme anti-Nicene actions in Africa Proconsularis, and elsewhere in the Maghreb. In the former region, where his leading followers were based, the persecution was at its most intense. Heather adds this was particularly important given the king deliberately chose to suppress the tribal organisation of his nobles there in favour of the Roman autocratic model he adopted to ensure the smooth running of his new kingdom.

Next, there were clear financial gains to be made for the Vandals by targeting the wealthy Nicene Church in the region. As Raven explained (1969, 169):

> Like all conquerors the Vandals were greedy for loot. The [Nicene] Church was rich: like the secular landlords, it was dispossessed of its finest estates, and had to give up its plate, its gold and its treasures of all kinds. But the Vandals had had no wish to cut down the olive trees or burn down the vines that were the basis of the prosperity they had every intention of enjoying themselves.

Thus the aggression against the church here was specifically targeted, and not part of a widespread policy of region-wide destruction. In short, for the Vandals, the wealth of the church was easy pickings.

The final contextual issue here is Donatism and its relationship with the Nicene Church, which remained highly confrontational. As O'Donnell explains (2009, 91):

> Many African Christians were still resentful of the forced unification of the churches when the [Nicene] Caecilianist faction won the support of the emperor against the Donatist faction.

This created an opportunity for the Vandals when they arrived in North Africa in AD 429, as they viewed the Donatists as another means of checking the power of the Catholic Church. In that regard, Raven suggests that some of the worst excesses of the Vandal conquest were actually private acts of revenge by Donatists on Catholics '...under the cover of invasion...' (1969, 196).

Reconquest

The peace agreement reached between the Vandals and the Western Empire in AD 442 proved ephemeral at best. Gaiseric, no matter how much he encouraged his nobles to embrace *Romanitas*, still ruled a Germanic military elite who were used to conquest and victory. To stay on the throne, he needed to keep them happy with the prospect of more plunder. Meanwhile, from a Roman perspective, recovering North Africa from the Vandals remained unfinished business. This economic jewel of their empire had been ripped from them, and any emperor who reclaimed it would match the achievements of any of his greatest forebears. This led to a number of failed attempts at reconquest, some huge in scale, before Justinian I finally succeeded through his general, Belisarius, shattering the Vandal kingdom in the process. Here I narrate the fractious relationship between the Vandals and Romans from AD 442 through to the end of Vandal Africa.

Pirates in the Mediterranean

Gaiseric's ability to project sea power had been steadily growing from the point he crossed to North Africa in AD 429. However, with his capture of Carthage a decade later, the Vandals became a first-rate sea power, able to match the Romans anywhere in the Mediterranean. As MacDowall details (2016, 90):

> With the great port...along with some of the best shipbuilders and sailors in the world now in their hands, the Vandals had all the capability they needed.

For the Romans, with their military raised on tales of famous victories at sea in the Punic Wars, it must have seemed as if the Carthaginians had risen from the dead, bent on revenge. An attempt by Theodosius II, perhaps with aid from Valentinian III, to recapture North Africa had already failed in AD 440 when the Roman fleet was recalled before reaching Sicily to deal with threats elsewhere in the empire. Then, after the AD 442 settlement, Vandal maritime predation became the norm for the next 37 years, as Procopius details (*The Vandalic Wars*, 3.5.21):

> Every year, at the beginning of Spring Gaiseric made invasions into Sicily and Italy, enslaving some of the cities, razing others to the ground, and plundering everything. When the land had become destitute of men and of money, he invaded the domain of the emperor of the east. And so he plundered Illyricum, most of the Peloponnese and the rest of Greece, and all the islands which lie near it. And then he went off again to Sicily and Italy and kept plundering and pillaging all places in turn. One day when he had embarked on his ship in the harbour of Carthage, and the sails were ready to spread, the pilot asked him against what men did he go? And he replied, 'Plainly against those with whom God is angry.'

As always, here we only have pro-Roman voices, in Procopius' case adding an extra layer of justification for the later Byzantine reconquest of North Africa. However, the archaeological record does show evidence for the Vandals causing widespread havoc across the Mediterranean in these decades. For example, a fleet of burnt cargo ships found in 2001 on the seabed of the harbour at Olbia in Sardinia was most likely the victim of a Vandal raid there.

Soon the Vandals moved from piracy to settlement, annexing parts of Sardinia, Corsica, and Sicily, if only seasonally. Faced with this challenge, Valentinian raised an emergency tax to pay for new troops and ships. He then ordered his *magister utriusque militiae*, Sigisvultus (earlier seen fighting Boniface in Chapter 5), to travel the length of the Italian coast, improving coastal defences as he went and rebuilding city walls where necessary. However, at this crucial moment Sigisvultus' own superior, the *magister militum* Aetius, departed for Gaul to campaign against raiding Visigoths and Burgundians with an army of Hunnic *foederates*. Valentinian now adopted a defensive footing in Italy, an uneasy stand-off following, with the Vandals continuing their raiding though on a lesser scale, and the Romans unable to stop them.

However, with Attila the Hun's death in AD 453, Valentinian decided a period of consolidation was needed in the west. In that context he determined the best way to deal with Gaiseric was through diplomacy, not military action. To settle matters he offered the hand of his daughter, Eudocia, to Gaiseric's eldest son, Huneric, at the same time asking the Vandal king to make Deogratias the new Catholic bishop in Carthage. Sadly for all, though, a new figure now emerged who set back relations between the Vandals and

Romans for decades, this being Petronius Maximus, soon-to-be emperor for a brief 12 weeks.

Maximus was born in AD 397 to a well-connected Senatorial family, enjoying a remarkable early career which included holding key posts in the *schola notariorum* (internal secret service) while still teenager. He then used his connections there to accrue a series of other key postings in the imperial administration, for example serving as the *comes sacrarum largitionum* between AD 416 and AD 419. This was a very powerful position indeed, giving him control of key sectors of the Roman economy, including the emperor's imperial estates, taxing Senators, raising custom duties, managing large scale *metalla* industries, running mills and textile factories, and controlling the imperial mints in the west (Scarre, 1995b, 231).

In AD 430 Maximus was then promoted to become the *praefectus urbi* (urban prefect) in Rome, giving him control of the municipal administration of the city. He later became the *praetorian prefect* at court, before returning as *praefectus urbi* again in AD 439. During this period he was also appointed *consul*. In the AD 440s he was then placed in charge of the entire *praetorian prefecture* of Italy.

Maximus was awarded a second consulship in AD 443, and then granted the official title *patrician*. This set him on a collision course with Aetius. To show his largesse and get one over on his rival for imperial attention, he then built his own *forum* in Rome in AD 445 on the Caelian Hill which he called the *Forum Petronii Maximi*. However, after Aetius' defeat of the Huns in AD 451 at the battle of the Catalaunian Plains, he found himself increasingly side-lined, and decided to act. Always at the heart of government, he persuaded the eunuch Heraclius, the emperor's *primicerius sacri cubicili* in charge of the imperial household, to become a fellow conspirator. Together they then convinced Valentinian that Aetius was planning a coup. Even Maximus was surprised at his own success when, without warning, the emperor himself stabbed Aetius to death in a fit of rage on 21 September AD 454, with Heraclius joining in (Goldsworthy, 2009, 333).

Sadly for Maximus there was no immediate reward for him. Valentinian had spent much of his reign under the control of others. First, his mother Gallia Placidia had long been his regent. Later, Aetius' enormous success as a military leader had overshadowed anything the emperor could achieve. Now free of his dominating *magister militum*, Valentinian was free to rule as he wished. Far from being the new power behind the throne, Maximus now found himself just another advisor. This did nothing to diminish his ambition, and soon the emperor himself became the new target for the ever scheming courtier.

Maximus convinced two palace guards called Optila and Thraus-tila, both Huns and former Aetian loyalists, to kill Valentinian. This they did on 16 March AD 455, also killing Heraclius in the process. The assassins then duly took the imperial diadem to Maximus, who the day after became emperor (Heather, 2005, 374). The former spymaster had now risen to the very top of the imperial tree, though it wasn't to last, with his fall dramatic and fatal.

In the first instance, Maximus quickly married Valentinian's widow, Licinia Eudoxia. However, he then made a huge mistake, cancelling the marriage of Eudocia to Huneric. Gaiseric, still a proud Germanic king despite adopting the trappings of *Romanitas*, took great offence at what seemed an arbitrary decision. Soon word reached Italy that Gaiseric was sailing with a vast fleet, his target: Rome. This caused panic there, with many inhabitants fleeing. At this point Maximus had a disastrous crisis of confidence. He chose to flee himself, hoping to reach Ravenna where he'd be secure behind its extensive marshes and wetlands. However, on 31 May, when he'd barely left Rome, his bodyguard abandoned him. Shortly after he was found by an angry mob, quickly set upon, and stoned to death. His body was then mutilated, and in a final humiliation his corpse was thrown in the Tiber.

By that point the Vandals had landed on the coast near Rome, and at the beginning of June they approached the city, destroying its key aqueducts on the way. On arrival Gaiseric learned of Maximus' death, and then received an envoy from Pope Leo I who begged the Vandal king not to destroy the ancient city. Gaiseric agreed, and the gates were thrown open to allow the Vandals in. However, while he kept his promise not to burn the city and slaughter its inhabitants, he couldn't prevent his followers from looting on a scale far greater than the Visigoth sack of Rome in AD 410 (Kneale, 2017, 90). They left two weeks later, with booty including the fine roof from the vast temple of Jupiter on the Capitoline Hill, hundreds of high quality marble statues, and tens of thousands of slaves. Also captured were Licinia Eudoxia and her daughters, Eudocia and Placidia, the last survivors of the Theodosian dynasty. They were taken to Carthage, with Eudocia finally marrying Huneric in AD 460, and Licinia Eudoxia and Placidia allowed to go to Constantinople two years later. Pohl emphasises the importance of this royal marriage to the Vandals, saying Eudocia '…conferred the prestige of the now ousted Theodosian dynasty on Gaiseric's family' (2004, 40).

Next came two serious, though ultimately doomed, attempts by the Romans to reconquer North Africa. First, in early AD 460 the Western emperor, Majorian, planned an assault using 300 ships staging through Cartagena in Spain, his aim to cross to Mauretania Tingitana and then target Carthage.

Simultaneously, another fleet under a general called Marcellinus would target Sicily, at that point under Vandal control. However, Gaiseric reacted with typical vigour, setting off with his own fleet and initiating a scorched-earth policy in each of his Mauritanian provinces as he progressed. He then led his ships against the Roman fleet at harbour in Cartagena. Here we have no real detail except the result, total victory for the Vandals, with Hydatius referencing treachery as a possible reason behind the Roman defeat (*Chronicle*, 80.2). Majorian was dead within a year.

Gaiseric's victory at Cartagena reset the power politics of the Roman Mediterranean. It was now clear the Western Empire was a spent force and unable to retake the North Africa. Indeed, with Huneric marrying Eudocia the same year, the Vandal king could even claim Theodosian legitimacy in the Roman West. However, Gaiseric now overplayed his hand and began to meddle in succession politics in Ravenna. In AD 465, after the death of the Western emperor Severus III, the Eastern emperor Leo I and the Western *magister militum* Ricimer cast around for a successor. Here Gaiseric thought he had a crucial advantage given Eudocia's sister, Placidia, was by this time married to a wealthy Senator called Ancius Olybrius. Kean and Frey say Gaiseric viewed Olybrius as '…a vassal kinsman to the Vandal king…' (2005, 257). However, the last thing Leo and Ricimer wanted was to hand more power to Gaiseric. In particular, Ricimer had form with the Vandals. The grandson of the Visigothic King Wallia who had almost wiped out the Silingi Vandals and the Alans in Spain, his mother was also Suebian. Further, in the aftermath of the sack of Rome he'd defeated a fleet of 60 Vandal ships off Corsica in AD 456. Both Leo and Ricimer now promoted another wealthy senator (this time from the east) called Procopius Anthemius to take the Western throne. This he did, arriving in Rome in the early spring of AD 467 with new troops under the command of Marcellinus, commander of the Illyrian field army, to bolster the armies in the west. He was then crowned in Ravenna on 12 April. Gaiseric reacted predictably, with a new wave of predation across the Mediterranean, particularly in the East. This prompted the final major attempt to retake North Africa in AD 468, which Kean and Frey say was Leo and Ricimer's plan anyway when installing Anthemius (2005, 256). Procopius is our best source here, saying (*The Vandalic Wars*, 6.4.1):

> The emperor Leo, wishing to punish the Vandals because of these things, was gathering an army against them; and they say that this army numbered 100,000 men. And he collected a fleet from the whole of the Mediterranean showing great generosity to both soldiers and sailors, for he feared lest from a parsimonious policy some obstacle might arise to hinder him in his desire to carry out his punishment of the barbarians.

This is an extraordinary number of men and clearly inaccurate, with Heather suggesting the Roman army was nearer 30,000, with an additional 20,000 sailors and marines manning over 1,000 ships (2005, 268). One figure isn't disputed though, the staggering cost of the expedition, which the primary sources suggest was around 60,000kg in gold.

At first the campaign went well for the Romans, with Marcellinus leading an assault on Sardinia where he drove out a Vandal army using it as a base to raid Italy. Another Roman army then landed in Tripolitania under the General Heracleius and defeated a small Vandal force there deployed on the border with Cyrenaica. However, Gaiseric was now forewarned and planned accordingly, gathering his own fleet and his best troops in Carthage, and positioning a chain across the harbour to prevent its use by the Romans.

The main Roman fleet, under the command of another general called Basiliscus, then sailed for Sicily where it reprovisioned, before heading south to North Africa. On arrival just off Carthage the Romans found the harbour entrance blocked by the chain and so headed to the nearest natural harbour able to accommodate the huge fleet. This was Cap Bon in modern Tunisia. The Romans now planned to unload their huge army as quickly as possible, and then strike overland at Carthage. However, they never got the chance, with Gaiseric making use of a favourable change of wind from the west to strike them at anchor with his secret weapon, fire ships. Procopius again takes up the story, which I recount in full. He says (*The Vandalic Wars*, 6.4.5):

> The Vandals, as soon as the wind had arisen for them which they had been expecting during the time they lay at rest, raised their sails and, taking in tow boats which they had made ready with no men in them, sailed against the enemy. And when they came near and their sails were bellied by the wind, they set fire to the boast which they were towing and let them go against the Roman fleet. And since there were a number of ships there, these boats easily spread fire wherever they struck, and were themselves readily destroyed together with those with which they came into contact. And as the fire advanced in this way the Roman fleet was filled with tumult, as was natural. With a great din that rivalled the noise caused by the wind and the roaring of the flames, the soldiers and sailors shouted orders to one another and pushed the fire-ships off with poles. They did the same with their own ships which were being destroyed by one and other in complete disorder. Already the Vandals too were at hand ramming and sinking the ships and capturing those soldiers, together with their arms, who tried to escape. There were also some attempts to fight by Romans who proved themselves brave men in the struggle. Best of all was Johannes, who was one of Basiliscus' generals. For a great throng having surrounded his ship, he stood on deck, and turning from side to side kept killing very great numbers of the enemy. When he saw his ship was being captured he then leapt into the sea in his full armour. And though Genzon, son of Gaiseric, pleaded with him not to do this, he did so anyway, saying he would never come under the hands of the dogs.

Despite such bravado, the result of this crucial naval battle was never in doubt, with the Romans suffering another shattering defeat. Four years later Anthemius was dead at the hand of Ricimer after a short but brutal civil war. The *magister militum* then put Olybrius on the Western throne, no doubt to the delight of Gaiseric, though he too was dead within a year, as was Ricimer.

As the AD 470s progressed the Romans again abandoned their policy of conflict with the Vandals, and by AD 476 Gaiseric had concluded a 'perpetual peace' deal with Constantinople. However, he then died on 25 January AD 477, aged 88. This giant of a late antique ruler was succeeded by Huneric, his eldest son. Sadly his rule was marked by unrest in the Maghreb interior, where our primary sources say the Berbers began a series of revolts which led to large areas of the Aures Mountains breaking away from Vandal control. Archaeological evidence backs this up, though perhaps not on the scale our pro-Roman authors suggest. Huneric then died in AD 484 of 'putrification', as Victor of Vita delights in telling us (*History of the Vandal Persecution*, 1.4). He was replaced by his cousin, Gunthamund, who ruled for 12 years. In that time the Vandals lost their last remaining territory in Sicily to Theodoric's Ostrogoths, and perhaps more land to the Berbers in the interior, though this is unclear. Gunthamund was succeeded by his brother, Thrasamund, who tried to take back some of the inland territory earlier lost to the Berbers, but in the only set-piece battle of the campaign suffered a disastrous defeat against a chieftain called Cabaon. He was then succeeded by Hilderic in AD 523, whose policy of rapprochement with the Byzantine empire set the scene for the final fall of Vandal Africa.

Enter Belisarius

Hilderic's real issue with his nobles was his unwarlike nature when compared to his forebears. A Germanic king was meant to lead from the front, as Gaiseric had done time and again. However, when the Vandals planned to tackle the breakaway Berber kingdoms to the south again, the new king appointed his young nephew, Hoamer, to take charge. At first his campaign was successful, the Vandals defeating a Berber chieftain called Abtalas in an engagement in Byzacena and driving him back to the Aures Mountains. However, Hoamer was then ambushed returning to Carthage with great loss of life. This proved the last straw for the Vandal nobility, already disgruntled by Hilderic's pro-Roman policies. Next in line for the throne was Gelimer, son of Thrasamund's younger brother, Geilaris. Procopius is again our best source, though as always comes with a health warning given the clear pro-Justinian narrative. He says (*The Vandalic Wars*, 9.1.1):

> Gelimer was thought to be the best warrior of his time but for the rest he was a cunning fellow and base of heart and well versed in undertaking revolutionary enterprises and laying his hands on the money of others…He was no longer able to restrain his thoughts, but allying himself with all the noblest of the Vandals, he persuaded them to wrest the kingdom from Hilderic, as being an unwarlike king who had been defeated by the Moors. Thus Gelimer seized the supreme power and imprisoned Hilderic, and also Hoamer and his brother Hoageis, after Hilderic had ruled the Vandals for seven years.

This was a usurpation worthy of the Romans, with Gelimer crowned in Carthage on 15 June AD 530. However, in the Byzantine emperor Justinian I he found his nemesis. Justinian was born Petrus Sabbatius in AD 483 to a peasant family in Tauresium near modern Skopje in the Republic of North Macedonia. He owed his rise to power to his uncle, the emperor Justin I. While still a young man, Justinian was adopted by Justin, who at the time was commander of an imperial guard unit, and then taken to Constantinople. He changed his name at the same time. In the imperial capital he received an excellent education, though given he was a native Latin speaker he spoke Greek with a strong accent throughout his life. When Justin became emperor in AD 518 he was elderly and childless, and increasingly relied on his adoptive son for guidance. In AD 525 Justinian was then made *caesar*, and in April AD 527 *augustus*. When Justin died in August AD 527 Justinian then became sole emperor, ruling until his death in November AD 565.

Justinian was always obsessed with legacy. Here he was remarkably successful, his codification of Roman law still of great importance in our world today where it is known as the Code of Justinian. However, it is his attempt to renew the Western Empire that still captures the popular imagination. On coming to power, his eastern field armies were fighting the Sassanid Persian King Kavadh along the Euphrates frontier. This was the conflict where his leading general, Belisarius, first made his name. When Kavadh died in AD 531 a peace agreement was reached with the new Persian king, Khosrow I, known as the Treaty of Eternal Peace. This was highly favourable to the Byzantines and emboldened Justinian, who cast around for more foreign adventures. He alighted on Vandal North Africa, the old jewel in the Western Empire's crown.

Justinian was angered when Gelimer seized the throne, given his improved relations with Hilderic. In a furious round of diplomatic activity, he demanded Gelimer reinstall Hilderic and wait his own turn on throne through natural succession. In reply, Gelimer blinded Hoamer which immediately removed him as a rival claimant to the throne. Aghast, Justinian then demanded Gelimer send Hilderic and Hoamer to Constantinople to live in exile. In reply, the Vandal king told him to mind his own business, using language equating Gelimer's kingship to that of a Byzantine emperor. Justinian reacted predictably and declared war, saying his intention was to put Hilderic back on the throne. So began the Vandalic War.

Justinian also knew he had a specific window of opportunity. His intelligence services had informed him that Gelimer planned to send his brother, Tzazo, with a large part of the Vandal army and fleet to deal with an uprising in Sardinia led by a Gothic nobleman. Further, another Berber uprising had also broken out in Tripolitania, this in response to Hilderic's overthrow given his popularity there. The emperor seized his chance, appointing Belisarius commander of a huge invasion force which now gathered in Constantinople. Thanks to Procopius, Belisarius' secretary and legal advisor for the campaign, we have exact details of the forces he commanded. These included 500 transport ships with 30,000 sailors, 92 *dromon* (warships) with 2,000 rowers and marines, 10,000 regular infantry, 5,000 regular cavalry, 400 Herul *foederate* shock cavalry, and 60 Hunnic *foederate* light cavalry.

With much pomp and ceremony, the Roman fleet set sail from Constantinople on 21 June AD 533. It then spent five days at Heraclea Perinthus on the coast of Thrace in modern Turkey while horses for the campaign were loaded aboard, awaiting a favourable wind. It next sailed west through the northern Aegean before stopping off at Methone near modern Thessalonica to gather a final contingent of troops for the campaign. Belisarius used his time there to acquaint his various differing contingents with each other so that once in battle they would all be aware of their capabilities. The fleet then sailed to the island of Zacynthus in the Ionian Sea, from where they crossed to the eastern Italian coast before heading south for Catania on the eastern coast of Sicily. There Belisarius received intelligence reports confirming Tzazon was now in Sardinia, while Gelimer himself was away from Carthage, heading inland to a town called Hermione to deal with a dispute. Indeed, the Vandal king seemed completely unaware that a huge Roman fleet was on its way. Seeing his chance, the canny Belisarius now ordered a lightning strike on Africa Proconsularis.

Sailing via Malta, the Roman fleet reached Cape Caputvada on the eastern shore of modern Tunisia 240km south of Carthage. Belisarius then held a council of war aboard his flagship where many of his officers argued in favour of a rapid advance on Carthage by sea while Gelimer was away. However, mindful of the fate of the AD 468 expedition and wary of an encounter with the Vandal fleet, Belisarius decided to disembark his army, building a series of fortified camps in case of any Vandal surprise attack. Once all were ashore he established a column of march and the following day set off north, targeting Carthage directly. He deployed John the Armenian to lead his vanguard of

300 horses, with the Huns on his left inland flank to provide cover there, and with himself at the rear with his own *bucellari*. The rest of his army marched by division in tight formation against the coast, with his fleet covering his right flank in the littoral zone there. Soon they reached a key town on the coast called Salakta (Roman Syllectum) which was captured using a ruse, giving Belisarius a port to begin disembarking his supplies for the campaign.

By this time Gelimer had learned a huge Roman army had landed. Aware of the severe danger he now faced given Tzazon was away in Sardinia, he ordered another brother called Ammatas to gather all the Vandal warriors in the region in Carthage. He then showed an unusual lack of confidence for a Vandal king, ordering his principal secretary, Bonifatius, to load as much royal treasure as possible on a ship there and be ready to sail for Spain if the Romans were victorious. He had Hilderic murdered at the same time. The king then headed for the coast, and soon caught up with Belisarius' sprawling column. However, given so many Vandal troops were away, he chose to shadow the Romans rather than force an engagement, ordering Ammatas to block Belisarius' line of march at a place called Ad Decimum near Carthage.

On 13 September Belisarius arrived at Ad Decimum. There he found Ammatas waiting for him, barring his way. Seeing this while trailing the Roman army, Gelimer ordered Ammatas to attack the Roman vanguard while sending another 2,000 horsemen under his nephew, Gibamund, to attack the Roman left. The king then attacked from the rear. Sadly for the Vandals, Gelimer's plan required tight coordination, which was lacking on the day. Ammatus charged too early and was killed, while Gibamund's force was intercepted by the Huns and wiped out, with Gibamund also killed. Unaware of these disasters, Gelimer struck out at the Roman rear-guard and was at first successful. However, he then came across his brother's body. Distracted, he gave Belisarius time to rally his troops and counterattack. Soon the Vandals were in full flight, with the engagement a crushing Roman victory.

After the battle Gelimer headed west to Numidia, leaving Carthage unguarded for Belisarius to enter the following evening. Soon his fleet was in the harbour too. When no Vandal force appeared to challenge him he then began a programme to bolster the city's defences, while sending his general, Solomon (soon to become the region's first Byzantine governor), to Constantinople to tell Justinian the good news.

Gelimer next based himself at Bulla Regia near present day Jendouba in Tunisia. There he gathered a new army, also recalling Tzazon from Sardinia and hiring large numbers of Mauri light cavalry. As soon as Tzazon arrived Gelimer made for Carthage, knowing the longer the Romans remained the more difficult they would be to remove. Hughes says his aim was to force a decisive meeting engagement as soon as possible, and that is what he got (2009, 100). Approaching the city, the Vandals cut the main aqueducts. This forced Belisarius' hand as he knew the city lacked provisions to withstand a lengthy siege, and so in mid-December he marched out to challenge the Vandals, targeting Gelimer's fortified camp at Tricamarum 28 km south of Carthage. The ensuing battle of Tricamarum was a cavalry affair, with John the Armenian playing the key role for the Romans and Tzazon the Vandals. The former led repeated charges into the Vandal centre, where after bravely holding the line Tzazon was finally killed. A Roman advance across the battleline then broke the Vandal army, with the survivors fleeing back to their camp. Gelimer, knowing all was lost, fled the battlefield with a few close guards and headed into the Numidian interior. Hearing this the remaining Vandals abandoned their camp which was promptly sacked by the Romans.

A Roman cavalry column then set off under John the Armenian, pursuing Gelimer for five days and nights, though the Roman leader was then killed in an accident when mistaken as a Vandal by one of Belisarius' bodyguards. When the Romans halted to mourn their leader Gelimer set off again, first to Annaba, and then to the Atlas Mountain stronghold of Medeus on Mount Papua. There he was blockaded by a force of 400 Byzantine cavalry under the Herul Pharas. Belisarius then arrived in Annaba, where the remaining Vandals surrendered. He also captured the Vandal royal treasure aboard the ship where it had been loaded by Bonifatius on Gelimer's instructions, and finally sent word to any Vandal outposts across the western Mediterranean that their king had been defeated.

Meanwhile Gelimer remained blockaded by Pharas, unable to escape. As winter dragged on the Herul tried to storm the fortress but was beaten back, losing a quarter of his warriors. However, the Vandal king's position was hopeless, and he eventually surrendered in March AD 534. Thus came to an end the *Regnum Vandalorum et Alanorum* in North Africa, not with a bang but with a whimper. Gelimer was then escorted back to Carthage.

Belisarius didn't remain in Africa for long, returning to Constantinople in the summer to prove his loyalty to Justinian after a number of his own Byzantine officers sent unfounded allegations to the emperor saying he was planning to establish his own kingdom in North Africa. He was accompanied by Gelimer and large numbers of Vandals who signed on as Byzantine *foederates*, eventually becoming regular troopers in five regiments of *Vandali Iustiniani*. In Constantinople Belisarius was then given a triumph, the first ever celebrated there. It was also the first for a private citizen in over 550 years. Centre of attention was Gelimer in all his regal finery, paraded for all to see as the defeated Vandal king, together with a vast amount of captured treasure including much the Vandals had seized when sacking Rome in AD 455. Afterwards Gelimer was treated well, retiring to estates in Galatia where he lived to an old age. Meanwhile Belisarius was named *consul ordinarius* for the year AD 535 which allowed him to celebrate a second triumph in which he was carried through the streets seated on a consular chair carried aloft by Vandal warriors.

Back in North Africa, Byzantine rule gradually rolled out across the former Vandal kingdom, with the Exarchate of Africa quickly established. However it took until AD 548 to pacify some of the Mauri tribes in the western Maghreb who still hoped for the return of Vandal rule. Sadly for them this never happened, with Justinian ordering any evidence of the Vandal kingdom destroyed. Those Vandals who remained in the region gradually merged back into wider North African society, a wretched end for a proud people who played a key role in the fall of the Western Empire, and for a time established their own heaven in North Africa.

Conclusion

The story of the Vandal kingdom in North Africa, and its dramatic fall, did not take place in isolation. It was part of a much broader picture set in the post-Roman West and Byzantine East. In short, in its prime it matched any Germanic kingdom emerging in Europe, indeed serving as a role model given its early founding. However, from a Vandal perspective it then suffered two catastrophes that effectively wiped its existence clean away from the Maghreb. These were Justinian's reconquest campaign which destroyed the kingdom in AD 534, and then the later Arab conquest which swept through the region, obliterating any surviving cultural remnants from the classical and late antique worlds in its path. Here in my conclusion I link the two, showing how Belisarius' great triumph helped set in place the conditions which allowed the Umayyads to so effectively rip North Africa from Byzantine control.

The Exarchate of Africa

After Justinian's death in AD 565 the Byzantine Empire found itself increasingly under pressure on all fronts, particularly along the Danube and in Syria. That meant its more remote provinces, particularly in North Africa, were left to fend for themselves for extended periods, often to the detriment of relations with the local population. This is evident in the archaeological record, where on my travels in the Maghreb I was much taken by the fact that the Byzantine occupation phase in key settlements often comprised a fortress or fort built in the centre of the old Roman town, often right on top of the old *forum*. Those I viewed were all constructed from reused Roman building material, often incorporating still-standing monumental buildings in their wall circuits. A fine example is that at Madauros in the Atlas Mountains where the Severan

theatre adjacent to the *forum* forms the Byzantine fort's north-west wall. Von
Rummel concurs, saying (2016, 114):

> The Byzantines devoted considerable resources and spent much energy in the construction
> of fortifications, many of which are still visible. Fortified complexes were built in urban,
> suburban and rural areas…and these had a major impact on existing urban layouts.

He talks of Byzantine fortifications large and small, citing those at
Haïdra (Roman Ammaedara) and Borj Helal (Roman Thunusuda) in Tunisia
at the upper end. I have seen similar and have a fond memory of waking in
Setif in Algeria to view the huge Byzantine fortress there from my bedroom
window. Earlier, Pringle carried out a detailed analysis of the fortifications of
Byzantine North Africa, saying (1979, 5):

> Some 80 sites that were provided with official works of fortification can be identified in
> Byzantine Africa by means of their surviving physical remains or from earlier written accounts.
> To these may be added another 40 of much less certain identification and several hundred
> more defensive works of an ad hoc character.

These remain the accepted figures today for the number of Byzantine fortifications in the Maghreb.

While inspecting those I visited on my own travels I was struck by two things.
First, they were full of horse-troughs, often re-using earlier Roman building
material as with the fortifications themselves. Clearly most were cavalry forts,
built to allow flying columns of horsemen to police the local population.
Second, most are not on the southern *limes* of the old Roman *diocese* or Vandal
kingdom, or on the border with Cyrenaica to the east. They are nearly all in
the lush coastal region or the Atlas Mountains. The key exception is the old
colonia at Timgad on the northern fringes of the Aures range which, having
been destroyed by the Berbers at the point of the Justinian conquest, features
a later Byzantine fort enclosing the town water supply (Blas de Roblès, Sintes,
and Kenrick, 2003, 189). The old adjacent legionary fortress at Lambaesis,
with its fine wall circuit, had long fallen out of use by that time.

Taken together, the fact most of the forts are for mounted units, and most
are in the heartlands of the old *diocese* and not the fringes, indicates to me that
the local North Africa population didn't welcome the eastern Romans back.
The Byzantine administration in Constantinople already had its well-earned
reputation for onerous autocracy that was later to define it. Indeed, when the
term Byzantinism emerged in the 19th century, it was a negative reference
for overly complex bureaucracies. Also note that the Vandal kingdom lasted
99 years and had seen off at least two serious Roman attempts at reconquest

before Belisarius succeeded. We are therefore talking of a population genera-
tions beyond any experience of Roman rule. Thus for the locals, especially the
Berbers who had been carving out a degree of autonomy under the Vandals,
Justinian's reconquest was a shock. This is an important new finding given it
forms a key feature of my closing narrative regarding the Arab Conquest in
North Africa.

Arab Conquest

The Arab Conquest of Sassanid Persia and much of the Byzantine Empire,
including all of the latter's territories in the Levant and North Africa, was a truly
shocking and unfathomable event to contemporary audiences. A key reason for
this response was the astonishing speed with which it happened, given it took
less than 100 years. In this short time, the two near-eastern superpowers of the
early medieval world fell with a whimper rather than a bang (in total in the case
of Sassanid Persia) to the most unlikely of protagonists, the Arab peoples of the
Arabian Peninsula. To that point, these warrior tribes were best known in late
antiquity as the Lakhmid allies of the Persians and the Ghassanid allies of the
Romans. Yet, by the mid-8th century AD, their new Caliphate (as the territory
controlled by the Arab conquests was known by that time) had conquered most
of their known world, including former Visigothic Spain.

When looking back at their remarkable success, many Arab scholars made
a specific link between piety and worldly power as they tried to explain their
forebears' incredible achievements. Tom Holland illustrates this well in his
thought-provoking *In the Shadow of the Sword*, where he explains this new,
all-conquering worldview (2013, 14):

> The Arabs…rejoiced in a rampant conviction that all their astounding victories were owed
> directly to the favour of God. Two centuries previously, so they believed, heaven had graced
> their ancestors with a stream of supernatural revelations: a dispensation that trumped those
> of the Jews and the Christians, and had set those who subjected themselves to it upon
> a road to global empire. Indeed, eight hundred years after the birth of Christ, it was as
> 'Muslims' – 'those who submit to God' – that most Arabs had come to identify themselves.
> The vast agglomeration of territories won by the swords of their forefathers, stretching from
> the shores of the Atlantic to the fringes of China, served as the ultimate monument to what
> God had demanded of them: their submission. 'Islam', they called it – shorthand for what
> had become, by the early 9th century AD, an entire civilization.

However, there were also a number of practical reasons why the Arab conquests
were so successful. Three I detail here, while the last two I consider when
concluding this section given the key roles the latter played in helping establish
the territories controlled by the new North African Caliphate.

The first is a simple case of classic misjudgement, though one with seismic results. In short, the Sassanid Persians and Byzantines completely underestimated their Arab neighbours. The huge, arid region the latter inhabited had always been the soft underbelly of their centuries-long superpower conflict, usually a secondary or even tertiary front when compared to the usual zones of engagement further north in Armenia and Syria. As Heather details (2018, 312):

> The Arabs of the desert fringe were the critical protagonists of the southern, desert conflict zone between the two great powers. Large conventional armies could not operate there, but the desert front offered many opportunities for profitable raiding and for distracting your opponent's attention from the heavily contested Armenian and Syrian fronts to the north, as practiced by [the Sassanid Persian king] Khavad I in AD 531 and Belisarius a decade later. Hence both sides recruited, paid, and armed [respectively Lakhmid and Ghassanid] allies to protect their provinces from desert raiders and to cause as much trouble as possible for the other side.

This view of the Arabs as compliant allies, there only to do the bidding of their superpower sponsors to the northeast and northwest, was not new. They had been similarly considered so for millennia by all the previous superpowers in the region, for example the Akkadians, Mitanni, Assyrians, Babylonians, Egyptians, Achaemenid Persians, and any of the Hellenistic kingdoms. This was now about to change, and in a very dramatic way.

The second factor was the timing given that, by the early 7th century AD, both the Sassanids and Byzantines were what a modern boxing commentator would call punch drunk. At the very moment an incendiary Arab uprising began in the Arabian Peninsula, the Sassanids and Byzantines were concluding the epic Byzantine–Sassanian War of AD 602 to AD 628. This had featured the titanic regional power struggle between Khosrow II and the emperors Flavius Phocas and, later, Heraclius, leaving both empires economically and militarily exhausted, with much of their territories devastated by the conflict. Worse, the region had also only just suffered a ravaging plague pandemic which had seen the dead piled in the streets in Constantinople and Ctesiphon. Given the dense nature of these and the many other sprawling population centres in the Levant, this had impacted the Mediterranean world to a far greater extent than it had the Arabian Peninsula.

The final reason is the socio-economic nature of the Arab Conquest. Early appreciations of its triumph tended to focus on the religious fanaticism of its warriors. However, more recent research has argued that, instead, many of the original Arab peoples involved were far more pragmatic, except perhaps the zealot core, and it was actually later recruits from the native populations in Mesopotamian, Syrian, and North African who proved the most fanatical adherents to their all-conquering cause. Many of these, having suffered severe economic dislocation as a result of the recent superpower conflict and pandemic, were unsurprisingly more than happy to throw in their lot with the new Arab invaders. Here Heather uses a most interesting analogy to provide context, arguing that in this regard, the Arab Conquest (at least early on) most closely resembled the earlier conquests of Attila the Hun. As he explains (2018, 313):

> Attila generated unity among a whole series of Rome's former European frontier clients and some of their neighbours from the deeper interior. All these groups had previously been just as likely to quarrel among themselves as fight the Roman empire...yet united under Attila, however unwillingly, in the 5th century AD they created a power bloc large enough to confront the empire directly.

Additionally, there is another important parallel between the armies of the Arab Conquest and Attila, this the quality of many of the natives recruited to the cause. Hunnic armies deliberately made use of the military skills of their vassal recruits, among others, including former Roman military personnel. The latter included engineers with experience in siege warfare, which made the Huns a far greater military threat as they plundered the Roman provinces in the east and west than, earlier, the Germans and Goths had been. No more could local populations sit behind their city fortifications to wait out the predations of the Huns.

In my opinion, the same was also true of the armies of the Arab conquests, perhaps to an even greater extent. Here in the Levant, these fast-moving Arab-led forces defeated huge Sassanid and Roman armies, often with ease, with many captives then recruited into their ranks. These locals were often ethnic Arabs themselves and included specialist Sassanid and Byzantine military engineers. Given the speed with which Jerusalem and many other cities in the region surrendered to the conquest armies, this was certainly a factor considered by regional municipal authorities when deciding whether to resist the Arab invaders, or stay loyal to Ctesiphon or Constantinople. Most chose the former.

Yet all these factors would have counted for nothing had it not been for a scorching religious conflagration lit by a desert prophet. Islam arose as a religious and political force in Arabia sometime around AD 610, with the Islamic Prophet Muhammad amassing a huge following. He then built a regional empire in the Arabian Peninsula after overcoming local persecution. The basic tenets of his new empire were that the military might of his followers was incontestable given they were doing God's bidding, and that its adherents should be humanitarian in how they treated conquered peoples. After his death in AD 632, his follower and friend Abu Bakr continued to expand the new empire westwards into the Levant, establishing the Rashidun Caliphate which lasted from AD 632 until AD 661. It was during this period that this brand new political and military power in the Middle East first challenged, and then to the astonishment of all, defeated in detail the Sassanids and Byzantines.

Abu Bakr was first alerted to the weakness of the Sassanid territories in Iraq and Syria by an Arabian chieftain called Muthanna ibn al-Haritha while leading his armies against rebel Arabian tribes in the Ridda Wars. A shrewd leader with an eye for the main chance, he quickly arranged a large raid into the rich upper Euphrates valley, catching the exhausted Sassanids completely by surprise. Here, huge numbers of the local population in the former Hellenistic cities and their hinterlands joined forces with the Arab raiders given the levels of discontent after years of fighting the Byzantines. They all sensed rich pickings were on offer, and so it proved. Abu Bakr's warriors then stayed in the region after the campaigning season ended, this marking the first expansion of the Arab Conquest out of the Arabian Peninsula.

Shortly afterwards, Abu Bakr sent a second invasion force to northern Syria, this to counter any interference there by the Byzantines while fighting his Euphrates campaign against the Sassanids. Inevitably this led to a war on two fronts for the new armies of Islam, one against the Sassanids in the east and one the Byzantines in the west. To ensure this dual narrative of conquest is easy for the reader to follow, I now deal with each in turn, rather than chronologically. I start with the war against Sassanid Persia.

In the first instance, after his initial success, Abu Bakr suffered a crushing reverse on the Euphrates against a Sassanid counterattack at the battle of the Bridge in October AD 634. However, the surviving Arab forces mounted an orderly retreat. They were then able to maintain control of their conquered territory on the western bank of the river. There the Arabs waited for the imminent arrival of reinforcements from Medina.

However, Abu Bakr died in AD 634. He was succeeded by Umar ibn al-Khattab as the second Caliph of the Islamic empire, and newly styled 'commander of the faithful'. The new leader swiftly reinforced his Mesopotamian front with new warriors, just in time to face off against a renewed attempt by the Sassanid Persians to regain their lost lands in the Euphrates valley. The Persian army here was led by one of the leading Sassanid generals, Rustam Farrokhzad, a legendary strategist who had come out of retirement to attack the entrenched Arab army on the Euphrates. Soon a major engagement took place at the battle of al-Qādisiyyah in AD 636. This was a see-saw affair, with the Arab army eventually winning decisively. The victory shattered Sassanid control over Mesopotamia, with its capital, Ctesiphon, quickly falling. The last Sassanid king, Yazdegard III, now raised one final, huge army to try to reverse the fortunes of his failing empire. However, two more defeats followed at the battles of Jalula and Nahavand in AD 637 and AD 642. After the latter, Sassanid resistance finally collapsed. Then, and despite capturing huge amounts of war booty including the Persian elephant corps, Umar ibn al-Khattab ordered his forces to consolidate their position in Mesopotamia, staying out of the Persian homelands in modern Iran. Sadly for him, though, his exemplary caution did not pay dividends, given a Persian slave called Lu'lu (who wished to avenge the loss of his kinsmen's kingdom) assassinated the Caliph in AD 644.

The next Caliph was named Uthman ibn 'Affan. He proved a more aggressive military leader, with the armies of the Caliphate soon on the march again. They pursued Yazdegard III to the northeast of his former territory, where he was murdered in AD 651 in Merv. This ended any remaining hope of successful Sassanid retaliation. The final Persian territories in the extreme northeast of their former empire, a region called Khurasan, then fell to the Arab Conquest by AD 653. With that, the once mighty Sassanid Persian empire was no more.

Back to Syria and the Byzantine front. Here the forces of Abu Bakr originally comprised four divisions under the leaders Shurahbil ibn Hasana, Yazid ibn Abi Sufyan, Amr ibn al-As, and Abu Ubaidah. All were specifically ordered by the Caliph to block any Byzantine interference in his Euphrates valley campaign against the Sassanids, but not to engage in open battle with the Byzantine field army in the region if possible. Further, they were told to avoid besieging any major Levantine cities and fortresses. However, Abu Bakr's hand was forced when the ailing Byzantine emperor Heraclius rashly ordered his brother Theodore to engage the Arab armies in Syria, his aim to relieve pressure on the Sassanids in Mesopotamia. The Caliph lost no time in responding, he using a clever stratagem in ordering his four divisions to move independently through the arid desert in the eastern Levant, using their camel trains to provide water. Here they were able to take advantage of the fact that, in their recent war with the Sassanids, the Byzantines had concentrated much of their expenditure on upgrading the frontier defences in northern Syria. This left the border defences running north-south along the Arabian frontier not only suffering from a lack of investment, but also undermanned. Soon, prompted by the Byzantine attack, the Arabs appeared on the fringes of Syria, their four columns uniting to surprise and comprehensively defeat the Byzantines at the battle of Ajnadayn in AD 634.

186 • VANDAL HEAVEN

Next, under the new Caliph Umar ibn al-Khattab, the Arab armies advanced northwards into the heart of the Levant and Syria. There they captured Damascus in AD 634, and then defeated another Byzantine army at the battle of Fahl in AD 635 before moving on to capture Homs (Roman Emesa) in AD 636. By now the Arab armies were very close to the huge metropolis of Antioch-on-the-Orontes, the regional Byzantine capital, where Heraclius himself was resident. The emperor was furious at Theodore's earlier defeat and dismissed the commander, gathering another huge army under the general Vahan of Armenia to face the victorious Arab army. The latter then retreated southwards beyond the Yarmouk River, this the largest tributary of the Jordan River. There the Arab army deployed on the river plain, drawing the Byzantine army into a wildly convoluted battle. This lasted a full six days in August AD 636. On the final day, sensing victory was imminent against a flagging and depleted enemy, the Arab leaders ordered a general advance. This enveloped the remaining Byzantine troops, massacring many and routing the rest in one of the greatest defeats in Roman history. Most of the Byzantine commanders were killed, either in the engagement itself, or while fleeing the battlefield.

With Byzantine resistance now broken in the Levant after such a shattering defeat, the whole of modern Syria, Jordan, Israel, and Palestine now fell to the victorious Arab forces, with Heraclius abandoning the region. It was this event which then allowed the Caliph to send reinforcements to bolster his campaign against the faltering Persians further south in Mesopotamia. Most notably, in the subsequent Syrian mopping-up operations, Jerusalem fell to Umar ibn al-Khattab's forces in AD 637 after a short siege, its leaders and citizens receiving a personal guarantee of safety from the Caliph which was well honoured.

Shocked, the Byzantines now adopted a purely defensive stance, hoping to stem the Arab advance. The two *praesental* field armies that had accompanied Heraclius to Antioch-on-the-Orontes were now withdrawn back to north-western Anatolia and Thrace, far from the Levantine front line and the all-conquering Arab armies. Meanwhile, the eastern Byzantine field army, which had been savaged in the recent battles, was divided into two under two new generals. These were titled the *magister militum Orientum* and the *magister militum per Armenian*. The two new armies were then renamed as the Anatolikon division and the Armeniakon division, with both deployed in Cappadocia in eastern Anatolia, their orders to hold the line there against any further incursions by the Arab-led armies. Meanwhile, to bolster the Byzantine forces defending Aegyptus, the European field army normally based in Thrace was then sent to help defend Byzantine North Africa from the new, existential threat to the east. This was placed under the command of a newly appointed *magister militum per Thracias*, and was soon in action.

After their successes in Mesopotamia and Syria, the Arab-led armies now paused, probing the Byzantine defences on the Cappadocian *limes* while consolidating their newly conquered territories to the south and east into the Caliphate. However, soon Amr ibn al-As, one of four commanders of the original Syrian campaign, sought an audience with Umar ibn al-Khattab. Here he proposed to renew the Arab Conquest, his plan to target North Africa. There, his intelligence sources had told him that the local population, especially the Berbers in the Maghreb, were dissatisfied with their Byzantine masters given the repressive policies instigated after the round of regional unrest that had followed recent Byzantine defeats in Mesopotamia and Syria. Further, the Exarchate of Africa who governed the region was dealing with yet another bout of religious in-fighting, this time due to the conflict between the region's Greek Orthodox Christians and the supporters of the newly arrived doctrine of Monotheletism, which held that Christ only had one will. An attempt here at compromise promoted by Heraclius in AD 638 had gone down badly with all parties, this no doubt resembling all of the earlier friction between the Nicene Church, Donatists, and Arians.

At first the caliph demurred. It took a great deal of persuasion by Amr to convince him otherwise. Finally, the general got his way and, reinforced with another army under Zubayr ibn al-Awamm, he swiftly invaded Egypt and won a major victory against the Byzantines at the battle of Heliopolis in AD 640. Within two years most of Egypt had fallen to the Arabs, an astonishing achievement, with a final Byzantine maritime counterattack at Alexandria in later AD 646 defeated with the help of native recruits keen to shake off their former masters. Next, with the assistance of a fleet built in Syria, Cyrenaica and Tripolitania were wrested from Byzantine control, especially after the decisive victory in the battle of Sufetula in AD 647. Cyprus fell soon afterwards after a short campaign in AD 649, followed by Rhodes in AD 654. Then at the battle of the masts in AD 655 the Byzantine fleet was crushed, leaving the Arabs the unlikely masters of the eastern Mediterranean. They then launched major raids against Crete and Sicily.

This initial period of rapid expansion was halted in AD 656 when Uthman was murdered by renegade soldiers. His successor was Ali ibn Abi Talib, who spent most of his reign trying to restore order to the huge empire he had inherited. A radical group called the Kharijites later murdered him in AD 661. On his death Mu'awiya I, the governor of Syria and his great rival, eventually assumed power, giving rise to the Umayyad Dynasty that flourished through to AD 750 when replaced by the Abbasid Caliphate. Once more the armies of the caliph went on the offensive, with the rest of North Africa falling by the early 8th century AD, the key city of Carthage having been captured by AD 695 (this the seat of the Exarch of Africa).

On a recent trip to the region I got a first-hand sense of how profound this dramatic change was. This was on a visit to the Sidi Okba Mosque near Biskra on the Saharan fringe in Algeria. There, in the oldest surviving mosque in the country, can be found the tomb of Uqba ibn Nafi, the nephew of Amr ibn al-As, a commander of the Arab army in the region who died fighting the Byzantine defenders in AD 683. Given the speed with which North Africa fell to the Arabs, his loss was not in vain.

However, that was not the end of the conquest, for the Umayyads then crossed into the Iberian Peninsula, in the first instance just a small raiding party that landed on Gibraltar in AD 711. Their exploits are just as remarkable as any in the Arab conquests, and within a few months this band of adventurers (together with Arab and local reinforcements) had succeeded in defeating the resident Visigoths in open battle, killing their king, and then capturing the Visigoth capital at Toledo (former Roman Toletum). To do this they first had to occupy the former Roman province of Baetica, and then traverse the Montes de Toledo mountains to penetrate central Iberia, where sat Toledo. As Holland says, this was 'deep in the vitals of Spain', and by AD 716 most of the peninsula had fallen to the Umayyads (2012, 395).

One is left here to reflect in astonishment at the success of the Arab conquests, which within 30 years of the end of the brutal Byzantine–Sassanian War destroyed the Sassanid Persian Empire and severely diminished the Byzantine Empire. As Holland explains, 'the balance of power that had for centuries divided the Fertile Crescent into two rival spheres of influence was no more' (2012, 299).

Earlier I detailed three factors that I believe played a key role in this amazing Arab success. To these we can now add two more specifically relevant to North Africa, having considered the Arab Conquest in detail. First, the administrative organization of the Byzantine Empire there provided a ready network for the Arab conquests to first infiltrate, and then take over. The Byzantine Exarchate of Africa, this region of control a legacy of the reconquest campaigns of Justinian I against Gelimer and the Vandals, remained a thriving if remote part of the Byzantine world. As detailed in Chapter 4, its system of administration dated back to the Diocletianic reformation, with additional reforms set in place by Justinian I. Each of its regions was run from a key city, within which sat the machinery of local administration. Leading examples included Alexandria, Cyrene, Leptis Magna, Carthage, and Tangiers. Therefore, as the tide of the Arab conquests swept east to west through North Africa, in simple terms all the incomers had to do was take control of the top level of administration in the key population centres. Their associated regions then fell to them by default. Such was the success of this Umayyad Arab takeover that it would be over a century before any serious administrative change was imposed on the region.

Finally, as detailed earlier, when the Byzantines reconquered North Africa, they clearly weren't welcomed as saviours from the Vandals given many natives there had thrived under their German rulers. This fractious relationship, especially with the Berbers, then worsened over time, especially after extra layers of Byzantine control were set in place in the Maghreb after the initial round of Arab victories in the Levant. Thus, as the unstoppable wave of Umayyad conquest washed through the region, more often than not they were welcomed as they arrived. And so today, this once crucial and indeed culturally central part of the Roman world is now a thriving part of the world of Islam.

Bibliography

Ancient Sources

Aeschylus, *Persians and Other Plays*. 2009. C. Collard, Oxford: Oxford World Classics.

Ammianus Marcellinus, *The Later Roman Empire*. 1986. W. Hamilton, London: Penguin.

Appian, *Punic Wars*. 1912. H. White, Harvard: Loeb Classical Library.

Apuleius, *The Golden Ass*. 2008. P. G. Walsh, Oxford: Oxford World Classics.

Aristotle, *The Politics*. 2009. E. Barker, Oxford: Oxford World Classics.

St Augustine of Hippo, *Select Letters of St Augustine*. 1930. J. Houston-Baxter, Harvard: Loeb Classical Library.

St Augustine of Hippo, *City of God*. 1989. G. E. McCracken, Harvard: Loeb Classical Library.

Marcus Aurelius, *Meditations*. 1964. M. Staniforth, London: Penguin.

Julius Caesar, *The Conquest of Gaul*. 1951. S. A. Handford, London: Penguin.

Marcus Cato, *De Agri Cultura*. 1934. H. B. Ash and W. D. Hooper, Harvard: Loeb Classical Library.

Cassiodorus, *The Variae*. 2019. M. S. Bjornlie., Berkeley: California University Press.

Cassius Dio, *Roman History*. 1925. E. Cary, Harvard: Loeb Classical Library.

Cicero, *Selected Works*. 2004. M. Grant, London: Penguin.

Claudian, *Works*. 1989. M. Platnauer, Harvard: Loeb Classical Library.

Flavius Cresconius Corippus, *De Bellis Lebycis*. 1998. G. W. Shea, New York: The Edwin Mellen Press.

Diodorus Siculus, *Library of History*. 1952. C. L. Sherman, Harvard: Loeb Classical Library.

Eusebius, *Ecclesiastical History: Complete and Unabridged*. 2011. C. F. Crusé, Seaside, Oregon: Merchant Books.

Eusebius, *de Vita Constanti*. 2011. C. F. Crusé, Seaside, Oregon: Merchant Books.

Flavius Eutropius, *Historiae Romanae Breviarium*. 1993. H. W. Bird, Liverpool: Liverpool University Press.

Quintus Horatius Flaccus (Horace), *The Complete 'Odes' and 'Epodes'*. 2008. D. West, Oxford: Oxford Paperbacks.

Hydatius, *The Chronicle of Hydatius*. R. W. Burgess, Oxford: Oxford University Press.

Julius Florus, *Epitome of Roman History*. 2017. D. Koryczan, Independently Published.

Sextus Julius Frontinus, *Strategemata*. 1969. C. E. Bennett, Portsmouth, New Hampshire: Heinemann.

Gaius, *Institutiones*. 1946. F. De Zulueta, Oxford: Oxford University Press.

Gildas, *De Excidio et Conquestu Britanniae*. 2010. H. A. Williams, Wokingham: Dodo Press.

Gregory of Tours, *History of the Franks*. 1974. L. Thorpe, London: Penguin.

Historia Augusta. 1921. D. Maggie, Harvard, Loeb Classical Library.

Herodian, *History of the Roman Empire*. 1989. C. R. Whittaker, Harvard: Loeb Classical Library.

Herodotus, *The Histories*. 2003. A. Selincourt, London: Penguin.

The Holy Bible, King James Version.

Homer, *The Iliad*. 1950. E. V. Rieu, London: Penguin.

Isidore of Seville, 2014. *Historia Gothorum, Vandalorum et Suevorum*. North Charleston, South Carolina: CreateSpace Independent Publishing Platform.

Silius Italicus, *Punica*. 1989. J. D. Duff, Harvard: Loeb Classical Library.

Jerome, *The Commentaries of Origen and Jerome on St. Paul's Epistle to the Ephesians*. 2002. R. Heine, Oxford: Oxford University Press.

Jerome, *Lettres*. 1949. J. Labourt, Paris: Les Belles Lettres,

Jordanes, *Getica*. 2014. Morrisville, North Carolina: Lulu Press.

Justinian, *The Digest of Justinian*. 1997. A. Watson, Philadelphia: University of Pennsylvania.

Justinian I, *The Digest of Roman Law*. 1979. Colbert, C., London: Penguin.

Libanius, *The Julianic Orations*. 1989. A. F. Norman, Harvard: Loeb Classical Library.

Livy, *The History of Rome*. 1989. B. O. Foster, Harvard: Loeb Classical Library.

Lucian of Samosata, *Works*. 2016. A. M. Harmon, St Albans: Wentworth Press.

Maurice, *Strategikon*. 2001. G. T. Dennis, Philadelphia: University of Pennsylvania Press.

Velleius Paterculus, *Roman History*. 1977. A. J. Woodman, Cambridge: Cambridge Classical Texts.

Olympiodorus of Thebes, *Historikoi Logio*. 1993. C. Chaffin, Lewiston, New York: The Edwin Mellen Press.

Orientus, *Orientii Commonitorium*. 1945. M. Tobin, Washington DC: Catholic University of America.

Paul the Deacon, *History of the Lombards*. 2015. Foulke, W., North Charleston, South Carolina: CreateSpace Independent Publishing Platform.

Paulus Orosius, *Seven Books of History Against the Pagans*. 1936. R. I. Woodworth, New York: Columbia University.

Pausanias, *Guide Greece: Central Greece*. 1979. P. Levi, London: Penguin.

Pliny the Elder, *Natural History*. 1940. H. Rackham, Harvard: Harvard University Press.

Pliny the Younger, *Epistularum Libri Decem*. 1963, R. A. B. Mynors, Oxford: Oxford Classical Texts, Clarendon Press.

Plutarch. *Lives of the Noble Greeks and Romans*. 2013. A. H. Clough, Oxford: Benediction Classics.

Polybius, *The Rise of the Roman Empire*. 1979. I. Scott-Kilvert, London: Penguin.

Possidius of Calama, *Vita S. Augustini*. 2022. H. T. Weiskotten, Ennis, Ireland: Dalcassian Publishing Company.

Procopius, *History of the Wars*. 1989. H. B. Dewing, Harvard: Loeb Classical Library.

Procopius, *Secret History*. 1989. H. B. Dewing, Harvard: Loeb Classical Library.

St Prosper of Aquitaine, *Defence of St Augustine*. 1995. P. de Letter, London: The Newman Press.

St Prosper of Aquitaine, *Prosperi Tironis Epitoma Chronicon*. 1892. T. Mommsen, Open Library.

Quintilian, *Institutes of Oratory*. 2015. J. Selby Watson, Scotts Valley, California: Create Space Independent Publishing Platform.

Salvian of Marseille, *De Gubernatione (On the Government of God, also including the relevant passages of Salvian's Ad Ecclesiam)*. 1930. E. M. Sanford, New York: Columbia University Press.

Second Maccabees. 2012. T. Horn, Crane, Michigan: Defender Publishing LLC.

Socrates Scholasticus, *Church Histories*. 1980. P. Schaff, Grand Rapids, Michigan: William B Eerdmans Publishing Co.

Statius, *Silvae*. 2004. B. R. Nagle, Bloomington: Indiana University Press.

Strabo, *The Geography*. 2014. D. W. Roller, Cambridge: Cambridge University Press.

Suetonius, *The Twelve Caesars*. 1957. R. Graves, London: Penguin.

Cornelius Tacitus, *Agricola and Germania*. 1970. H. Mattingly, London: Penguin.

Cornelius Tacitus, *The Annals*. 2003. M. Grant, London: Penguin.

Cornelius Tacitus, *The Histories*. 2008. W. H. Fyfe, Oxford: Oxford Paperbacks.

Theodoret of Cyrrhus, *The Questions on the 'Octateuch': On Leviticus, Numbers, Deuteronomy, Joshua, Judges, and Ruth*. 2008. J. Petruccione, and R. C. Hill, Washington D.C: Catholic University Press of America.

Albius Tibullus, *Catullus. Tibullus. Pervigilium Veneris*. 1989. F. W. Cornish, Postgate, J. P. and Mackail, J. W., Harvard: Loeb Classical Library.

Aurelius Victor, *De Caesaribus*. 1994. H. W. Bird, Liverpool: Liverpool University Press.

Vegetius, *De Re Militari*. 1993. N. P. Milner, Liverpool: Liverpool University Press.

Victor of Vita, *History of the Vandal Persecution*. 1992. J. Moorhead, Liverpool: Liverpool University Press.

Wolf, H. *Corpus Historiæ Byzantinæ*. 2018. London: Forgotten Books.

Zosimus, *New History*. 1982. R. T. Ridley, Leiden: Brill.

Modern Sources

Barker, P. 1981. *The Armies and Enemies of Imperial Rome*. Cambridge: Wargames Research Group.

de la Bédoyère, G. 2017. *Praetorian: The Rise and Fall of Rome's Imperial Bodyguard*. New Haven: Yale University Press.

Benseddik, N. and Potter, T. W. 1993. *Fouilles du Forum de Cherchel*. Algiers: Agence nationale d'archéologie et de protection des sites et monuments historiques.

Berndt, G. M. 2016. *Arianism: Roman Heresy and Barbarian Creed*. London: Routledge.

Bidwell, P. 2007. *Roman Forts in Britain*. Stroud: Tempus.

Birley, A. R. 1999. *Septimius Severus: The African Emperor*. London: Routledge.

Bishop, M.C. 2016. *The Gladius*. Oxford: Osprey Publishing Ltd.

Blas de Roblès, J. M., Sintes. C. and Kenrick, P. 2003. *Classical Antiquities of Algeria*. London: Silphium Press.

Bonifay, M., 'Africa: Patterns of Consumption in Coastal Regions Versus Inland Regions. The Ceramic Evidence'. *Late Antique Archaeology*, 2014, Volume 10 (1), 529–566.

Breeze, D. J. and Hodgson, N. 2020. 'Plague on Hadrian's Wall?' *Current Archaeology*. Issue 365, V.30, 28–35.

Brown, P. 2012. *Through the Eye of a Needle: Wealth, the Fall of Rome and the Making of Christianity in the West, 350–550 AD*. Princeton, New Jersey: Princeton University Press.

Burgess, R. W. 1993. 'Principes cum Tyrannis: Two Studies on the Kaisergeschichte and Its Tradition.' *The Classical Quarterly*. V.43, 491–500.

Bury, J. B. 1923. *History of the Later Roman Empire from the Death of Theodosius I to the Death of Justinian*. London: MacMillan.

Cameron, A. 1993. *The Mediterranean World in Late Antiquity*. London: Routledge.

Carroll, M. (2009). 'Cologne.' in M. Gagarin, ed. *The Oxford Encyclopaedia of Greece and Rome*. Oxford: Oxford University Press, 251–260.

Connolly, P. 1988. *Greece and Rome at War*. London: Macdonald & Co (Publishers) Ltd.

Cornell, T. J. 1993. 'The End of Roman Imperial Expansion.' in J. Rich, and G. Shipley, G. eds. *War and Society in the Roman World*. London: Routledge, 139–170.

Cornell, T. J. and Matthews, J. 2006. *Atlas of the Roman World*. Oxford: Phaidon Press Ltd.

Courtois, C. 1964. *Les Vandales et L'Afrique*. Aalen: Scientia Verlag Und Antiquariat.

Cowan, R. 2003a. *Roman Legionary, 58 BC–AD 69*. Oxford: Osprey Publishing.

Cowan, R. 2003b. *Imperial Roman Legionary, AD 161–284*. Oxford: Osprey Publishing.

Cowan, R. 2007. *Roman Battle Tactics 109 BC–AD 313*. Oxford: Osprey Publishing.

Crawford, D. J. 1976. 'Imperial Estates.' in M. I. Finley, ed. *Studies in Roman Property.* Cambridge: Cambridge University Press, 35–70.

Cunliffe, B. 1988. *Greeks, Romans and Barbarians. Spheres of Interaction.* London: Batsford Ltd.

D'Amato, R. and Sumner, G. 2009. *Arms and Armour of the Imperial Roman Soldier.* Barnsley: Frontline Books.

D'Amato, R. 2009. *Imperial Roman Naval Forces 31BC–AD500.* Oxford: Osprey Publishing.

D'Amato, R. 2016. *Roman Army Units in the Western Provinces (1).* Oxford: Osprey Publishing.

D'Amato, R. 2018. *Roman Heavy Cavalry (1).* Oxford: Osprey Publishing.

D'Amato, R. 2019. *Roman Army Units in the Western Provinces (2).* Oxford: Osprey Publishing.

Darlington, J. 2023. *Amongst the Ruins.* New Haven: Yale University Press.

Dodd, L. 2016. *Kinship, Conflict and Unity Among Roman Elites in Post-Roman Gaul: The Contrasting Experiences of Caesarius and Avitus.* London: Routledge.

Dowley, T. 1997. *The Atlas of the Bible and Christianity.* Oxford: Candle books.

Drinkwater, John F. 1998. 'The Usurpers Constantine III and Jovinus.' *Britannia.* V.29, 269–98.

Elliott, P. 2014. *Legions in Crisis.* Stroud: Fonthill Media Ltd.

Elliott, S. 2016. *Sea Eagles of Empire: The Classis Britannica and the Battles for Britain.* Stroud: The History Press.

Elliott, S. 2017. *Empire State: How the Roman Military Built an Empire.* Oxford: Oxbow Books.

Elliott, S. 2018a. *Septimius Severus in Scotland: The Northern Campaigns of the First Hammer of the Scots.* Barnsley: Greenhill Books.

Elliott, S. 2018b. *Roman Legionaries.* Oxford: Casemate Publishers.

Elliott, S. 2019. *Julius Caesar: Rome's Greatest Warlord.* Oxford: Casemate Publishers.

Elliott, S. 2020a. 'Clash of the Titans: The Battle of Lugdunum, AD 197.' *Ancient Warfare,* XIII-3, 27–35.

Elliott, S. 2020b, *Romans at War.* Oxford: Casemate Publishers.

Elliott, S. 2020c. *Pertinax: The Son of a Slave Who Became Roman Emperor.* Barnsley: Greenhill Books.

Elliott, S. 2021a. *Roman Britain's Missing Legion.* Barnsley: Pen & Sword.

Elliott, S. 2021b. *Roman Conquests: Britain.* Barnsley: Pen & Sword.

Elliott, S. 2021c. *Pertinax: The Son of a Slave Who Became Roman Emperor.* Barnsley: Greenhill Books.

Elliott, S. 2021d. *Ancient Greeks at War.* Oxford: Casemate Publishers.

Elliott, S. 2022. *Legacy of Rome.* Stroud: The History Press.

Elliott, S. 2023. *Roman Special Forces and Special Ops.* Barnsley: Pen & Sword.

Erdkamp, P. ed. 2013. *The Cambridge Companion to Ancient Rome.* Cambridge. Cambridge University Press.

Fournier, E. 2017. 'The Vandal Conquest of North Africa: The Origins of a Historiographical Persona.' *The Journal of Ecclesiastical History.* V.68, 687–718.

Garrison, E. G. 1998. *History of Engineering and Technology: Artful Methods.* Boca Raton, Florida: CRC Press.

George, J. 2004. 'Vandal Poets in Their Context.' in A. H. Merrills, ed. *Vandals, Romans and Berbers.* London: Routledge, 3–28.

Gibbon, E. 2010. *The History of the Decline and Fall of the Roman Empire.* New York: Random House.

Goldsworthy, A. 2000. *Roman Warfare.* London: Cassell.

Goldsworthy, A. 2003. *The Complete Roman Army.* London: Thames and Hudson.

Goldsworthy, A. 2009. *The Fall of the West.* London: Weidenfeld & Nicholson.

Green, P. 1990. *Alexander to Actium.* London: Thames & Hudson.

Haldon, J. 1999. *Warfare, State and Society in the Byzantine World 565–1204.* London: UCL Press.

Haywood, J. 2009. *The Historical Atlas of the Celtic World.* London: Thames & Hudson.

Head, D. 2016. *Armies of the Macedonian and Punic Wars*. London: Wargames Research Group.

Heather, P. 2005. *The Fall of the Roman Empire*. London: Macmillan.

Heather, P. 2007. 'Christianity and the Vandals in the Reign of Geiseric.' *Bulletin of the Institute of Classical Studies*. V.50, 139–140.

Heather, P. 2009. *Empires and Barbarians*. London: Macmillan.

Heather, P. 2013. *The Restoration of Rome*. London: Macmillan.

Heather, P. 2018. *Rome Resurgent: War and Empire in the Age of Justinian*. Oxford: Oxford University Press.

Herrmann-Otto, E. 2013. 'Slaves and Freedmen.' in P. Erdkamp, eds. *The Cambridge Companion to Ancient Rome*. Cambridge: Cambridge University Press. 60-76.

Hingley, R. 2005. *Globalizing Roman Culture—Unity, Diversity and Empire*. London: Routledge.

Holder, P. 2003. 'Auxiliary Deployment in the Reign of Hadrian.' in J. J. Wilkes, ed. *Documenting the Roman Army. Essays in honour of Margaret Roxan*, Bulletin of the Institute of Classical studies Supplements. London, 101–146.

Holland, T. 2013. *In the Shadow of the Sword*. London: Little, Brown.

Holland, T. 2015. *Dynasty*. London: Little, Brown.

Holland, T. 2019. *Dominion*. London: Little, Brown.

Hornblower, S. and Spawforth, A. 1996. *The Oxford Classical Dictionary*. Oxford: Oxford University Press.

Horsted, W. 2021. *The Numidians*. Oxford: Osprey Publishing.

Howard-Johnston, J. 2021. *The Last Great War of Antiquity*. Oxford. Oxford University Press.

Hughes, I. 2009. *Belisarius: The Last Roman General*. Barnsley: Pen & Sword.

Hughes, I. 2012. *Aetius: Attila's Nemesis*. Barnsley: Pen & Sword.

Hughes, I. 2013. *Imperial Brothers: Valentinian, Valens and the Disaster at Adrianople*. Barnsley: Pen & Sword.

Hughes, I. 2014. *Belisarius: The Last Roman General*. Barnsley: Pen & Sword.

James, S. 2011. *Rome and the Sword*. London: Thames and Hudson.

Jestice, P. G. 2008. 'Introduction.' in P. G. Jestice, ed. *Battles of the Bible*. London: Amber Books, 6–18.

Jones, B. and Mattingly, D. 1990. *An Atlas of Roman Britain*. Oxford: Oxbow Books.

Kean, R. M. and Frey, O. 2005. *The Complete Chronicle of the Emperors of Rome*. Ludlow: Thalamus Publishing.

Keppie, L. 1984. *The Making of the Roman Army, from Republic to Empire*. London: Batsford.

Kiley, K. F. 2012. *The Uniforms of the Roman World*. Wigston: Lorenz Books.

Kneale, M. 2017. *Rome in Seven Sackings*. London: Atlantic Books.

Kolb, A. 2001. 'The Cursus Publicus.' in C. Adams and R. Laurence eds. *Travel and Geography in the Roman Empire*. London: Routledge, 95–106.

Kulikowski, M. 2007. *Rome's Gothic Wars*. Cambridge: Cambridge University Press.

Kulikowski, M. 2016. *Imperial Triumph: The Roman World From Hadrian to Constantine*. London: Profile Books.

Lambert, M. 2010. *Christians and Pagans*. New Haven: Yale University Press.

Lambshead, J. 2022. *The Fall of Roman Britain*. Barnsley: Pen & Sword.

Lavan, L., 'Local Economies in Late Antiquity? Some Thoughts.' *Late Antique Archaeology*, 2014, Vol. 1, 1–11.

Le Bohec, Y. 2000. *The Imperial Roman Army*. London: Routledge.

Lillington-Martin, C. and Turquois, E. *Procopius of Caesarea: Literary and Historical Interpretation*. London: Routledge.

Luttwak, E. 1976. *The Grand Strategy of the Roman Empire: From the First Century AD to the Third*. Baltimore: John Hopkins University Press.

MacDowall, S. 2016. *The Vandals*. Barnsley: Pen & Sword.

Machiavelli, N. 1961. *The Prince*. London: Penguin.

Mason, D. J. P. 2003. *Roman Britain and the Roman Navy*. Stroud: The History Press.

Mattingly, D. 1995. *Tripolitania*. Ann Arbor, Michigan: University of Michigan Press.

Mattingly, D. 2006a. *An Imperial Possession, Britain in the Roman Empire*. London: Penguin.

Mattingly, D. 2006b. 'The Garamantes: the First Libyan State.' in D. Mattingly, S. McLaren, K. Gadgood, E. Savage, and Y. Al-Fasatwi eds. *The Libyan Desert: Natural Resources and Cultural Heritage*. London: Society for Libyan Studies, 1–10.

Mattingly, D. 2011. *Imperialism, Power and Identity—Experiencing the Roman Empire*. Princeton: Princeton University Press.

Matyszak, P. 2009. *Roman Conquests: Macedonia and Greece*. Barnsley: Pen & Sword.

Matyszak, P. 2022. *Forgotten Peoples of the Ancient World*. London: Thames & Hudson.

Merrills, A. 2004. 'Introduction.' in A. H. Merrills ed. *Vandals, Romans and Berbers*. London: Routledge, 3–28.

Merrills, A. and Miles, R. (2010). *The Vandals*. Hoboken, New Jersey: John Wiley & Sons.

Millett, M. 1990. *The Romanization of Britain*. Cambridge: Cambridge University Press.

Moorhead, S. and Stuttard, D. 2012. *The Romans Who Shaped Britain*. London: Thames and Hudson.

Moss, H. 1947. *The Birth of the Middle Ages*. Oxford: Oxford University Press.

Murphey, R. 1951. 'The Decline of North Africa Since the Roman Occupation: Climatic or Human?' *The Annals of the Association of American Geographers*. V.41, Issue 2. 116–132.

Newark, T. 1985. *The Barbarians: Warriors & Wars of the Dark Ages*. Poole: Blandford Press.

Nikita, E. 2011. 'Activity Patterns in the Sahara Desert: An Interpretation Based on Cross-Sectional Geometric Properties.' *American Journal of Physical Anthropology*. V.146. 423–434.

O'Donnell, J. 2009. *The Ruin of the Roman Empire*. London: Profile Books.

Oleson, J. P. 2009. *The Oxford Handbook of Engineering and Technology in the Classical World*. Oxford: Oxford University Press.

Oosthuizen, S. 2019. *The Emergence of the English*. Leeds: ARC Humanities Press.

Parker, P. 2009. *The Empire Stops Here*. London: Jonathan Cape.

Pausche, D. 2009. 'Unreliable Narration in the Historia Augusta.' *Ancient Narrative*. V. 8. 115–135.

Pitassi, M. 2012. *The Roman Navy*. Barnsley: Seaforth.

Pohl, W. 2004. 'The Vandals: Fragments of a Narrative.' in: A. H. Merrills ed. *Vandals, Romans and Berbers*. London: Routledge, 31–48.

Pollard, N. and Berry, J. 2012. *The Complete Roman Legions*. London: Thames & Hudson.

Potter, D. 2009. *Rome in the Ancient World: From Romulus to Justinian*. London: Thames & Hudson.

Pringle, R. 1979. *Sixth-Century Fortifications in Byzantine Africa*. Doctor of Philosophy (PhD) Thesis. Unpublished: University of Oxford.

Raven, S. 1969. *Rome in Africa*. London: Routledge.

Rodgerds, N. and Dodge, H. 2009. *The History and Conquests of Ancient Rome*. London: Hermes House.

Rosenblum, M. 1961. *Luxorius: A Latin Poet Among the Vandals*. New York: Columbia University Press.

Scarre, C. 1995a. *The Penguin Historical Atlas of Ancient Rome*. London: Penguin.

Scarre, C. 1995b. *Chronicle of the Roman Emperors*: London: Thames and Hudson.

Shanzer, D. 2004. 'Intentions and Audiences: History, Hagiography, Martyrdom, and Confession in Victor of Vita's *Historia Persecutionis*.' in A. H. Merrills ed. *Vandals, Romans and Berbers*. London: Routledge, 271–290.

Shaw, B. D. 2004. 'Who Were the Circumcellions?' in A. H. Merrills ed. *Vandals, Romans and Berbers*. London: Routledge, 227–258.

Sheldon, H. 2010. 'Enclosing Londinium.' *London and Middlesex Archaeological Society Transactions*. V.61, 227–235.

Sheppard, S. 2020. *Roman Soldier versus Parthian Warrior*. Oxford: Osprey Publishing.

Starr, C. G. 1941. *The Roman Imperial Navy 31BC–AD 324*. New York: Cornell University Press.

Stathakopoulos, C. 2007. *Famine and Pestilence in the Late Roman and Early Byzantine Empire*. London: Routledge.

Stevens, S. and Conant, J. 2016. *North Africa Under Byzantium and Early Islam*. Washington D.C: Dumbarton Oaks Research Library and Collection.

Todd, M. 1981. *Roman Britain 55 BC–AD 400. The Province Beyond the Ocean*. Glasgow: Fontana Press.

Von Rummel, P. 2016. *The Transformation of Ancient Land and Cityscapes in Early Medieval North Africa*. Washington D.C: Dumbarton Oaks Research Library and Collection.

Walas, A. H. 2022. 'New Perspectives on the Roman Military Base at Bu Njem.' *Libyan Studies*. V.53, 48–60.

Watson, G. R. 1969. *The Roman Soldier: Aspects of Greek and Roman Life*. Ithaca, New York: Cornell University Press.

Weber, W. 1907. *Untersuchungen zur Geschichte des Kaisers Hadrianus*. Leipzig: B. G. Teubner.

Whitby, M. 2002. *Rome at War AD 293–696*. Oxford: Osprey Publishing.

Wickham, C. 2010. *The Inheritance of Rome: A History of Europe from 400 to 1000*. London: Penguin.

Wilkes, J. J. 2005. 'Provinces and Frontiers.' in A. K. Bowman, P. Garnsey, and A. Cameron eds. *The Cambridge Ancient History Vol. XII, The Crisis of Empire, AD 193–337*. Cambridge: Cambridge University Press, 212–268.

Williams, T. 2022. *Lost Realms*. London: William Collins.

Wilson, I. 1999. *The Bible of History*. London: Weidenfeld & Nicholson.

Wilson, A. 2002. 'Urban Production in the Roman World.' *Papers of the British School at Rome*. V.70, 231–273.

Windrow, M. and McBride, A. 1996. *Imperial Rome at War*. Hong Kong: Concord Publications.

Wolff, C. 2015. 'Units: Principate.' in Y. le Bohec ed. *The Encyclopedia of the Roman Army Vol. 3*. Hoboken, New Jersey: Wiley and Blackwell. 1,037–1,049.

Index

Ad Decimum, battle 176
Aetius, Flavius 137, 143, 152, 168, 195
Africa, *diocese* xi
Africa Proconsularis xi, xx, 130, 135, 152, 162, 166
agentes in rebus 83
Agricola, Gnaeus Julius 18
ala Ulpia Contariorum 51
Alans ix, xxii, 59, 87, 88, 97
Albinus, Clodius 57
Alexander Severus xiv, 16
Annaba 136, 139
Anthemius, emperor 171
Antonine Plague 52
Aquileia 51
Arab Conquest viii, xi, xiii, 6, 7, 21, 125, 189
Arabian Peninsula 181, 183, 184
Arcadius, emperor 136
Arianism 27
Arles 102
Arminius 42, 69
Aspar 153
Athaulf 136
Atlas Mountains vii, xii, 15
Attecotti 84
Attila the Hun 115, 137, 168
Augustus, emperor xv, 13, 40
Aures Mountains vii, 24, 131
Auxilia 12, 40, 42, 51, 53
Auxilia Palatina 111

Baetica 107, 116, 147
bagaudae 111

Ballomar 51, 53, 54
Bassus, Marcus Iallius, governor 51
Batavi 69
Batavian Revolt 46
Bavaria 51
Belisarius vii, viii, xviii, 155, 156, 173, 177, 178
beneficiarii consularis 2
beneficiarii procuratoris 2
Berbers 122
Beremudius 136
Béziers 102
Boniface, *comes* ix, 116, 138, 140, 142
Bonifatius 177
Boudicca 42
Boulogne-Sur-Mer 101, 103
Britannia, province 31, 62
Britanniae, *diocese* 85
Bructeri 42
bucellari 136, 139

Caerleon 2
Caledonians 84
Caligula, emperor 128, 131
Cantabrian Wars 40, 106
Capitoline Hill 170
Capitoline Triad 10
Caracalla, emperor 4
Carnuntum 50, 52, 53, 56, 91
Cartagena 106, 118, 170
Carthage ix, x, xiii, 21, 25, 103, 139, 159
Carthaginians 128
Carthaginiensis 116
Castinus, Flavius 116

Catalaunian Plains, battle of 115
Catholic Church 13
centinaria 132
Centurion 2
Chatti 42
Cherchell 15
Cherusci 69
Classis Britannica 2, 194
Classis Flavia Moesica 54, 92
Classis Flavia Pannonica 52, 92
Classis Germanica 90
Classis nova Libyca 131
Claudius, emperor 88, 128
Claudius Gothicus, emperor 79
Clemens, Sextus Cornelius 77
comes Africae 139
comes Domesticorum 138
comes Rei Militaris per Britanniarum 42
Commodus, emperor 57
commitatus 68
comitatenses 95
Constitutio Antoniniana 4
Constantine, city viii
Constans, emperor 23
Constantine I, emperor xiv, 10, 16
Constantine III, usurper 85, 98, 103
Constantinople xiv
Constantius II, emperor 27, 28
Constantius III, emperor 109
contos 56
Corpus Historiæ Byzantinæ xiv
Council of Arles 16
Council of Chalcedon 19

Dacia 51, 56, 61, 78, 80, 81
Danube, River 12, 28, 33, 45, 51
Darius 150
Djemila viii, 16, 17
Didius Julianus, emperor 55
Dio, Cassius xv
Diocletian, emperor xi, xiii, 15, 16, 93, 106
Diocletianic persecutions 25

Diocletianic Reformation 93, 106
Dominate xiv, 3, 10, 19
Domitian, emperor 15
Donatism 21
Donatus Magnus, bishop 21

Elbe, River 40
Emesa 133, 186
Eudocia 170
Eudoxia, Licinia 170
Eutropius, Flavius xv
expeditio sarmatica 56
Exuperius, bishop 103

fabricae 89, 197
Felix of Aptungi, bishop 22
Felix, Flavius 138, 139, 140, 152, 163
foederates 138
Fort xviii
Fortlet xviii
Fortress xviii
Frontinus, Sextus Julius 191
Fronto, Claudius 53

Gaiseric, king vii, ix, x, 118, 121, 150, 155
Gallaecia 116
Gallia Aquitania 89
Gallia Belgica 88
Gallia Lugdunensis 89
Gallia Narbonensis 89
Gallia Placidia 136, 169
Garamantes 123
Gelimer, king x, 155, 166, 176, 178, 188
Germania 40
Germania Inferior 88
Germania Superior 88
Germanicus Julius Caesar 44
Getae 70
Gildas 84
gladius Hispaniensis 193
Governor 2, 13, 31, 33

Greece xxiii, 53, 168, 192, 193
Guerilla warfare 25
Gunderic, king ix, 99, 114, 115, 141
Gunthamund, king 165, 166, 173

Hadrian, emperor 15, 31, 98, 132, 158
Hasdingi Vandals ix, 54, 77, 79, 82
Herodian v
Hoamer 173, 174
Hilderic, king 165, 166, 173, 176
Hispaniae, *diocese* xi
Historia Augusta xv
Honorius, emperor 136
Huneric, king 165, 168, 170, 171, 173
Huns xxii, 51, 62, 63, 71, 76

Iazyges 51

Jerome xvii
Joannes, emperor 137
John the Armenian 175
Julian, emperor 18, 23
Julius Caesar 40, 51, 55
Juno 10
Jupiter 10, 12, 45, 170
Justinian I, emperor vii, x, xvi, 9, 165,
    167, 175

Kingdom of the Vandals and Alans 155

Lacringi 51, 78
Lambaesis viii, xviii, xx, 23, 131, 135,
    180
legate xix, 24, 41, 55, 137
legio I *Adiutrix pia fidelis* 12
legio III *Augusta* 133
legio XII *Fulminata* 12
legio III *Italica concurs* 92
legion 36, 38, 40
Legiones Comitatenses 111
Leo I, Pope 170
Libya xi, 14, 121, 123
limes 41, 54, 56, 60, 70, 77

limes Germanicus 51, 95
limes Tripolitanus 132, 133, 180
limitanei 95
Lincoln 16
lorica hamata 148
lorica segmentata 42
lorica squamata 148
Lucius Verus, emperor 52, 64, 129
Lusitania 116
Lugdunum 89
Lugdunum, battle of 120

Madauros x, xxi, 8, 179
magister equitum 83
magister militum 83, 84, 85, 115, 138,
    152, 168
magister peditum 83
Mainz 42, 43, 73, 89, 90
Majorian, emperor 112, 170, 171
Mansuetus of Urusi, bishop 151
Marching camps xviii, xix
Marcian, emperor 19, 112
Marcomanni 45, 50
Marcomannic Wars 12, 35, 50
Marcus Aurelius, emperor 11, 12, 15, 52,
    53, 54, 79
Mauri 126
Maxentius, emperor 16
Maximinus Thrax, emperor 61
Mercury 12
Meung-sur-Loire 103
Miltiades, Pope 22
Milvian Bridge, battle of 16
Minerva 10
Moesia 53

Nero, emperor 15, 16, 18
Noricum 54
Notarii 83
Numidians 125, 126

officium consularis 2
Oporto 117

Oriens, diocese xi
Ostrogoths 51, 70, 85

Pampinianus of Vita, bishop 151
Pannonia 51, 52, 56, 88
Pannoniae, *diocese* 91
Parthia 62, 132
Paulus Orosius xvii
Petronius Maximus, emperor 169
Pertinax, emperor 4, 53, 53
Niger, Pescennius 57
Picts 84
Pompeianus, Claudius 54
Pompeii 11
praefectus urbi 169
praetentura Italiae et Alpium 54
Praetorian Guard 9
Praetorian Prefect 53, 56, 108, 109, 137, 169
primicerius notariorum 137
Princeps xiii, 9
Principate xiii
Procopius viii, 64, 137, 142, 144
Procurator 2, 53, 93
protectores divinis lateris 83
protectores domestici 83
Przeworsk culture 75

Quadi 12, 50, 51, 56, 57

Raetia 61, 79, 82, 91, 92
Ravenna 138
Regional Fleets 2, 90
Regnum Vandalorum et Alanorum 155
Rhine, River ix, xxii, 33, 35, 40, 44, 50
Rhine crossing ix, 74, 84, 95, 98
Ricimer 171
Rome 6, 8, 11, 12

Sahara Desert xx, 25, 122, 131
Saragossa 109
Sassanid Persia 11, 28, 174
Sarmatians 51, 52, 70

Septimius Severus, emperor 12, 31, 131
Severan dynasty 16
Seville 118
Sigisvultus 139
Silingi Vandals 11, 54, 80
Suebi ix, xxii, xxiii, 51, 88, 96
Stilicho 84, 85

Tarraconensis 111
Teutoberg Forest 35
Theodosius I, emperor 136
Theodosius II, emperor 8
Thrasamund, king 165, 173
Tiberinius 12
Tiberius, emperor 44
Timgad viii, 8, 24, 133, 180
Tiw 72
Toulouse 103
Trajan, emperor 15, 61, 70, 88, 91, 92
Tricamarum, battle of 177
Tuisto 72
Tisza, river 77
Tzazo 175

Uzès 102

Varian Disaster 35, 45, 46
Valentinian I, emperor 19
Valentinian II, emperor 18
Valentinian III, emperor 8, 137
Vandals vii, x, 26, 30, 33, 51, 57, 77, 78
Vandal language 74
Vandali Iustiniani 177
Varus, Publius Quinctilius 41, 42, 45
Vexillation 132, 133
Vexillation fortress xviii
Victor, Aurelius xv
Visigoths ix, xix, xxiii, 75, 85, 95

Wallia ix, 114, 171
Wōden 72

York 16